Evelyn Sharp

Manchester University Press

Aubrey Beardsley's design for the spine of Evelyn's first book, *At the Relton Arms*, published in John Lane's Keynote Series in 1895

Evelyn Sharp
Rebel Woman, 1869–1955

ANGELA V. JOHN

Manchester University Press
Manchester and New York

distributed in the United States exclusively
by Palgrave Macmillan

Published by Manchester University Press
Oxford Road, Manchester M13 9NR, UK
and Room 400, 175 Fifth Avenue, New York, NY 10010, USA
www.manchesteruniversitypress.co.uk

Distributed in the United States exclusively by
Palgrave Macmillan, 175 Fifth Avenue, New York,
NY 10010, USA

Distributed in Canada exclusively by
UBC Press, University of British Columbia, 2029 West Mall,
Vancouver, BC, Canada V6T 1Z2

British Library Cataloguing-in-Publication Data
A catalogue record for this book is available from the British Library

Library of Congress Cataloging-in-Publication Data applied for

ISBN 978 0 7190 8014 2 *hardback*

ISBN 978 0 7190 8015 9 *paperback*

First published 2009

18 17 16 15 14 13 12 11 10 09   10 9 8 7 6 5 4 3 2 1

The publisher has no responsibility for the persistence or accuracy of URLs for external or any third-party internet websites referred to in this book, and does not guarantee that any content on such websites is, or will remain, accurate or appropriate.

Typeset by Servis Filmsetting Ltd, Stockport, Cheshire
Printed in Great Britain
by the MPG Books Group in the UK

In Memory of my Grandmother:

EVELYN SCOTT
(1881–1971)

Contents

List of illustrations

Every effort has been made to trace copyholders; these efforts were unsuccessful in relation to 5. The following illustrations are reproduced by permission of: The Bodleian Library, University of Oxford, 1, 7, 8; The British Newspaper Library, Colindale, 11; Llyfrgell Genedlaethol Cymru / The National Library of Wales, 14; The Bodley Head, Random House, frontispiece, 3, 4, 6, 9, 10; Lutterworth Press, 12, 13; Estate of Sir William Rothenstein, National Portrait Gallery, London, 15.

Preface

As with my previous biographies, this book is structured thematically. It covers Evelyn Sharp's life (1869–1955) in a broadly linear fashion but, after an opening chapter exploring her early years, subsequent chapters address a particular issue or subject of interest to her. They examine her relationship to this through her actions and writing. To aid the reader, the main events of her life are set out at the start of the book on pages xiv–v. A list of her major publications is given in Appendix 1. Appendix 2 gives an example of one of her many short stories. Taken from the *Daily Herald* (6 August 1923) this, typically, has a domestic setting though its subject is international. It gently challenges expectations about gender, age and nationality.

This book is best read alongside my earlier life of Evelyn Sharp's husband, the radical war correspondent, Henry W. Nevinson (*War, Journalism and the Shaping of the Twentieth Century: The Life and Times of Henry W. Nevinson*; I. B. Tauris, 2006). These books explore what I call biographical history. This volume is intended to illuminate our understanding of, for example, women's suffrage in the Edwardian and First World War years and writings on childhood in the 1920s, as well as to explore the story of a remarkable individual.

Evelyn Sharp's long life encompassed enormous changes, from the narrow Victorian world in which she was raised and the experimental and rebellious years of the 1890s and 1900s, to the upheavals of two world wars and the very different and difficult demands that they made on peacetime. Following Evelyn Sharp's responses to both the upheavals and the more subtle shifts she witnessed over so many years personalises and helps to explain the story of a period as well as a person.

Tracing the contours of a Victorian woman's life involves determination, perseverance and some good luck. During my research I was

fortunate enough to have assistance from many individuals and institutions. They helped to ensure the pleasure that also comes from such
work though I am solely responsible for its outcome. As with my recent
biography of Henry Nevinson (to which this life of Evelyn Sharp is a
companion) my initial research began with a Charter Fellowship at
Wolfson College, Oxford. I am grateful to the President and Fellows of
Wolfson and the School of Humanities at the University of Greenwich
for making this possible. The Department of Special Collections and
Western Manuscripts at the Bodleian Library, University of Oxford,
where the Evelyn Sharp Nevinson Papers and Henry Nevinson Papers
are kept, was the engine house for this research. I thank this department, especially Colin Harris, for expert support and courtesy. I am
indebted to the Michael Ayrton Estate for permission to use these
papers.

I am especially grateful to the staff of the North Reading Room in
the Llyfrgell Genedlaethol Cymru / The National Library of Wales for
their efficiency and helpfulness. Thanks are also due to the following:
Aberystwyth University; the Society of Antiquaries of London; Bristol
University Library Special Collections; the BBC Written Archives
Centre Caversham Park; the British Library; the British Newspaper
Library, Colindale; the British Library of Political and Economic
Science Archives Division; Cumbria Record Office Carlisle; Devon
Record Office; Ealing Local History Library; English PEN; the Fales
Library and Special Collections New York University; Friends House
Library, London; Hull University Archives; Isle of Wight Record Office;
IndependentAge; Local Studies Kensington Library; the Liu Clinic,
London; News International; Provost and Scholars of King's College,
Cambridge; The Board of The National Library of Ireland; National
Portrait Gallery Library; Harry Ransom Humanities Research Center,
University of Texas at Austin; University of Reading Special Collections
Service; the University Librarian and Director, The John Rylands
University Library, The University of Manchester; Director of Culture,
Sheffield City Council, Sheffield Archives; Society of Authors (literary
representative of the Estate of John Masefield); Master and Fellows of
Trinity College, Cambridge; the Vaughan Williams Library English
Folk Song and Dance Society, the Vaughan Williams Charitable Trust
and the Women's Library.

Many have helped with queries but I must mention the following: Johanna Alberti, Harish Chandra Banazi, Mike Barlow, Paula
Bartley, Tom Buchanan, Susan Chitty, Hugh Cobbe, David Crew,

Leonore Davidoff, Teresa Doherty, David Doughan, Iris Dove, Lis Evans, Edward Fenton, Imogen Forster, Michael Gaum, Jennian Geddes, Myrna Goode, June Hannam, Wendell V. Harris, John Havard, Ann Heilmann, Fred Hunter, Bob Jones, Ann Keen, David Lazell, Marian Löffler, Jen Llywelyn, Alan Maizels, Dominique Marshall, Kate Murphy, Nancy Nichols, Sue Nott, Richard O'Riordon, Sowon Park, Mark Pottle, Ellen Ross, Dorothy Sheridan, Kathy Stansfield, Naomi Symes, Malcolm Taylor, Linda Walker, the late Ursula Vaughan Williams, Stephanie Ward, Revd. Juliet Woollcombe, Kathy Young. Special thanks are due to Liz Bellamy for photographic work and to the fine biographers Sheila Rowbotham and Judith P. Zinsser for their valuable advice.

I am grateful to my readers and to Emma Brennan and the team at Manchester University Press. Finally, thanks to the Universities of Aberystwyth, Cambridge, Cincinnati, Hull, Keele, New Mexico and Southern California where I have tried out some of my ideas about Evelyn Sharp.

Angela V. John, Pembrokeshire, Wales
(www.angelavjohn.com)

List of abbreviations

DORA	Defence of the Realm Act
EFDS	English Folk Dance Society
EFDSS	English Folk Dance and Song Society
FEWVRC	Friends Emergency and War Victims Relief Committee
NCCL	National Council for Civil Liberties
NUWSS	National Union of Women's Suffrage Societies
PEN	Poets, Essayists, and Novelists
SCF	Save the Children Fund
SCIU	Save the Children International Union
TUC	Trades Union Congress
WIL	Women's International League
WILPF	Women's International League for Peace and Freedom
WSPU	Women's Social and Political Union
WWSL	Women Writers' Suffrage League

Evelyn Sharp's life

1869	Born in London, England
1877	Family moves to Weston Turville, Buckinghamshire
1889	Essay on Fairy Tales published
1894	Moves to London: lodgings, part-time teaching
1895	First novel published (*At the Relton Arms*)
	Publishes stories in the *Yellow Book*
1896	Publication of *Wymps and Other Fairy Tales*
1901	Publication of *The Youngest Girl in the School*
	Meets Henry Nevinson
1904	Begins writing for the *Manchester Guardian*
1906	Joins the National Union of Women's Suffrage Societies
1907	Joins the Women's Social and Political Union (WSPU)
1909	Lectures in Denmark for the WSPU
1910	Secretary of the Kensington WSPU (until 1913)
	Publication of *Rebel Women*
1911	Imprisoned in Holloway Gaol after breaking windows
1912	Takes over editorship of *Votes for Women* (until 1918)
1913	Imprisoned again in Holloway
1914	Helps found United Suffragists
1919	On staff of *Daily Herald* (until autumn 1923)
	Publication of *Somewhere in Christendom*
1920	Relief work for Quakers in Berlin
1921	Investigating the Terror in Ireland
1922	Famine Relief in Russia (with the Quakers). Starts writing for *Manchester Guardian*'s new Women's Page (continues until 1934)

1923	Investigating conditions in Germany
1927	Publication of *The London Child*
1931	Publication of *The African Child*
1933	Marries Henry Nevinson
	Publication of autobiography *Unfinished Adventure*
1936	Publication of libretto for Vaughan Williams's *The Poisoned Kiss*
1940	Bombed out of Hampstead, Nevinsons move to Chipping Campden
1941	Nevinson dies. Moves back to Kensington, London
1955	Dies in London

Introducing the Rebel Woman

Evelyn Sharp disliked labels. Yet decades of achievements as an author and journalist (the description she chose for her passport) and commitment to social and political movements saddled her with plenty of them. She was called a feminist, pacifist, socialist and much else. Wary of being pigeonholed and conscious that, although sensitivities shift over time, place and specific circumstances, epithets tend to stick, she declared, with characteristic wit, that 'The worst kind of label is the adhesive label'.[1] But there was one label that she willingly and consistently embraced: that of the Rebel Woman.

Evelyn's retrospective accounts of her childhood invariably cast her as the sole rebel in a large, respectable Victorian family.[2] She saw herself as less conventional than the rest of the Sharps, including her brother Cecil who became a famous folk song and dance expert. She delighted in sharing a birthday with the Romantic poet Shelley. Much of her time was spent writing stories, weaving fairy tales about changelings, spells and magic, with princesses who know their own minds. Evelyn felt that her family did not appreciate the ambitions of the modern young woman.

Determined to make a career as a writer, she became one of the infamous *Yellow Book* contributors in the 1890s, insisting that the journal lacked 'enough impropriety to cover a sixpence'.[3] The following decade she joined the militant wing of the women's suffrage movement, the suffragettes, rebelling against both her background and her times, and on behalf of others as well as herself. She was twice imprisoned and gained considerable experience in speaking in public.

Research has revealed a world of ordinary suffrage campaigners alongside the famous Pankhursts. Yet 'celebrity suffrage' has dominated the story of suffragette leadership.[4] The contribution of the less flamboyant but equally committed Evelyn Sharp deserves much greater attention especially since, unlike Emmeline and Christabel Pankhurst, Evelyn carried on her suffrage work throughout the First World War. She was the last woman to refuse to pay her taxes because she had no vote. But it was pacifism that increasingly appealed. International peace and harmony became her leitmotif, perhaps best demonstrated in her remarkable utopian fantasy of 1919, *Somewhere in Christendom*. This book, and the experience of working with students in war-ravaged Germany, helped seal the transition from total dedication to women's rights to a wider humanitarian engagement, though she always remained sensitive to women's needs.

Although she never joined the Society of Friends, Evelyn worked with the Quakers in Germany and in 1922 in Russia's Volga valley where she helped famine victims in harrowing conditions and freezing temperatures. Her practical work had further benefits since, as a well-known writer, she could publicise her findings at home and so help raise vital funds. Her stories and articles for the *Daily Herald* and other papers enlightened and informed. But her writing was not polemical. In place of statistics and preaching she told good stories, invariably laced with humour.

The interwar years also saw Evelyn become the first in a distinguished line of regular contributors to the *Manchester Guardian's* iconic Women's Page. In fact she wrote for the paper, which she saw as the best in the world, for much of the first half of the twentieth century. She had become famous for her 1890s schoolgirl fiction which focused on the daughters and families of the privileged, most notably her novel *The Youngest Girl in the School*, and was described in the United States as one of England's most popular writers of books for young people.[5] In the 1920s she became an expert on the inner-city working-class child. How children were treated became, for Evelyn, a barometer for measuring the worth of a society.

This versatile writer published over thirty books including fifteen novels, many volumes of short stories, the libretto for a comic opera by Vaughan Williams, a history of folk dancing (she recognised the potential for international harmony in dance), a life of the physicist Hertha Ayrton and the official account of a seminal conference in Geneva on the African child.

Evelyn never gave up easily. She remained passionate and principled into old age, deeply saddened by the rise of fascism. She further defied tradition by marrying for the first time in her sixties. Her husband was Henry Nevinson, the renowned war correspondent, essayist, diarist and fellow rebel and campaigner. Her complicated relationship with the handsome Nevinson, nicknamed the Grand Duke, dated back to the start of the century. He was the love of her life. By the early 1940s this elderly married couple were facing bombs and the dislocation of war. Then Evelyn lost her husband of eight years. But she carried on writing, displaying a real talent for shrewd commentary as well as friendships. When the artist Frieda Harris sketched Evelyn at seventy-five, she aptly named her drawing 'The Observer'. Evelyn suggested instead 'A Modern Rebel'.

This is the first biography of that indefatigable rebel. Inevitably, some aspects of Evelyn's life were better recorded than others. Despite extensive research, there is less verifiable documentary evidence available about her childhood and the final half-dozen years of her life than for the years in between. Although an admiring Naomi Mitchison told Evelyn 'You have long been a great name to me', and Vera Brittain declared 'you have always fought so bravely for all the things I care for most',[6] Evelyn was a self-effacing individual. Readers of her autobiography *Unfinished Adventure* could not deduce from it just how much she achieved. Soon after her death in 1955, her old friend Frederick Pethick-Lawrence commented that 'she never forsook her innate humility'.[7] Unlike Henry's triple-decker autobiography – he was a skilled self-publicist – Evelyn's volume is modest, mentioning few of her books by name. She described it as 'selected reminiscences'. Although the 'series of leaps and bounds' by which it proceeds is probably truer to how lives are lived than is the impossibly neat parcelling of most autobiographies and, indeed, biographies, it leaves out as much as it includes. Nevertheless, it is a rich and compelling account by a woman described by A. S. Byatt as 'perspicacious, witty and a very good writer'.[8]

Evelyn's biographer can also draw on a wealth of printed material, including many hundreds of newspaper and magazine articles. Moreover, her papers in the Bodleian Library contain drafts of her writing and a voluminous correspondence that show us other people's opinions and assessments. And there are her diaries. They include holiday diaries that give an insight into how Evelyn enjoyed herself and show how she combined her writing and her recreation. They demonstrate her love of travel. This was also the theme of her autobiography, which takes physical journeys and combines them with the symbolic life journey and her adventurous quest for a better life for others.[9] The diaries reveal Evelyn's curiosity about people and places that we can then see translated into her fiction.

There are two Russian diaries, displaying the first-hand and frightened reactions of a compassionate woman plunged into a terrifying world of disease and death. A diary of the General Strike gives us a fresh angle on a much-documented subject, showing the outlook of an observant and sympathetic woman who travelled round London during those nine days and recorded people's behaviour. Evelyn also kept perceptive diaries of her visits to Germany in the interwar years. They are informative and poignant and can be usefully set alongside Henry Nevinson's powerful diary which also charts German privations. It is revealing and occasionally surprising to compare these diaries with their better-known autobiographies and articles.

Then there are the magnificent war diaries of Evelyn's later years. After Henry's death in 1941, Evelyn took on the role of chronicler. Her diary account of life as an elderly widow in Kensington is a valuable piece of social history. Thanks to those involved in Mass-Observation[10] and other recorders, we are not short of first-hand experiences for these war years. But Evelyn's comments are particularly valuable. She not only possessed a writer's curiosity but also held views that were at variance with those of the majority. Moreover, her diary did not end with peace but takes us into the often neglected second half of the 1940s. And throughout all of this we can see how the writer chose to draw upon certain experiences for her fiction. The diary became in those lonely later years a welcome companion as well as the fascinating personal record of a woman more usually glimpsed through her public utterances.

Evelyn's published work is revealing for historians and literary critics as well as having a wider appeal. Henry Nevinson once described her qualities as a writer: 'Her humour goes to the very root of life, her satire is the reverse side of loving-kindness, her politics are illuminated by imagination.'[11] This combination makes her stories sparkle. Some are now in print again: her fairy tales with their feisty heroines are finding a new audience whilst *The Making of a Schoolgirl* has a modern readership appreciative of her pioneering approach.[12]

In the early years of the twentieth century much of Evelyn's literary work was dedicated to women's suffrage: 'This insatiable Cause'.[13] She took over the editorship of the popular newspaper *Votes for Women* when Christabel Pankhurst fled to France in 1912 and kept it going until 1918. The actress, writer and suffragette Elizabeth Robins declared, in one of the first histories of the movement, that Evelyn made 'the largest sacrifice of time, ambition, health and most of the outward things that sensitive, proud-spirited women prize'.[14] Many of Evelyn's suffrage stories have been reprinted. Her book *Rebel Women* has recently been described as 'the finest collection of short stories written about the daily activities of ordinary suffragettes'.[15]

Her *Manchester Guardian* journalism displays wit and wisdom. For example, in 1928 she remarked that the advent of the bobbed head and artificial silk stockings had destroyed class distinctions more effectively than any revolution.[16] Her more serious reportage from Germany deserves attention since it tracks the fortunes of Weimar Germany from the viewpoint of someone determined not to demonise those who had so recently been the enemy. Evelyn first visited the country in 1920, and returned twice in both 1923 and 1931. These visits make possible valuable comparative perspectives. As Wendell Harris has noted, she was one of a 'prophetic minority'[17] who foretold the disastrous consequences of retribution in both Germany and Ireland. Her fact-finding mission in Ireland brought her face to face with another kind of rebel.

Evelyn deplored warfare and violence but endured two world wars. She also married a war correspondent[18], though one whose attitudes towards war and militarism were as complex and equivocal as were her own views on pacifism. Deeds mattered too. Never afraid to explore in fiction the ironies and inconsistencies of the human spirit or to celebrate its triumphs, she participated in the causes she advocated in print. Evelyn wrote to her friends Bessie and George Lansbury[19] just after women first won the vote in 1918, assuring them that she would continue to hold herself 'pledged to the cause of human justice and equality'.[20] The Rebel Woman was a consummate observer and communicator who became, and remained to the end of her long life, an international humanitarian.

1

From Evie to Becky Sharp

Evelyn Sharp did not have to look far to find the big, boisterous families that inhabit the pages of her children's stories. Born on 4 August 1869, she was the ninth of eleven children and the youngest of the four daughters of Jane and James Sharp. Every child had Jane or James as a middle name.[1] Brothers played a prominent part in Evelyn's fiction and life. The older ones evoked especial pride. Llewelyn (known as Lewen), the cleverest brother in Evelyn's view, became an architect and designed the Apollo Theatre. A Liberal, he sat on the London County Council for nine years and introduced the bell on fire engines. Ronald, one above Evelyn in the family order, was the source for one of her first published stories, 'My Favourite Brother', which appeared in the popular girls' magazine *Atalanta* in September 1894.[2] But it was the eldest son and third child, who achieved the greatest fame: Cecil Sharp, folk song and dance collector.

Their father, James Sharp, was a Gladstonian Liberal and reluctant businessman. His older brothers died young and at the age of sixteen he took control of the family firm, a slate business in London's Tooley Street. His real interests were books, architecture, old coins and classical music. His sons wished that he had hoarded modern rather than ancient coins.[3] Many of Evelyn's children's stories include a clever, absent-minded but kindly father, responsible for a crowd of rowdy youngsters.

Evelyn's mother Jane (née Bloyd) was the youngest daughter of a City lead merchant originally from north Wales. She boasted Italian ancestry on her mother's side and was tall and elegant. Her grandfather had worked in the Army Ordnance Department and lived in the Tower of London. The young Evelyn used to visit her great-aunts there, one of whom, Mary Anne Angell, was 'a supporter of women' and a secret writer of fairy tales.[4] Evelyn enjoyed watching people's reactions when Mrs Sharp used to tell her daughter 'You grow more like an Angell every day'.

Quintessentially Victorian in her attitudes and accomplishments, Jane Sharp excelled at modelling wax flowers. Her husband's interests and politics differed from hers but Evelyn was convinced that their marriage was a happy one. Jane Sharp had eleven children in eighteen years with gaps of only one or two years between all but the two youngest children. So she must have had little time or energy to pursue wider interests. She was twenty-six when she married and had her last child in her late forties.[5] The family lived in a large white Georgian house half-way up Denmark Hill in south London. Evelyn suspected that her mother liked the location because it was fashionable and that her father tolerated it since Ruskin lived there.

In 1869 James Sharp persuaded his wife that they should travel on the continent. They did so, accompanied by eight children under thirteen. Evelyn was a tiny baby. Most of the first year of her life was spent in Europe, an appropriate start to a life full of travel and adventure. Evelyn later called this it a 'grand tour of my infancy'.[6] But tragedy struck the family not long after leaving England. In Paris, a few weeks before the outbreak of the Franco-Prussian War, five-year-old Oswald died of croup (another child, Neville, had earlier died in infancy). Yet after burying this 'fine little fellow' in Père Lachaise cemetery and sending the older children home, the Sharps kept going, through France and into Germany. Little Evie, as she was known, came too:

> a mere lump of animated putty, over-dressed in unhygienic clothes, probably hated for the strength of my lungs wherever I went, and almost certainly one of the most expensive items in the hotel bills'.[7]

With them was the faithful Nurse, Eliza Brown. Evelyn's collection of stories called *Lessons* was dedicated to her.[8] She became Evelyn's lodestone and stayed with the family until she died aged ninety-three. In the 1920s Evelyn recalled that her death left 'a blank that no affection or loyalty from any other friend could ever fill'.[9] In a family where the nursery seemed to form a world of its own and where Evelyn was dominated by boys, it was fortunate that her strict but kind nurse won approval.

The family firm had been left in the hands of a manager. It folded soon after the family returned from abroad. The Sharps now rented 84 Cornwall Gardens, a substantial six-storey corner building. Overlooking a small park, its Ionic columns and imposing front entrance commanded respect. Looking back (in the 1920s) on her childhood, Evelyn painted a picture of an austere, regimented home life where young children were not much seen by parents and certainly not heard unless they were playing music. Her book *The London Child* opens with a lonely girl wistfully peeping out from the top floor nursery window to the lively world of the square below. Evelyn's boisterous older brothers were away in boarding school for much of the year. The younger ones were too small for company but she was too young to join her older sisters' activities. As she put it, 'the Victorian family fell by sheer force of numbers into groups'[10]. She had the misfortune to head the youngest group comprised of little Sharp boys. 'God knows', she wrote years later, 'you can be lonely in a large family'.[11]

There were, though, occasional childhood treats such as Hengler's circus, the pantomime at Drury Lane, an annual visit to the Crystal Palace and instructive lectures at Regent Street Polytechnic on topics such as turning the cocoa pod into chocolate. Most cherished by the imaginative youngster who loved fairy tales were the trips to the Egyptian Hall of Mystery in Piccadilly to see the magician. And in the summer a month was spent in the care of Nurse at Brighton with Evelyn's two little brothers. Later came holidays when the whole family decamped to a country house. But most of the time young Evie, with hair in plaits and dressed in hated blue serge with black worsted stockings, was taught by sisters Ethel and Bertha. 'Our Eldest', as Mabel was known, shouldered responsibility in a family where her mother was pregnant for much of the time. Mabel was charged with overseeing the children's spiritual state and took her duties very seriously, teaching Bible stories on Sunday afternoons.

Then came a significant break. When Evelyn was twelve she went to Strathallan House School in nearby Bolton Gardens, becoming a boarder for her last four terms since her restless father had moved the family to Buckinghamshire. Unlike her friends, Evelyn found boarding school positively liberating: 'the only supremely satisfactory experience of childhood'. 'School was', she wrote, 'the great adventure of late Victorian girlhood, where girls for the first time found their own level'.[12] At home the boys were dominant and favoured. Evelyn lacked her family's musical talent. School enabled this 'book-worm' to study, escape from being the little sister and enjoy the companionship of girls of her own age. Her fictional Miss Strangways, a liberal, kindly

1. Evelyn aged fourteen

headmistress, is based on Miss Spark who ran Strathallan House with her sisters.

Evelyn's sisters attended a finishing school abroad but she had to look after her two younger brothers. This created an unfortunate pattern. Decades later Lancelot and Algie still expected Evelyn to provide emotional and financial support.[13]

In the early 1880s the Sharp family moved to Weston Turville, a village between Aylesbury and Tring with about five hundred inhabitants where they occupied the handsome redbrick Manor House. This three-storey Georgian building was the third Manor House erected on what had been the site of Weston Castle. Flanked by the remains of a Norman motte and bailey, it boasted a rambling garden, orchard and grass meadows; the nearest building was the Early English church. Recalling her home in later years, Evelyn remembered most vividly the shabby schoolroom, the feminine boudoir and the out-of-bounds smoking room 'where men demonstrated that they were men'.[14] James Sharp now played the part of the kindly squire, concerned (according to his daughter) about his tenants' rights[15] and the cultivation of land.

This daughter did not relish the statutory roles required of young 'gentlewomen'. In one of her novels Dolly protests that 'If you're a girl, you can't do anything but sit at home and be expensive'.[16] Practising music and paying calls held no appeal for Evelyn. She deplored the way daughters were expected to practise 'one passage of the Moonlight Sonata for half the morning in order to play it very badly after dinner in the evening'[17] and felt superfluous with three unmarried older sisters at home. She later described these years as 'the denial of everything I had hoped to do'.[18]

When she revisited Weston Turville in 1921, former neighbours at the Rectory recalled Evelyn as a beautiful young woman of about seventeen in a sunbonnet with a book under her arm, 'staring dreamily'. Her response to this romantic image was to stress how differently she was perceived by her family who 'brought me up in a Spartan theory of life in which compliments simply did not exist' and whose 'jibes and snubs' ensured that she lacked self-confidence.[19] Although there were times when she praised the virtues of a large family with especially lively boys, Evelyn became increasingly critical of the strictures of the Victorian household, its parental authority and hierarchies and, in particular, its gendered implications. Mrs Sharp appeared to illustrate well the Victorian lady, wedded to notions of acceptable female

Manor House, Weston Turville,

2. Evelyn's home at Weston Turville

behaviour, just as Evelyn represented the new generation with its hopes for women's employment and rights. Yet, as we shall see, Mrs Sharp was capable of surprising her daughter and herself.

The young Evelyn sought refuge in studying – and passing – the Cambridge Higher Local Examination in history. She spent four months in Paris attending lectures at the Collège de France, staying at a boarding house for ladies with Ethel and Mabel. Whenever she ventured out, she found 'an elder sister planted on each side'.[20]

Evelyn's brothers were treated very differently. Cecil, for example, boarded in Brighton, then spent five years at Uppingham (where Henry Nevinson's son would later be miserable) before being coached for Cambridge where he read mathematics. As a girl Evelyn was given no such opportunities. She began to resent being one of a sex that was told to be good rather than clever and was soon advocating women's higher education.

She was an avid reader of *Atalanta*. This popular magazine had been founded by the prolific children's novelist L. T. Meade in 1887. Its contributors included Rider Haggard, Mrs Molesworth, Grant Allen and the suffragist Mrs Fawcett. *Atalanta* lasted only eleven years but this was long enough to have a profound influence on Evelyn and other aspirant lady writers, Angela Brazil included.[21] In 1890 Evelyn's indignant response to Robert K. Douglas's article on the deleterious effects of higher education on the female sex was printed. She stressed that reading had 'raised my woman's ideal higher and higher, as a being who is neither the rival nor the inferior of man'.[22]

Evelyn participated in the 'Atalanta Scholarship and Reading Union'. Articles on literary figures were accompanied by essay questions. For 5s a year, a reader could have her monthly essays assessed. The best writers were cited in an 'Honour List'. Evelyn achieved this in 1888 for essays on Robert Browning, George Eliot and Tennyson. For three years she diligently composed essays on subjects such as 'Show as far as you can wherein lies the special excellence of G. Eliot as a novelist'. She qualified for the final competitions, just missing a two-year scholarship worth £40.[23]

In October 1893 *Atalanta* published the first of Evelyn's seven fictional contributions. 'The Sufferings of the Artist's Friend' adopted, not entirely successfully, a humorous tone. A young woman on holiday on the east coast of England encounters artists. She is soon carrying easels, bribing little boys to remain in the same position for half an hour, making small girls sit on damp grass and smile and posing patiently herself in the teeth of the wind.[24]

Most of Weston Turville's population was engaged in rather different work. 'Duckers' bred the famous Aylesbury ducks for the London market. Over twenty thousand birds were sent to London by rail each year, selling for 16s a pair. Evelyn had her own links with the locals. At the bottom of the Manor House's drive was an empty lodge. Here, for over four years, she taught village lads two evenings a week for several hours. They sat on benches listening to her Shakespearean readings and tales from history. On a blackboard she set out the basic principles of natural science. Geology was especially popular since some of the young men were working on the extension of the Metropolitan Railway.

Thirty years later a former pupil told Evelyn that she had inculcated in him a lifelong taste for reading. She ended each class by telling one of her own fairy stories. She later claimed that in these young men she witnessed 'undeveloped intelligence' and a thirst for knowledge surpassed only by the peasants of all ages whom she saw 'flocking to the schools' after the Russian Revolution.[25]

Telling stories enabled Evelyn to use her imagination and to inhabit a world free from siblings and society. In time story-telling became story-writing and before long, sitting under the mulberry tree in the garden, she began her first novel. *At the Relton Arms*, for adults rather than children, appeared over a decade later on the recommendation of John Davidson and Richard Le Gallienne.[26] It was published by John Lane's Bodley Head Press which had a reputation for literary trend-setting. Evelyn later described the acceptance letter of November 1894 (for what was initially called *At the Relton House*) as 'the most thrilling letter I ever received'.[27]

'Small, fat and pontifical', her publisher Lane became a close friend. But he initially presumed that Evelyn Sharp was a man and invited her to a smoking evening held by the Odd Volumes Literary Society of which he was president. [28] The book sold for 3s 6d. It was volume XIII in Lane's Keynote Series, named after the book of short stories by the New Woman[29] writer who called herself George Egerton. Each volume boasted the author's own Keynote designed by Aubrey Beardsley.

Evelyn's novel is a comedy of manners about two sons: one a prodigal son spoilt by his family, the other musical and spoilt by society. They are part of a family of eleven children, have an idealistic, impractical father and live in the centre of duck-breeding at Murville Manor.[30] Both sons become entangled with an older forty-three-year-old single woman but neither can match her worldliness and wariness. The musician underestimates his seemingly naive wife Norah (Ibsen's play *A Doll's House* in which the 'doll-wife' heroine Norah eventually leaves home, slamming the door on her husband and children, had a huge impact on late Victorian women writers). The novel takes a wry look at the Marriage Question, a topic that was provoking debate on both stage and page. Evelyn's tongue-in-cheek comments, such as 'morality is mainly a question of circumstance, and largely dependent on the chances of detection', were taken too seriously by some.[31] The *Bookbuyer* noted that its morals were hardly what 'our grandmothers called "nice"'.[32]

Early in 1894 Evelyn had tried her fortune in London, as had other aspiring young women writers of the decade. She later wrote that she 'ran away from home'.[33] Whether her departure was quite so dramatic is uncertain but, whatever the manner of it, she caused consternation in Weston Turville. Several of her stories feature daughters from country houses who leave home to become artists. In 'Susan the

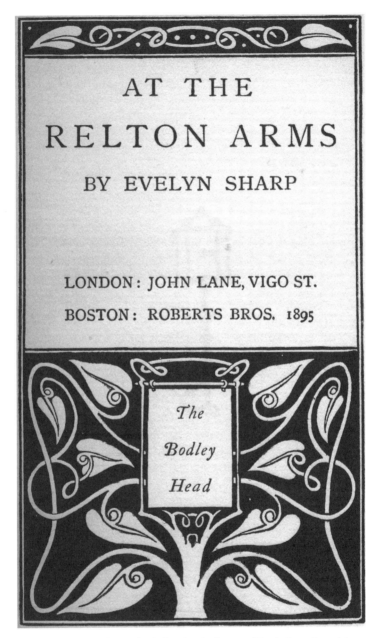

3. The title page for Evelyn's first book, designed by Aubrey Beardsley

Indispensable' the mother of the eponymous heroine admits that parting with a daughter who is getting married is no hardship. Yet she cannot spare the daughter who wants to leave to pursue a career painting. It is her duty to remain at home. Susan later confronts her mother with this inconsistency:

'My dear', said Mrs. Wilbraham, bewildered, not to say a little shocked. 'My dear, going away to be married is not the same thing as going away to be a painter in London, just as if you were a man! What extraordinary things you do say!'[34]

Evelyn had saved £5 and borrowed another £5 from Lewen – the Sharp family fortunes were now relatively precarious. She secured work coaching an architect's daughter in Bedford Square. Miss Spark also found some schoolteaching for her and hostel lodgings at Brabazon House in Store Street, Bloomsbury. A book of thirteen short stories by Evelyn published in 1904 (all but one had previously appeared in periodicals such as *Temple Bar*) drew attention to the difficult position governesses and teachers faced with young charges and anxious parents.[35] Its title, *Lessons*, had already been used by the famous advocate of women's rights and education, Mary Wollstonecraft. Wollstonecraft's *Lessons* had been written for her daughter, the future Mary Shelley.

In the evenings Evelyn wrote by candlelight in a tiny curtained cubicle with no table. Kitty, the heroine of her novel *The Making of a Prig* (1897), is a country clergyman's daughter who has to learn to share her cramped space with post office workers, shorthand clerks and many other working women from respectable but less refined backgrounds than her own. Meanwhile she teaches in a school near Paddington run by a widow who knows more about etiquette than education. Her classes include Gothic architecture. Evelyn was drawing closely on her own experience. Her personal papers include ten lectures on this subject.[36]

The acceptance of Evelyn's first novel and a story for the most talked-about periodical of the day, the *Yellow Book* enabled her to move to Piccadilly's Victorian Club with its attic bedrooms for professional women, their own reading room and reserved table in the dining room.[37] She was one of its original members. They included a professional singer, a milliner and two French teachers. Netta Syrett, another *Yellow Book* writer, occupied the room next to Evelyn. The niece of Grant Allen (author of the popular novel *The Woman Who Did*), she would become a prolific writer. The young women's rooms were so small and close together that Evelyn and Netta talked to each other by leaning out of their windows.[38]

The *Yellow Book* was an illustrated quarterly that appeared in thirteen volumes from April 1894. The brainchild of Aubrey Beardsley and the American Henry Harland, it was published by John Lane and (initially) Elkin Mathews and perceived as daring and decadent. *Punch* quipped that 'Uncleanliness is next to Bodliness'. Distinctive in its binding designed to look like French 'yellow-back' novels and not afraid to experiment with style and taste, it ceased publication after three years owing to its wrongly assumed links with the disgraced Oscar Wilde. But during its short, significant life it included many of the promising and the prominent writers and artists of the day. Here talented newcomers could showcase their work. Over a third of its contributors were women.

Six of Evelyn's stories appeared in the *Yellow Book*. Her first story, 'The End of an Episode', came out in January 1895 but had been written before Evelyn left home. Its subject was the unusual one of how people react to blindness. In 'The Other Anna', published in the last number of the periodical in April 1897, along with poems by Yeats and Henry Nevinson, Evelyn subverts the usual story of the artist's model presumed to be sexually available. This and another story, 'In Dull Brown' (January 1896), implicitly question presumptions about class and gender based on appearance.[39] 'A New Poster' (July 1895) was reprinted at the end of the twentieth century as an example of fin de siècle fiction.[40] Its targets were self-absorbed men and women in London Society. Here Evelyn exposed social and artistic pretensions. She also derided those who affected to care about the less fortunate without understanding them. Similarly, in the most powerful section of *The Making of a Prig*, she derided philanthropists who romanticised women's employment.[41]

Like many young women of her class and age, Evelyn was however keen to understand a world far removed from her own experience. She did some settlement work in Hoxton,[42] regaling children in play hours with her fairy stories. She also helped the Women's Industrial Council investigate the sweated trades in which women worked for a pittance in shocking conditions. She joined the Anti-Sweating League, another step in her political education.

At the same time Evelyn frequented the social circles of artistic London. She visited (as a guest) the quintessential 'advanced' club for the New Woman of the early 1890s, the Pioneer Club. It made her feel 'almost raffish'.[43] Evelyn believed the notoriety of the *Yellow Book* set to be undeserved and could not understand why some thought the journal indecent. But perhaps because of its reputation and its fate, she later defiantly presented its heyday as a sort of prelapsarian dream of intellectual searching and promise.[44] The gregarious Henry Harland and his musical wife Aline entertained on Saturdays in their pink drawing room in the Cromwell Road.[45]

One tea party was graced with an especially distinguished contributor, introduced by Harland as 'Mon maître': Henry James. Evelyn recalled how:

> He behaved grandly, as a lion should, living up to his reputation for meticulous choice of language, pacing sometimes up and down the room in his agonised search for the right word.[46]

James's short story in the first number of the *Yellow Book* was called 'The Death of the Lion'. It attacked the vogue for women writers.[47]

The Irish writer and politician Stephen Gwynn later recalled that Evelyn had an 'absurdly boyish figure'. But, he added, she had 'brown eyes bigger than grow in any boy's head'.[48] She inherited her mother's prominent nose but not her height, being just 5 foot 3 inches tall and slim with brown hair. But those large, expressive brown eyes were remarkable. A rather romanticised portrait of her by the artist E. A. Walton appeared in the *Yellow Book* in January 1897.

Evelyn and her friends dined cheaply in Soho, drinking wine that tasted of sulphuric acid. They queued for hours for cheap seats to hear a Wagner opera at Covent Garden and attended the equivalent of today's 'fringe' theatre for pioneering and controversial plays by Henrik Ibsen. The fiction of the self-styled Baron Corvo includes a pen portrait of Evelyn as thin, thirty and wide-mouthed. She was 'coy and silent', with huge black eyes yearning for the secretary of a bank.[49] This was a reference to Kenneth Grahame, also a *Yellow Book* contributor but best remembered today for *The Wind in the Willows*. This shy, sensitive Scot, whom Evelyn judged extremely handsome, 'simply hated being lionised'. Evelyn once remarked that he looked 'as if he thought you might be going to bite if he wasn't very careful'.[50] She told him that the little girls in his stories lacked the credibility that was evident in his fictional boys. Grahame became Secretary of the Bank of England in 1898, and even Evelyn's eldest sister Mabel

4. Evelyn as depicted by E. A. Walton in the *Yellow Book*

approved of this member of the notorious *Yellow Book* circle. When he died in 1932, Henry Nevinson's diary alluded to the 'real love' he had felt for Evelyn, claiming that Grahame would have married her had he not felt bound by 'false fidelity' to honour an engagement that 'spoilt his work & life'.[51] In July 1899 Grahame had married Elspeth Thomson.

Meanwhile, Lane sought in vain to partner Evelyn with the *Yellow Book* poet William Watson. Given her surname, her literary friends had chosen for her nickname that of Thackeray's heroine, so she was now known as Becky.[52] She accompanied the Harlands and Kenneth Grahame to Brussels one Christmas and to Boulogne the following year. Several summer holidays were spent in Dieppe, meeting friends like Ella D'Arcy (Harland's factotum and, along with him, the *Yellow Book*'s most frequent contributor). It was a world away from Weston Turville, with residents such as the artist Walter Sickert and a 'lovely personage' dressed in blue linen who called himself 'Narcisse'.[53] Evelyn stayed with her friends the Hannays (whose children she taught) at a villa by the castle. But 'The most exquisite of them all' was Max Beerbohm, 'without whom', she wrote, 'Dieppe would have been mere Brighton'.[54]

Evelyn, the illustrator Mabel Dearmer – a 'brilliant creature with flaming red-gold hair' – and her husband, the Rev. Percy Dearmer, spent a month cycling through Normandy.[55] Evelyn also stayed with the Dearmers at several country rectories in the mid-1890s, usually accompanied by Laurence Housman and the socialist writer Jo Clayton who would be a good friend in years to come. Percy Dearmer was writing about Gothic architecture and Anglican ritual, and Evelyn cycled with him in search of churches. One long journey in 1897 took them from Somerset to Reading by bicycle.

In these years Evelyn survived financially by teaching – every morning and two afternoons a week at one stage – and reviewing or writing middles (short essays on topical subjects) as well as composing verses about children. Her work appeared in respected newspapers such as the *Morning Leader* and *Daily Chronicle* and in journals.[56] She also read manuscripts for the Bodley Head. One was called *Journalism for Women: A Practical Guide*. Although it criticised female journalists as unprofessional in many ways, it argued that the situation would change with better educational opportunities for women. Its author was the editor of *Woman* magazine, Arnold Bennett, soon better known as a novelist. He was delighted with Evelyn's 'glowing report'.[57] She was interested in his subject.

In the mid-1890s Evelyn had begun renting rooms. Ellen D'Arcy briefly shared a flat with her in Knightsbridge at Park Side, Albert Gate. But the unhealthy state of the building prompted Evelyn to move to Marjorie Mansions in the Fulham Road. Her younger brother Lancelot joined her and they each had a sitting room. According to

Henry Nevinson, this was not a success: Lancelot drank until Evelyn could 'endure it no more'.[58] She moved to Kensington, renting a flat on her own at Mount Carmel Chambers in Dukes Lane close to the High Street. It was home for over a decade. 'Petticoat' Lane was notoriously slow in paying his employees. Evelyn tried to prod him, relating how her dressmaker 'comes and sits on the doormat here every morning and expects to be paid'. But she was now helped by a small family annuity which supplemented her income from writing and freed her from teaching. Although there were rejection slips, the turn of the century saw her gain success as an author of children's and fairy stories. She earned a minimum of two guineas per thousand words for original stories published in British periodicals and magazines and commanded much higher rates in the United States. Most of these stories then appeared in book form in both countries. Evelyn's reputation as a journalist and author was spreading. There was, however, a price to pay. On more than one occasion at the turn of the century her doctor ordered a rest. A spell in Brighton usually helped recovery.

Evelyn had joined a profession that had transformed itself over the previous couple of decades.[59] Women journalists were part of that modernisation though their numbers were modest. The Institute of Journalists (initially called the National Association) had been formed in 1885. Five years later it had just sixteen women members. Emily Crawford, who wrote for the *Daily News* for fifty-five years and was their foreign correspondent for more than two decades, was the only woman working full-time for a national newspaper. However, the anti-feminist Eliza Lynn Linton (who wrote a novel called *The Rebel of the Family* about a young woman from Kensington) had been the first full-time woman journalist in England in the 1840s.

In 1893 Flora Shaw (who also wrote children's fiction) became the first member of the professional staff of *The Times* and the highest-paid woman journalist, commanding an impressive £800 a year. She had written her first article for the *Pall Mall Gazette* whose most famous editor had been the crusading journalist W. T. Stead (who paid women journalists the same rate as men). Evelyn also contributed to this well-known paper in the 1900s. When Flora Shaw (later Lady Lugard) was making her name on *The Times* as its colonial editor, there were seven women members of the Institute of Journalists on the staff of London dailies. Six more worked for provincial papers and a couple were attached to a London news agency. Mary Howarth of *The Lady* later edited the *Daily Mirror* which began life in 1903 as the first daily newspaper for women. She was one of a dozen women members working on women's periodicals and a further dozen were regularly employed on other periodicals. The Society of Women Journalists was started the following year. It had only sixty-nine members in 1900 but within five years their number had risen to 236. So Evelyn's timing was promising.

Some women journalists, such as Emilie Marshall (Peacocke from 1909), came from newspaper families. Starting as a reporter on her father's *Darlington Northern Echo*, she became the *Daily Mail*'s first woman staff reporter, inaugurated the *Daily Telegraph*'s women's department and was depicted in Philip Gibbs's 1909 novel *The Street of Adventure*. But Evelyn had a little more in common with another editor's daughter, Ella Hepworth Dixon.[60] The seventh of eight children, for five years she was an art critic on the *Westminster Gazette* (to which Evelyn contributed), had a story in *The Yellow Book*, a weekly column in the *Lady's Pictorial* and briefly edited the *Englishwoman*. Although primarily a journalist, she too was a novelist. *The Story of a Modern Woman*, published in 1894 when the label 'New Woman' came into vogue, has a journalist heroine. It underscores the importance of women working together to help each other. The idea of women acting collectively increasingly appealed to Evelyn.

One of the ways in which she and other kindred spirits came together was through the first literary club for women: the Women Writers' Club. It was founded in 1892 above a teashop in the Strand but soon moved to premises in Norfolk Street. The women met on Friday afternoons where they provided 'solid scones, strong tea'. Evelyn later recalled the initial welcome they gave to an 'unknown country mouse'.[61] For a guinea a year members had a meeting place, a reference library and writing materials. They also held dinners. Its first president was the popular novelist Henrietta Stannard who also owned and edited an illustrated penny weekly for women.[62]

Lacking family contacts in the trade, Evelyn had come to journalism via fiction. Four years after she had taken the plunge and left home for London, the 'School of Journalism' section of *Atalanta* magazine, started by Nora Vynne, told how girls might elect to try their fortune in London or 'make a tentative venture from a quiet country home'.[63] Evelyn had bravely done both though her home had never been quiet. *Atalanta* was cautious about such methods, however, recommending instead that an article be submitted to the local paper on a local subject. Evelyn had not taken that path. Neither had she attended one of the new journalism schools such as the London School of Journalism. Her route to success and to writing for national papers was through her own publications. She poured out spirited fairy tales and books for and about children. Small numbers of women were now at last getting some opportunities in higher as well as secondary education. But Evelyn Sharp's literary career was based on only three years of formal schooling.

2

Writing for the young

Evelyn's first publication had been not a modern story for the *Yellow Book* but a defence of traditional fairy tales. 'Fairy Tales. As They Are, As They Were and As They Should Be', an essay of seven pages, was published in 1889 when she was twenty.[1] Somewhat conservative in its approach, this essay nevertheless made clear her conviction that imagination and a sense of magic mattered when writing for children. Evelyn's appeal to what she called 'the marvellous in their minds' helped to make her a successful writer of schoolgirl fiction and family adventure stories as well as fairy tales.

She wrote two books about girls' boarding schools. Shifts in the legal definitions of the age and dependence of childhood, along with the upsurge in popular magazines and an expansion of schooling for girls, made the late nineteenth century a good time for schoolgirl stories. Her first effort was initially serialised in *Atalanta* magazine in six parts from October 1896. It was then published as a novella called *The Making of a School Girl* in 1897,[2] the second of John Lane's six Bodley Booklets (Max Beerbohm wrote the first) costing just a shilling.[3] Beverley Lyon Clark's Introduction to its 1989 reprint hails Evelyn's story as a neglected masterpiece, even comparing it favourably with *Tom Brown's Schooldays*.[4]

Although Sarah Fielding (sister of Henry) had written in the mid-eighteenth century about young girls at a female academy, the editor of *Atalanta*, L. T. Meade, prolific author of school stories about Lavender House, had been the first woman writer to make school the real centrepiece of novels for girls.[5] Evelyn continued this tradition but was less concerned about moral development than Meade and more interested in the transition from the private world of home to the public school.[6] She explored the effect of boarding school on gender identity and awareness. A new girl (called Becky) comes to her girls' boarding school fresh from a home dominated by boys and their preconceptions about their sisters, preconceptions which, as Evelyn knew from experience, would have been reinforced by rigorous training in masculinity in their own single-sex preparatory and public schools. In one of her short stories a father sends his son Wilfred away to 'prep' school as it is 'time he learned to be a man'. Now his point of comparison will be with his own gender: 'when you've been with boys – big chaps like Marson major, who really *know* things', sisters seem 'so slack'.[7] Evelyn showed sensitivity towards the bravado of such boys and their changing relationships with younger sisters. Her early short story 'My Favourite Brother' expresses the bewilderment and loss experienced by a younger sister when her beloved brother exchanges home for boarding school with its exclusive rituals, rules and friendships that effectively mark the end of their closeness.[8]

The puzzled, plucky girls of *The Making of a School Girl* were deposited in somewhat sentimentalised all-female communities that were becoming old-fashioned. They did not reflect modern, large, girls' public schools but suggested rather the intimate atmosphere of Strathallan House, the small, genteel school that Evelyn had attended and loved.

Nevertheless, some of her depictions suggested changing values. In Evelyn's account of the gymnastics competition in *The Youngest Girl in the School*, the Canon, representing traditional concerns, provides the prize books. The humane and, in many ways, progressive headmistress would have preferred all thirty-two of her girls to have been given prizes. This was also a time when German and Swedish methods in physical education were being debated. Evelyn had a German gymnastics master at Strathallan House so modernity is signalled via the hockey playing and the account of the girls' gymnastics. Their display opens with step-marching, followed by orchestrated feats on horizontal bars and vaulting-horses. An expert from a pioneering college (which really existed), Madame Bergman Österberg's Hampstead College of Physical Training, established in 1885, is one of the judges though the German teacher knows about music, not physical movement. There is an accident rather than competition resulting in victory.[9]

It was this second book about a girls' boarding school that made Evelyn's name. Stephen Gwynn was working for Macmillan and helped to effect the first of her many contracts with that publisher. *The Youngest Girl in the School* appeared in Britain and the United States in

1901. It sold for 6s and Evelyn received a 15 per cent royalty. It was translated into a number of languages and was reprinted a decade later in a cheap edition.

This story prefigured later titles by prolific popular authors such as Angela Brazil and Enid Blyton. Brazil was Evelyn's exact contemporary. Her first book was published in 1906, five years after *The Youngest Girl*. Given the subsequent popularity of the genre, it is perhaps difficult to appreciate today just how refreshing Evelyn's stories must have been. Publicity for her later books invariably mentioned that she was the author of *The Youngest Girl*. She became sought after as a reviewer and commentator on children's literature and her earlier adult fiction was largely forgotten. In a telling comment, *The Youngest Girl* was hailed as the first book for girls where the writer 'dared to be manly instead of maudlin!'[10] It was portrayed as a model for writers of children's stories.[11] Nearly all of its excellent reviews commented on what the former actress and writer Elizabeth Robins once described as 'Miss Sharp's invincible humour'.[12] For the *Daily Chronicle* reviewer this 'rich, sensitive, radiant' humour pervaded her book 'like a joyous elemental spirit'.[13] Evelyn's 'delicious irony'[14] replaced much of the mawkishness that so characterised earlier writers of schoolgirl stories. Her use of dramatic irony in, for example, depicting an adult romance alongside the preoccupations of the youngsters, also helped her to appeal to adults as well as children.

Yet both of these stories depict a harmonious world in which relations between staff and pupils and amongst the girls were far removed from the harsh discipline that characterised many schools. Evelyn was adept at delineating the clannishness, intensity and interiority of the boarding school, the consequent liminality of day-girls and the authority of the Head Girl.[15] She explored well the rituals and difficulties of acclimatising to the total institution. But her limited and fortunate experience with the Spark sisters at Strathallan House produced actions and sentiments far removed from the experience of many young women who went away to school. The reader for Macmillan was impressed by the story but suggested that 'three girls of eleven and twelve would hardly have swarmed up a water butt and robbed the Principal's larder to "feed the poor", intending to claim her sympathy and approval next day!!'[16] *The Making of a Schoolgirl* is dedicated to Evelyn's former headmistress, 'A Maker of Schoolgirls', and her fictional headmistresses are remarkably tolerant and understanding.[17] Miss Finlayson, the headmistress of Wootton Beeches in *The Youngest*

Girl, hates punishment and has 'a way of looking at a girl that gener-ally made a friend of her at once'.[18]

Just under a third of this book is set in a domestic rather than school environment, amongst the Berkeley children. The moment when siblings are separated as school beckons had already been explored in Evelyn's short story 'My Favourite Brother'. It was also used in her two schoolgirl books. *The Youngest Girl* confounds gendered expecta-tions as Evelyn would frequently do. Nineteenth-century life and literature show, time and again, sisters left with governesses as boys are sent away to school.[19] Evelyn, however, at the start of the twenti-eth century, chooses a setting in which the sole girl goes to boarding school but two of her brothers are tutored at home.

Babs Berkeley is the only girl in a family of five boys. Their mother is dead. Charlotte Yonge's famous domestic novel *The Daisy Chain* (1856) was by no means alone in depicting large families lacking mothers. The incomplete family often featured in family adventure stories for juveniles. In *The Youngest Girl* the children live with their unworldly, intellectual father.[20] It is this masculine environment that has made eleven-year-old Babs (hovering between the Babe and Barbara) a tomboy who slides down the school banisters, whooping in delight. Evelyn uses irony to depict her character's hopes. Babs harbours romanticised notions of what schoolgirls will be like, based, presum-ably, on reading rather than real knowledge of boarding school. Simultaneously intellectually precocious and ignorant of many of the rudiments of education, when Babs has to choose a topic for an essay she selects a comparison between the position of women in the eight-eenth century and the present. However, adept at distracting herself, she gets no further than the title. Babs's imagination enables her to seek refuge in a dream world of fairy tales. She also learns to make new friends. She adapts to her environment just as her school chums get used to her spirited ways. The youngest girl becomes the most popular girl in the school.

After her schoolgirl books Macmillan published three novels by Evelyn in rapid succession, each concerned with the adventures of brothers and sisters from privileged backgrounds. *The Other Boy* (1902) received a somewhat critical reader's report suggesting that the subject matter was becoming a trifle hackneyed.[21] It had already been serialised in Cassell's weekly girls' magazine, *Little Folks* (to which Angela Brazil also contributed). Somewhat dismayed by Mrs Jebb's report, Evelyn reworked it but held out for – and got – her 15 per cent royalty.[22] She was never afraid of negotiating with publishers about payment. And less than a year later Maurice Macmillan was reporting to the New York office on her growing reputation.[23] Publishers recognised that money was to be made from childhood. E. Nesbit's stories about the young Bastables had been so popular in 1898 that over the next few years she produced three more 'Bastable' novels.

At first sight Evelyn's novel *The Other Boy* offers yet another formulaic tale with the usual tribe of privileged children exclaiming 'Pax!' and 'Honour Bright!' What gives this novel some interest for the modern reader, though, is Evelyn's depiction of a newcomer to the family circle. Tony is an effete, artistic young Londoner, with a limp handshake. Charlotte (who wishes she were a boy) complains that 'If he was a girl he wouldn't be so bad' but that 'as it is, you can't call him anything!' Her brother agrees that 'he certainly isn't a boy'.[24] His courage is eventually and predictably revealed. Tony is best understood in the context of debates about sexuality and a pathologising of homosexuality in the wake of the Oscar Wilde trials which was challenged by progressive thinkers on sexuality. The latter included Evelyn's friend the gay writer and socialist Edward Carpenter, who explored the concept of an 'intermediate sex'.[25] *The Other Boy* seems an apt title.

The Children Who Ran Away (1903) is about orphans who, like a number of Evelyn's characters, abscond in a remarkably safe (fictional) world. *Micky* (1905) has the familiar trope of an absent mother and an absent-minded, liberal writer-father having to cope with boisterous boys (aided, of course, by servants). The mother, whose presence connotes harmony and patience, returns from Australia just in time to complete the happy ending. Most of Evelyn's children's books involve a *deus ex machina*. In several instances a relative returns from Africa. Empire, like mothers in these stories, may not be present but can be assumed to be part of the smooth running of society. Nevertheless, a dissenting note gradually creeps into Evelyn's stories. In 'Wilfred', related from the viewpoint of the former governess, we are shown, through Wilfred's conversation, how the teaching of history at boarding school has made this boy believe in white supremacy. The narrator gently seeks to undermine his jingoism.

Evelyn's perceptions of social class shifted over time but during the late Victorian and Edwardian years her children's stories reflected the exclusive world that she had known as a child. The foreword to a 1991 American reprint of *The Child's Christmas* (1906) describes it as a 'guidebook to the way Christmas used to be' in England and misleadingly explains how it begins after Thanksgiving.[26] The family enjoying the Twelve Days of Christmas was hardly representative of English family life. Evelyn was writing about those she knew best: the English gentry. Most of her stories were set in manor houses. The urban middle class is ignored. Yet this expanding section of society sought acceptance through the emulation of customs traditionally associated with the gentry. So how children were nurtured in wealthy traditional households *was* of interest to those with aspirations.

Evelyn's few working-class characters are thinly drawn and tend to be either servants to the main protagonists or vehicles for plot development. The poor are usually very poor and in some cases signal danger. In *The Youngest Girl* they convey the possibility of disease in the form of scarlet fever though the harshness of this message is mitigated by the implication that good works often amount to misguided interference. Servants reinforce social hierarchies.

In 'The Amenities of Domestic Life', serialised in *Atalanta* in eight parts in the mid-1890s, Evelyn attempted to satirise a young woman's initiation into daily married life in the suburbs.[27] The serial's title was presumably intended to reflect the lack of excitement of such an existence. Here the cook's ideas of manners and customs are much more rigid than are her young employer's. Nell, the newly married narrator, does not know how to run a home and is hindered by her patronising husband. This serial needs to be seen in the light of the popularity of works such as the 1888 edition of Mrs Beeton's *Book of Household Management*.[28] Produced over two decades after the author's death, it had been expanded into a more formal, elaborate commentary on social conduct as well as cookery than in its original form.

In a sense Evelyn was putting her own gloss on prescriptive literature. Rather than telling young women what to do and how to behave, she suggested how the newly married wife might feel and react. Although she had no first-hand experience of such domestic dilemmas, she was pointing to the gap between theory and practice. We also get a glimpse of what became her trademark: humour blended with a plea for appreciating women's needs. Nell soon learns that the less she tries to impress others, the more she is likely to succeed. Four years earlier Evelyn had been deeply impressed by seeing Ibsen's devastating new play *Hedda Gabler* on the London stage with the American actress Elizabeth Robins as the eponymous, equivocal 'heroine'. In Evelyn's story Nell's husband Tom works in the City but writes manuscripts

that are rejected. Nell is no Hedda but she does resent being infanti-
lised by Tom and the reader is left feeling that the future does not look
rosy for Nell.

Evelyn's writings suggest that she took an interest in gender issues
long before her involvement in women's suffrage. This can be seen
even in her stories for very young children. In 1903 she produced
three small volumes of Readers for Macmillan. The simple stories and
rhymes in Book II, for example, suggest what girls can't do and what
boys want to do when they grow up. 'The Other Side' opens with the
words:

> To be a little girl of ten
> Seems nice enough – to boys & men;
> I wonder if they've ever tried
> To argue from the other side![29]

But it was during the Edwardian years that Evelyn's feminism
became most clearly expressed in her books and plays. She wrote at
least eighteen plays, and manuscripts survive of many of these, dating
from the mid-1890s onwards. Most remained unpublished but a few
were turned into short stories or books. *The Rebellion of Nicolete*, a four-
act comedy about a modern young woman artist, formed the basis of
Evelyn's novel *Nicolete*. The heroine shocks her aunt who thinks she is
living with a man. She has rejected the old-fashioned Dick who claims
he had missed her company when he was in the swamps of Africa. On
his return he gets to know her much more traditional younger sister,
Sally, a 'true woman'. He is relieved that 'With all these suffragettes
about', Sally likes 'a man to be a man'.[30]

In 1912, a crucial year for suffragette fortunes and a time when
Evelyn was deeply involved in promoting their cause, *The Victories
of Olivia* appeared.[31] Some of its nine tales had already seen the light
of day in publications as varied as *Girls' Realm*, *Temple Bar* and the
Manchester Guardian. Olivia is the heroine of the first story (almost
a hundred pages long). She, like many women of her time, lacks an
appropriate job. She is a Greek scholar with a First in 'Mods' from
Oxford University – Evelyn makes a point about women still not being
awarded their degrees there – and, when her father wishes her to run
his household, she becomes a governess. Evelyn was well aware of
the irony of an educated woman determined to earn an independent
living having to take on a surrogate family in order to retain respectability. But her employer Mrs Widrington makes it plain that Olivia's

father should never have taught his daughter to think 'if he didn't mean you to rebel'.[32]

Most of the subjects of these stories are young women. Changes in definitions of childhood through legislation concerning, for example, the age of consent, along with the Edwardian discovery of adolescence (usually discussed as though it were a male phenomenon) provided an opportunity to explore territory that was only too familiar to Evelyn. Conscious of the tension between home and ambition for young women, she portrays them as hopeful artists (rather than writers) whose goal is freedom from domesticity.

In two stories young women artists realise their ambitions and are shown as contented individuals. 'Susan the Indispensable', in contrast, has sacrificed a career as an artist and lost Brian, a prospective husband, to the Empire because she is responsible for her widowed stepmother and stepbrothers and sisters. The burden of duty is made greater by her caring for those who are not blood relatives. Perhaps too the use of the stepmother, so often parodied, enables Evelyn to sound a harsher note than if Susan had been resentful of her own mother. Susan is forty-one 'but all unmarried women were "girls" to Mrs Wilbraham, unless they had to leave home and earn their living, in which case they became "poor things"'.[33] Thanks to the intervention of Prue, Susan's appreciative young stepsister, Brian returns from South Africa after fifteen years and the couple are reconciled.

An unpublished script of 'Susan the Indispensable' as a one-act play has a very different ending. Susan (here aged forty-three) admits that 'There had been a time when I could have been a flaming rebel, when I wanted to let loose fire and sword in the land for the sake of making it better for the other women'.[34] But it was now too late. Her future was to be that of generations of middle-class women 'whose spirit has been killed', one of those 'calm and very peaceful and quite, quite colourless' women evoking pity: 'People will be kind, and they'll ask me out to tea when they are alone.' Twenty-year-old Prue, eager to train in medical gymnastics, is saddened by Susan's sacrifice. She maintains that 'a woman isn't free to choose the right sort of man unless she has a career that makes her independent of marriage'. Prue shocks Brian and Susan by declaring that she and Bobby, a medical student, are determined to be together, to qualify and earn their livings, to keep one another but not to marry until they are in a position to do so. She is the young rebel woman who offers hope for the future.

Rebellion is also intrinsic to Evelyn's fairy tales. Yet her 1889 essay had taken a traditional approach, questioning 'delusive discourses in which the old-fashioned magician is an argumentative Free Thinker, and the time-worn dwarf is a Home Ruler in disguise'. She had been raised on the Brothers Grimm and Hans Christian Andersen.[35] Indeed, reviewing Evelyn's collection of stories *All the Way to Fairyland* (1898), the *St James's Gazette* mentioned these writers, adding that 'now room must be made in that select company for the tales of Evelyn Sharp'.[36]

In the same year that Evelyn expressed her initial thoughts on fairy tales, the prolific and versatile Scottish writer Andrew Lang, aided by his wife Leonora, published *The Blue Fairy Book*, the first volume in his series of 'colour' books. Although the 1860s had seen an outpouring of fairy fiction in Britain (often in magazine stories by women), between 1889 and 1910 Lang's series, along with Christina Rossetti's poem 'The Goblin Market', played an important part in reviving and codifying fairy tales.[37]

Fairy paintings had been very popular in Victorian society, from Richard Dadd's fantastic scenes to Celtic representations of folk tales. Evelyn's stories were brought to life by highly skilled artists such as Charles Robinson, who illustrated Robert Louis Stevenson's *A Child's Garden of Verses*. Nellie Syrett (Netta's sister) was the artist for Evelyn's collection *The Other Side of the Sun* (1900).[38] This was one of the four volumes of fairy stories written by Evelyn, each with eight stories and accompanying pictures, beautifully produced by John Lane at the Bodley Head. *Wymps and Other Fairy Tales* (1896) and *All the Way to Fairyland* (1898) are now collectors' items with their stunning coloured plates and jackets in bright green, red, yellow and orange, designed by Mabel Dearmer.[39]

The cover of *Round the World to Wympland* (1902) by Alice B. Woodward had Wymps frolicking round to the back of the book. Described by the *Spectator* as 'delicious', Wymps (devised long before 'ET') were Evelyn's pixie-like creations, little bald creatures with huge eyes living in the land of yellow fog on the other side of the sun. 'Worthy of the creator of Alice's Adventures' is how the critic in *New Age* described them.[40] They travelled on slippery sunbeams and were brimming with mischief. Yet they only mocked those who had not learned to laugh.

In contrast to Oscar Wilde's children's stories, humour was central to Evelyn's tales. A king sits in his study trying to make ice-pudding out of moonshine. He has been trying to do this for the last fifty years.

A table walks. Why else would it have four legs? A page teaches a cat to stand on its head. There is a sense of the absurd along with magic and a confounding of expectations. A relatively young giant of five hundred years lives on beech-nuts so his voice sounds like a mowing-machine. When he tells Boy that he eats boys for his supper, Boy says he doesn't believe it and this puts the giant, who had never actually eaten a boy, in 'an awkward fix'.

Evelyn encouraged children to use their imaginations. When she sent young Geoffrey Dearmer her lavishly illustrated book *The Story of the Weathercock* (1907) for Christmas, he told her that it was 'absolutely ripping'. He added 'I now know that there are such things as fairies and that they are to be seen if you have enough sense to look for them'.[41] The weathercock has come from the Fairy Queen's farmyard and he and babies can communicate with each other. But once a baby starts speaking human words, the communication with the language of the fairies is lost. In Evelyn's stories childhood is not innocent though it is a state that exists defiantly apart from adolescence and the strange world of adulthood.

Long before C. S. Lewis created *The Chronicles of Narnia*, Evelyn invented Nonamia. It appears in the first story in *All the Way to Fairyland*. But she had already conjured up this magic land ruled by a Queen (with the king merely known as her husband) in 'The Restless River' published in *The Yellow Book* with its adamantly adult readership.[42] J. M. Barrie's immensely popular, yet complex, *Peter Pan* was first performed at the Duke of York's Theatre in December 1904.[43] Evelyn too could appeal to adults. Kenneth Grahame praised the stories in *All the Way* for their humanity and the way that each one 'bubbles with wit, tenderness and fancy'.[44]

Evelyn's fairy tales do contain some lessons. We must not be deceived by appearances. Self-pity is a sin and we should appreciate what we already have. Children who respect nature on their quests are rewarded later. Despite the somewhat pious claims of her 1889 essay, Evelyn increasingly took advantage of her subject matter to make political points and challenge conventional wisdom. She did not yet call herself a pacifist but in 1900 she was already questioning what constitutes bravery. For Princess Winsome, the bravest boy in the world is Kit the Coward who understands animals and doesn't fight like other boys.[45] A later story tells of a prince who had been given an enquiring mind by the family witch: 'This pleased her parents very much indeed, for there had never been such a thing in the family before.' He rejects the idea of a perfect princess, seeking instead a cobbler's daughter. Unlike conventional tales, this young woman has no desire to live in a palace.[46]

Since transformation is its subject, the fairy tale was an effective medium for a writer like Evelyn who sought changes in female fortunes. Women's fairy tales for publication date back to the French salons of the 1680s. The twists and attitudes expressed in Evelyn's accounts of feisty princesses invite comparison with modern-day writers of fairy tales such as Babette Cole or the American storyteller Nancy Schimmel.[47] Nevertheless, marriage, albeit after pride and fall, is almost invariably the goal and outcome in Evelyn's stories even though one princess questions why the prince always goes out into the world to find a princess. Why shouldn't the princess do the finding for a change? Evelyn's witches include wise women of the woods and Blarnie the beautiful little witch of the Plain. For five minutes of fun she turns a tyrant king into a mouse and the private secretary he bullied into a cat. Then there is the lazy but likable little Firefly in 'The Spell of the Magician's Daughter' (reprinted in 1987). She has resolved to marry a prince rather than become a witch. But in finding her prince she creates spells that confirm her as a witch and enable her 'to this day' to 'do what she likes with the king's son'.[48]

In 'A Fool's Way with the World' the Princess rescues herself 'by walking out at the door of her lonely tower (as she might have done any moment in the last hundred years)'.[49] Evelyn delights in confounding expectations and subverting her genre. Her one-act drama 'The Green Enchantress', in which a king falls in love with a scullery maid, plays with the Cinderella story. It also derides hunting (which the king prefers to balls) as a cruel sport.[50] Nature and anthropomorphism play a large part in Evelyn's fantastic stories, from characters such as Wriggles, the exceptional tadpole, to intellectual pigs. A serious prince who knows long words like 'isothermal' and 'municipality' cannot understand life and win a princess so long as he does not laugh or see the dew on the rose leaves or the flash of the swallow's wing. And of course there are dragons such as Salamander who features in *The Naughty Little Princess*, Evelyn's 'fairy comedy' in three acts.

This play was performed for three nights in Hampstead in 1907, produced by Mabel Dearmer and starring her sons Christopher and Geoffrey. As well as 'A really nice dragon' there were other characters typical of Evelyn's fairy stories: Malarius, the Professor of Bad

Weather, Dodo the Professor of Extinct Facts and an unmanageable princess, Tormentilla.[51] But Evelyn seems to have been more adept at writing short stories than plays and found it difficult to get her work staged. In 1910 John Masefield commented on a script she had sent him.[52] He told her that she had a 'rare and admirable gift for writing dramatic dialogue' and 'a keen eye for stage effect'. But although there was plenty of action, a play should be 'a thought reduced to such simple terms that it stands out into the mind, apart from its constituents, as a thing with a life of its own'. Here she failed. The theme was not sufficiently dramatic, being 'more of a story than a clash', and the way to Fairyland was made too easy for the characters. There was insufficient suspense. It should be 'the soul of drama'.

The wisdom of Masefield's critique can be seen in the different versions of Evelyn's tale about a blind princess (one of several stories with disabled children).[53] She falls in love with an ugly poet who helps her to see again and to recognise that 'The power of sight is not the gift of seeing' which comes from the soul.[54] As 'The Little Princess and the Poet' the short story (published first in *Atalanta* then in *All the Way to Fairyland*) works well but as a one-act play called *The Poet Whom Nobody Wanted* it lacks drama and appears didactic.

But Evelyn had no trouble getting at least fifty fairy tales published. Most appeared in book form at the turn of the century. A few were published in journals and newspapers in the 1920s. Her papers include several versions of 'The Hundredth Birthday' set 'in the very beginning of time' in the Land of Happy People, which she hoped to publish as part of a collection as late as 1948.[55] The heroines in her domestic and school stories also weave fairy tales. The boys, in contrast, tend to imagine they are involved in historical battles or brave chivalric deeds.

Just as Evelyn's books about families revolve around youngsters from country houses, so too her fairy tales show toys coming alive in the sort of nursery that was familiar to her and other privileged children. Her fairy tales are frequently about royalty. We meet a few commoners in the service of the king and are introduced to some foolish prime ministers and puzzled professors but most stories focus on princes or princesses. They set off on quests and discover an unknown world beyond the palace. They encounter people who are themselves 'out of time': beggars, woodcutters' children, gardeners' boys, inhabiting an enchanting (in both senses of the word) fairy-tale world where all things can be or be made 'bright and beautiful'.

Yet, despite Evelyn's imaginative subversion of many plots and female-centred focus, these fairy tale figures *and* the children and young women of her 'realist' prewar stories were hardly typical of the early twentieth-century world. The twenty-first-century reader can easily criticise her somewhat arch style. Yet these tales need to be appreciated in the context of her period. Evelyn told a good adventure story and her tone would have been refreshing for many youngsters. A review of *The Children Who Ran Away* explained that here was a story in which they would be able to detect 'no sinister desire to improve their minds and morals'.[56]

Evelyn once commented that a writer should approach children as equals and 'make them feel on a level with the author'.[57] This belief and her evident success in writing for young people may have been linked to the fact that, like a number of eminent children's writers, Evelyn Sharp never had any children of her own.

3

Fellow traveller: meeting Henry Nevinson

On Monday 30 December 1901 Evelyn and two journalist friends went ice skating at Prince's Skating Rink in Knightsbridge. They were members of the Ottawa Club which met there twice weekly. On the ice Evelyn collided with another, rather accomplished, skater. This was her introduction to the war correspondent Henry W. Nevinson.[1] Her life would never be quite the same again. Skating, like dancing, permitted immediate physical contact between men and women meeting each other for the first time. Forty-two years later, after Henry's death, the elderly, lonely Evelyn reflected on the 'journey' they began that day 'when he took my hand in his & we skated off together as if all our life before had been a preparation for that moment'.[2]

Nevinson, who had published a poem in the *Yellow Book*, already knew Evelyn's companion Clare who drew fashion plates for the press. Her husband Clarence Rook (who gave the English language the word 'hooligan' after a family name in his East End fiction) wrote for the *Daily Chronicle*. Nevinson was the paper's literary editor. Evelyn also contributed to the renowned Literary Page of this influential Liberal daily and for the past few years had corresponded with and written reviews for Nevinson though they had never met. He found the company at the rink 'very delightful' and five weeks later met Evelyn there again.[3] He noted in his diary that she was 'talking very prettily'.[4] In early March a further encounter prompted Evelyn to invite him to a tea party at her flat. This 'gathering of wits', he wrote, was 'a gallant thing for a young girl'.[5] Evelyn was actually thirty-two but Henry Nevinson was in his mid-forties and smitten.

Evelyn was a sociable person. She had enjoyed the literary evenings held by the Harlands and eagerly attended the gatherings hosted by Wilfred and Alice Meynell at nearby Palace Court, Kensington, home for another poet, Francis Thompson. She now hosted her own tea

5. Henry Nevinson

parties, a blend of old customs and modernity. Her old nurse came to pour tea, a reminder of the correct and genteel world of Evelyn's childhood, whilst women and men, mostly journalists, discussed the latest developments in the arts. Henry admitted that he came away with his brain whirling. At the end of April he sailed to South Africa. As a war correspondent he spent long periods abroad and it was seven months before Evelyn saw him again at the ice rink. Then, just before Christmas, he arrived before anybody else at her tea party. Evelyn was suffering from writers' cramp and needed to dictate her stories so they discussed this difficulty.

But it was in late 1903, after further tea parties and meeting at plays and dinners with mutual friends like the journalist Hamilton Fyfe, that Evelyn got to know Henry rather better. On 19 September, after listening to Netta Syrett talking about plays, he stayed on alone at Evelyn's flat, 'unwitting'. His diary relates how Evelyn unexpectedly told him: 'The first time I saw you I knew you wanted something you have never got.'[6] He left suddenly, but regretted it. She was, Henry wrote, 'both pretty & wise – exquisite in every way she seemed, with eyes singularly brilliant'. That evening would mark an anniversary for them. Two months later Henry hosted a dinner at Previtali's for his *Daily Chronicle* reviewers. They included the journalist L. F. Austin who later told Evelyn that 'old Nevinson was sublime' and had remarked that, despite her 'terrifying wit', she was 'too nice to run away from'.[7]

Both were preoccupied over the following months. Evelyn's elderly parents had returned to London to live at 83 Brook Green, Hammersmith. James Sharp had been in poor health recently and in November died of pneumonia, aged seventy-seven. Sister Ethel had married and neither Bertha nor Mabel could be at home following his death. So Evelyn sublet her flat and, for about nine months, dutifully lived with her mother. Henry and Evelyn now read each other's work. Commenting on Charles Masterman's praise for Henry's collection of stories called *Between the Acts*, Evelyn wrote:

> Of course, the book is like you, I know – that is why I love it so, but I didn't realize how much like everything I know & like in you, till I read that review . . . I've been trying to think what it is I like best in you & I think I know.[8]

She called Henry's 'St George of Rochester' (a romantic tale set on a barge and part of his collection of cockney stories called *Neighbours of Ours*) 'the most inspired fairy tale I have ever read'.[9] He read her children's stories, admitting in his diary that, although witty and sweet, some were a little too sweet and 'overwitty' for his taste. He nicknamed Evelyn the Wymp.[10] She declared that the magician had bewitched her for all time.

With characteristic directness, probably encouraged by the fact that their meetings were now frequently shared with the elderly Mrs Sharp, Evelyn admitted in her letters to Henry how much she cared for him. When he away giving lectures on Macedonia, she wrote: 'I think if you had gone away for a whole year just now I sh. have given up all hope & wanted to die. You do make beautiful heavenly interludes that keep me going.'[11]

But Evelyn was ignorant of just how many 'beautiful heavenly interludes' Henry enjoyed. She was only too aware that he was married. His wife Margaret, a highly intelligent woman with a flair for languages – she taught for a while at Hampstead High School – had been a childhood friend of Henry's in Leicester. He was the son of a Leicester solicitor though his family had strong connections with Hampstead. Margaret's father was a clergyman, originally from west Wales. Henry and Margaret shared a love of the classics. Henry had discovered his passion for classical Greek and Greece when at Shrewsbury School, and Christ Church, Oxford had developed it further. The couple had married in 1884 and had immediately gone abroad to Germany, their stay at Jena University camouflaging from family and friends the fact that Margaret was pregnant and enabling Henry to pursue his postgraduate study of German philosophy and literature. On their return they spent several years living in the East End of London with their small daughter Philippa. They taught classes at nearby Toynbee Hall. To pay the bills Henry lectured young ladies in history at Bedford College. He wrote stories and articles for pleasure and a little profit.

After moving to Hampstead (where he was based for almost all his long life) Henry became part-time secretary to the Playing Fields Association. He was unhappy in this job and the Nevinson marriage was also in trouble. After the birth of their son Richard, who would find fame as the artist C. R.W. Nevinson, Margaret suffered from what we now know as post-natal depression. The couple had long been incompatible and Henry, at least, appears to have resented his marriage from the outset.

In the 1890s, however, two events dramatically altered his prospects and perspectives. In the spring of 1897, on the eve of war between Turkey and Greece, he seized an opportunity to act as a war correspondent for the *Daily Chronicle* in his beloved Greece. It signalled the start of a long and distinguished career reporting wars from all over the globe. It earned him fame and made him more restless than ever.

The other event was his meeting with Nannie Dryhurst, a beautiful and highly politicised Irishwoman living close by in Hampstead, married to a man who worked at the British Museum. Henry and Nannie probably met for the first time in February 1892. They soon became lovers and Nannie became the overriding passion of Henry's life. His interest in Irish nationalism, along with a wider concern about the self-determination of small nations, was fuelled by her. A number of women seem to have found Henry irresistible. Nannie, who could be passionate one day yet tantalisingly aloof the next, guaranteed Henry's interest. Both partners found out about Henry and Nannie's passionate affair but although evidence suggests that their marriages remained unsatisfactory for all concerned – something it is impossible to judge clearly in retrospect or, indeed, for anybody outside these relationships to understand fully – Henry and Margaret did not part. Quite apart from the stigma and infrequency of divorce in these years, Margaret was from a clerical family (one brother became a canon). Unlike her husband, she was a deeply religious Anglo-Catholic. And, as Nannie was well aware, four children's lives were involved. She already had two daughters, one of whom became the poet Sylvia Lynd.

Margaret appears to have been most adversely affected by the situation. Her autobiography and other publications, for she too was a writer, exude bitterness and imply loneliness. Yet her involvement in the women's movement, most notably in suffrage, supplied networks of friendship and she remained close to a few relatives. She seems to have spoilt her son who became an extremely self-centred adult whilst, in contrast, both parents were sparing in their praise for their daughter who was a talented musician.[12]

On 4 October 1901, a couple of months before Henry met Evelyn, he and Margaret purchased jointly a new home at 4 Downside Crescent, just off Haverstock Hill, Hampstead. It was a modern semi-detached house that seems to have reflected their lives inside it. Henry's diary shows that he had his own rooms there. Margaret and Henry now took separate holidays at home and abroad and, with Henry often working nights, eating out most of the time (often in the National

Liberal Club) and spending many months abroad most years, they seem to have existed as independently as possible whilst remaining nominally married for forty-eight years.

Margaret was already a school manager and within a few years was putting considerable energy into a new commitment as a Poor Law Guardian for Hampstead. After the First World War she would become one of the first women Justices of the Peace. Yet because the sources are heavily weighted – Margaret left nothing comparable to Henry's voluminous diary – evidence about how Margaret and Henry navigated their often tempestuous marriage is skewed and anyway inevitably incomplete. What is evident, both from Henry's diary and from that of his nephew John, is that tensions and scars remained in what was a sad marriage. Both partners espoused different viewpoints on most issues and there was considerable resentment on both sides.

Evelyn was taking on a lot. Henry was judged by men and women to be exceedingly good-looking, He offered an unusual combination of military bearing and adventurous international lifestyle with a knack for sensitively appreciating women's perspectives. A sensual man, he was especially popular with progressive women and was easily flattered. He spent much of his life travelling and acted as though he were not married. Apart from a sustained flirtation with Jane Brailsford (married to his colleague Noel Brailsford), and one or two other intense female 'friendships', it was Nannie and Evelyn who monopolised his emotions. Then in 1912, a quarrel with Nannie, in the offing for some time, ended their intimacy. Unknown to almost all his friends, it was this love affair that he called 'the event of my life'.[13]

Henry's diary shows him juggling his multiple relationships. Occasionally his worlds unwittingly came together. In October 1904, for example, to Henry's chagrin, Nannie and her daughter, Evelyn and Jane Brailsford attended a production of *Hippolytus* at the (Royal) Court Theatre. Interested in the arts and 'advanced' ideas, Evelyn and Nannie met on a number of occasions. Evelyn, who seems to have possessed – perhaps as a necessary protection – an element of 'adamant innocence', does not appear to have been aware of Henry's protracted affair with Nannie at the time. She even suggested in 1904 that he lacked the passionate mind, 'I suppose because you are so much older'. But she discovered how susceptible he was to attractive women and how they responded to him.

The passing years did not help since Henry aged remarkably well.[14] After his death Evelyn sent a little notebook to Nannie's daughter Sylvia.

She had found it amongst Henry's possessions and, as she told Sylvia, would not have read any of it had she not initially thought it 'the skeleton of a projected book'. What it contained is not spelt out but Evelyn's words suggest that it may well have belonged to Sylvia's mother and revealed something of her relationship with Henry. Evelyn told Sylvia: 'I hope it will not sadden you: if it does I shall wish I had destroyed it without saying anything to you about it. And what I have read I have forgotten.' [15] Sometimes it was easier for Evelyn to try to forget.

Evelyn lived alone but was involved with Henry for over thirty years before she was finally able to marry him. Quite how awkward she found the situation we cannot tell. Propriety dictated that she could not easily discuss her situation openly, particularly in the years before the war when, despite her association with the bohemian world of the *Yellow Book*, Evelyn was not only identified as a writer for young people but also had to consider the feelings of her elderly mother and other relatives. A woman who could display strong ethical and moral opinions, Evelyn had to accept that Henry remained married to Margaret.

Occasionally Evelyn's fiction suggests some of the tensions in her life. After the First World War she was on the staff of the *Daily Herald* and wrote weekly short stories for the paper. In one, entitled 'Old Age', a young woman and her lover are talking about the chaos in the world. Her elderly aunt begins musing about the man she had wanted to marry when she was young. Aunts feature frequently in Evelyn's stories, symbolising both wisdom and a position from which to survey what is happening in the world around them. Here the aunt's musing recalls a man with humorous eyes and a brilliant mind, with a heart that 'loved the just and the unjust' (Henry was renowned as the champion of lost causes) and a spirit that was 'always too fine to despair'. He reminds her of the 'magnificent rage & despair of Carlyle and Goethe and Ruskin' (Henry greatly admired these writers. One of his finest essays was called 'Where Cruel Rage'). The aunt worries about the famine and distress in the world. Her old lover tells her how some men and women 'have learnt to put things of the spirit first', to care for freedom before comfort, and fraternity before prosperity' (the word 'freedom' features in four of Henry's book titles, and one of his best-known sayings was that 'Freedom, like love, must be conquered for ourselves afresh every day. The battle of freedom is never done; that field is never quiet.'). The old lover declares that they have been lucky for, as they have grown older, they have stumbled upon 'the eternities'.

He suggests that she tells the young folk 'about us'. But Evelyn had spent much of her adult life unable to talk about her relationship with Henry and she ends her romantic tale with the aunt telling the young people that he is a figment of her imagination. They suspect senility but she knows better.[16]

As Evelyn and Henry spent more and more time together advocating issues they felt strongly about, so friends came to appreciate the situation. When Evelyn died, S. K. Ratcliffe explained in the *Manchester Guardian* that, although they were not able to marry for many years, her 'devotion' to Henry was 'well known among her friends'.[17] Elizabeth Robins organised a dinner in honour of Henry's suffrage work in 1918 and Henry felt obliged to point out the circumstances (Evelyn, not Margaret, attended but Robins knew Margaret from the Women Writers' Suffrage League). Henry's diary admits: 'told her of my great difficulty: wh she pretended not to have suspected'. He then dined with the theatre critic and translator of Ibsen, William Archer, Robins's secret lover for many years.

Although, as we shall see, Evelyn was fortified by strong friendships with suffrage friends, she must have found the situation difficult in the years before the war. She and Margaret were mainly involved in different suffrage societies (Margaret's commitment was to the Women's Freedom League and the Cymric Suffrage Union) but Evelyn was a founder member and vice-president of the Women Writers' Suffrage League and Margaret its national treasurer. Both women were speakers at its monthly 'At Home' on 4 May 1909 at the Waldorf Hotel. Henry too was present and said a few words.

Henry tried to act discreetly. Yet the emotional swings between elation and despair expressed in his diary (depending on how Nannie was reacting or Jane Brailsford tantalising him) suggest a volatility that cannot have been easy for those at the receiving end. In mid-October 1905 he started replacing the initials ES with D when referring in his diary to private meetings with Evelyn.[18] He already used coded initials for Nannie (EW) and Jane Brailsford (O). He was about to leave England for revolutionary Russia. As always, his partings were protracted. He spent his last evening with Evelyn. He sent her a farewell telegram and wrote a note to Jane before Nannie came to see him board the *Irkutsk* at Millwall docks. During his assignments abroad Henry would write to the women in his life. On the way to Angola he posted letters to 'The Three & Phil'.[19] Now, he 'Wrote to D, EW & O' before setting off on a long train journey to Kiev.[20] When he told Evelyn that he had purchased a pair of 'revolutionary goloshes' in Moscow she responded: 'I cd love you in anything but galoshes & I do love you, terribly, madly.'

Henry suffered from recurring bouts of illness. He was haunted by the aftermath of malarial fever in Greece, South Africa and Angola. When he was in agony, with rashes on arms and legs after returning from Russia, it was Evelyn who provided comfort. She was already suffering from pleurisy and a dilated heart.

To aid recovery she spent May recuperating in the mountain air of Sallanches in the French Alps, staying at the Belle Vue Inn whilst Henry returned to Russia. This had been his idea. In September 1888 when Henry and Margaret still took holidays together, they had stayed in this hotel. Each morning they had been awakened early by the tramp of heavy boots pacing up and down the bare boards above them and wondered who this crazy person might be. On discovering that the man they had been cursing was John Ruskin (one of Henry's hero since his student days) they sent him a cyclamen and were rewarded with an invitation to his room. He told them how beauty and sublimity were combined at Sallanches and that he liked to view Mont Blanc before sunrise. Ruskin was already troubled with mental health problems and, although a few days later he wrote the epilogue to the final edition of *Modern Painters*, this was to mark the end of his active years. Sallanches remained deeply significant for Henry. He later wrote several versions of that encounter (with hints of Ibsen's *John Gabriel Borkman*) and the month after his father died he returned there with his sister Marian.

With an introduction to the proprietors from Henry, Evelyn was placed in Ruskin's former room with its glorious view. She caused something of a stir as a single and self-sufficient woman and had to deal tactfully with the unwelcome attention of travelling salesmen such as Monsieur Beauvais who 'travelled in scent' and his Swiss rival 'whose interests were in drapery', determined she should sample local liqueurs.[21] Henry covered the opening and lengthy meetings of the first Duma and Evelyn's letters entertained him with stories from Sallanches. But she also wondered why she should have 'only scraps of magnificent happiness at the expense of so much torment & desolation'.[22] In a long letter she told Henry:

> If I loved you less I sh not care whether you were in danger or not whether you were brave or a coward. Oh I am so glad I love some one

who cd never make me feel ashamed of what I have given him so freely.[23]

Soon after this he was back in London and reunited with Nannie. Evelyn returned home. She was still unwell. Henry found her full of 'fears & anxieties & vague terrors of lonely illness'. He wrote to reassure her. She declared that she would keep his letter:

as long as I live. If it isn't true that you love me it isn't true that the sun shines or that my heart beats quicker when I hear you at the door. My heart is only ill because you put a smile into it that will never die, and my heart had not learnt to smile before.[24]

Yet there was a lot to stop her smiling. She hated the secrecy of their relationship, admitting that she would give up all her literary fame to 'belong to you openly & fairly'.[25] Typically, she blamed herself: 'I have brought you no happiness & complicate your life & perhaps spoil your career.' She wondered whether he had been happier before her 'tormenting spirit' came into his life. If so, she wrote (yet did not mean) 'I will really give you up this time'.[26] Henry, who was far away in Georgia – three weeks earlier Nannie had been there with him – wrote in response in his diary: 'It is not true that one love drives another out.'[27]

In March 1907 Evelyn told Henry that:

All through I have wanted you so terribly to be sure that I sh never disappoint you. It is a magnificent thing to be made a Queen by the man who made me a woman. But for you I sh never have discovered the meaning of womanhood . . . I have never done anything to deserve that life sh have given me you.[28]

But there was sadness 'that love cannot have its natural end'.[29] The subject of childhood dominated her fiction. Her journalism in the *Manchester Guardian* included advice on subjects such as children's parties, and its focus on children's lives would sharpen over time.[30] Yet Evelyn admitted privately that 'I can hardly bear to look at a baby now'.[31] Henry commented on her longing for motherhood in the springtime and admitted in his diary that he had a strong desire to have another child, 'to produce a life with a beloved woman'.[32] But Evelyn was almost thirty-eight and both were well aware that it was more than time that militated against her assuming the responsibilities of motherhood. As well as 'longing for the impossible' she was adamant that she would 'sooner go on the streets' than marry a man simply because she wanted a child.[33]

Evelyn came to accept that her relationship with Henry was too strong for her to surrender him willingly. Henry, meanwhile was devoting rather more attention to her. Although the final rupture with Nannie was in 1912 (ostensibly after a quarrel over women's suffrage),[34] since parting from her in Georgia in late 1906 the personal comments in Henry's diary had been dominated by references to Evelyn. He was spending considerably more time with her as they both threw themselves into women's suffrage. He was frequently at her flat and could now telephone her. Her number '1683 Western' sounded, she declared, like a Stuart Rising.[35]

In July 1909 they met in Paris, Evelyn having told her mother that Henry was to 'see her through the dangers of France'. They took an overnight train to Savoy and stayed in Chambéry. Evelyn then travelled on to Italy to stay with her ailing sister Bertha in a hotel at Rapallo. Henry went cycling and found his way back to Sallanches. A few weeks later he was sent to a barricaded Barcelona. According to his diary, Henry was 'Pining' for Evelyn when he received a letter 'full of sad sweetness & love & regret' from her in Rapallo. She wrote how she missed feeling 'your arms around me', adding that: 'Even when you tear my heart in two, I wd be torn in pieces rather than stop loving you'. Henry had a lonely dinner, 'wrote to D & thought & longed'.[36]

Long periods of enforced separation necessitated by Henry's work as a correspondent enhanced his longing for those who loved him as well as encouraging him to express his emotions in letters. Unfortunately such correspondence is incomplete. We do not have Henry's letters though his voluminous diaries dissect his feelings. Here he uttered remarkably frank statements for a Victorian though we are, of course, only party to what he chose to reveal in his daily musings. Importantly, we have reproduced in these diaries sections of the letters from his lovers, sometimes unattributed (though largely identifiable from comparing internal evidence with other sources and facts) but usually given his coded initials for them. Although Henry did not replicate the letters in their entirety, choosing what to record and, just as significantly, what to omit, we are nevertheless permitted a rare insight into an aspect of early twentieth-century living and loving that is often hidden and dismissed as the stuff of fiction.

Evelyn's reality was made more uncomfortable by family problems. In 1907, with a characteristic mixture of humour and sadness, she told Henry 'It is very stupid, the way one gets pitchforked out of the unknown into the wrong family, and it means a terrible lot of unhappiness for somebody. I can trace all the bitterness of my own soul to it.' Changelings and mix-ups were integral to her fairy stories but she often felt out of step with the values of the Sharps. In a story called 'The Wrong Sort of People', set in a village full of duckers and farmers, she discusses the impact of the coming of the railway on the community and how different social groups react to this change and thereby reveal their own petty snobberies. The Squire exclaims that all sorts of dreadful people now appear on bank holidays, and retired shopkeepers and others beneath his dignity try to buy land. The narrator, who had herself once lived in the village, decides that rather than protest and get dismissed as a socialist, it is better to say nothing and hope that there was 'just a chance, a glorious chance', that the little daughter of the manor house would one day 'grow up and go out into the world and meet the wrong sort of people to whom real things happen'.[37]

Evelyn had been close to her father. She got on well with Lewen (she spent holidays with him in the Canary Islands and Normandy) and would later be reconciled with her mother and share some interests with Cecil, but her letters sent to India (where Henry was working in early 1908) told of unhappy family affairs, exacerbated by her father's will. This had named Evelyn and Ethel's husband Malcolm McCall as executors and trustees of a complicated trust fund. The fund was not divided equally amongst the Sharp children, discriminating against Algernon because of his marriage and conversion to Catholicism. It led to prolonged family wrangles. Henry noted how Evelyn was sometimes 'sunk in gloom over the follies of that disastrous family'.[38] In 1912 Algie and his wife had serious financial problems. Lancelot, who had lived with Evelyn at Marjorie Mansions for four years and accompanied her on cycling holidays, was drinking heavily again. Her favourite sister Bertha was dying of cancer. To help bail out Algie, Henry gave £26 to one 'infernal moneylender', paid off money he owed a friend and rent owed by that 'most hopeless of that hopeless family'.[39]

Henry showed little patience with Evelyn's younger brothers who, in great contrast to the older ones, were dogged by problems: 'one drinking himself to death, the other plunging deeper into hopeless debt, driving the mother to rage & helpless misery' whilst Evelyn was more and more upset and worn out by their demands which led her into financial and other troubles 'from which she is never free'.[40] In 1913 when she was also exhausted by suffrage work, Henry privately denounced the greed of all five 'damned & helpless brothers' as the source of Evelyn's 'deep & incurable unhappiness'.[41] He was just as critical of her sister Mabel who disapproved of her suffragette actions.[42] That autumn Mrs Sharp had a stroke. Henry realised that Evelyn seemed to be battered on every side: 'God is hard in way of family, friendship, lover, career & cause, & there seems no outlook of hope.'[43]

He empathised with her, not least because of his own family. He had rejected his parents' Evangelic outlook and faced problems with his eldest brother. Basil George Nevinson had gone to Oxford and became a barrister but never practised. He was an extremely talented cellist. Variation XII of what is known as the *Enigma Variations* is called 'B. G. N.' and was Edward Elgar's tribute to Basil. Elgar called him 'a very dear friend',[44] appreciating his artistic and entomological achievements. In contrast, Henry saw Basil as a failure and burden and had little sympathy with his Tory politics. The early death of his wife led to depression. He lived for years with the other Nevinson brother, the architect Edward Bonney, who became guardian to Basil's children. Basil gambled at the Savage Club, became an alcoholic and died in 1909 aged fifty-seven. Evelyn and Henry also had to cope with the fact that in their own lifetimes their fame was gradually eclipsed by the achievements and public adulation accorded to close relatives: Cecil Sharp and C. R. W. Nevinson.[45]

Evelyn and Henry also shared a strong commitment to writing, inspired by both a love of literature and financial need. Already well connected in the world of journalism, Henry was able to introduce Evelyn to R. H. Gretton, London editor of the *Manchester Guardian*, and to C. P. Scott. Evelyn came to see Scott as the greatest of editors (as did Henry). They did publicly disagree over militant suffrage but Scott told Henry that Evelyn was 'the ablest & best brain in the movement'.[46] Gretton provided some valuable critiques of Evelyn's stories. Commenting on *Nicolete* (1907) he wrote, 'You *can* tell a story. It all goes splendidly, and there isn't an awkwardness anywhere in the telling . . . It's *very* full of life, and of ideas, and of the frightful hampering of women.' He added that he almost felt as if he could 'get on with children now. At least, I'd know how *not* to get on with them.'[47]Gretton seems also to have been aware of Henry and Evelyn's relationship. After Henry's first suffrage speech, Evelyn noticed that a 'discreet lunch' for two had been deliberately laid out in Gretton's room.[48]

Evelyn began contributing to the *Manchester Guardian* in 1904. Women had written for the paper for some years. In the 1870s Rachel Cook had done reviews. Flora Shaw had been an accredited correspondent for the *Guardian* in the following decade and Helena Swanwick who, like Evelyn would soon edit a suffrage newspaper, was contributing when Evelyn began. Swanwick had initially reviewed books then contributed articles on domestic matters. From 1908 Evelyn was writing regularly for the paper's back page. Arnold Bennett told her that he was a fervent reader of the paper: informing her in 1910 that he 'read and copy your articles therein each week'.[49] She wrote features on topics such as 'Dress and the New Drama' (challenging the notion that the modern woman dressed to please men).

In the autumn of 1905 Evelyn began covering events outside London for the paper. Assigned to report from Norfolk on the centenary of Nelson's death, she felt 'desperately inadequate'. Suddenly and unexpectedly, Henry turned up at the station to see her off. 'He took it for granted that I could do it' and so gave her the confidence she needed. Years later he told Evelyn that he never forgot 'the joy in my face' when she spotted him.[50] Evelyn travelled in a very slow and cold train to Nelson's birthplace, Burnham Thorpe. She joined villagers for beef and plum pudding in the schoolroom.

Another celebratory event was held that autumn at Aldeburgh, Suffolk, where the poet George Crabbe was being commemorated by British and French scholars. There at the house party in Strafford House, the holiday home of the literary banker Edward Clodd, Evelyn met Thomas Hardy.[51] Her chief impression of him was his modesty. She admired his intolerance of oppression, evident in his ever-watchful eyes.[52] Evelyn's memoirs also casually mention Henry Nevinson's presence at this gathering! Clodd was a good friend of Henry's and a trusted reviewer. For the previous few years Henry had visited him at this seaside house. But the stimulating weekend of talks and sailing in 1905 was spoilt by the news of the death of L. F. Austin, *Daily Chronicle* contributor and Henry and Evelyn's friend. They returned to London 'in bitter sadness'.[53]

The year 1905 also saw the inauguration of the Saturday Walking Club. Henry and Evelyn were two of its most enthusiastic members. From the late nineteenth century many intellectuals enjoyed organised weekend walks. For example, Leslie Stephens founded the Sunday Tramps. These male writers, lawyers and academics would leave

London by train on alternate Sundays for long countryside walks in the colder half of the year.[54] The members of the Saturday Walking Club explored the Buckinghamshire, Surrey and Kent countryside on Saturdays. Its stalwarts were writers and artists: the Rooks, Norah and W. K. Haselden (the cartoonist), Hamilton Fyfe and Lewis Hind. For the few years before immersion in women's suffrage absorbed time and energy and established new networks, Evelyn and Henry (when he was not working abroad) spent a lot of time roaming the countryside. In town their social life largely revolved around the theatre (Henry wrote a number of theatre reviews) and dining in West End restaurants which had become an important public space for socialising.[55] Although Evelyn and Henry were serious walkers, both the Saturday Walking Club and dining with friends afforded the opportunity to be together in public in a manner that was acceptable. When the club went to Ightham Mote in Kent, Henry wrote that Evelyn was 'charming' and 'the rest unimportant'.[56]

Evelyn and Henry also influenced each other's writing and even the production of their books. In the second volume of her Macmillan's *Readers*, an illustration for the story 'The Man in the Wood' shows three children, and Henry posing as a squire[57] On one occasion he had to alter a joke in the middle of one of his tongue-in-cheek fictional stories about the absent-minded intellectual Mr Clarkson since he found that Evelyn had already used it in her article in the *Manchester Guardian*. Some of their more pointed political commentaries show, if not a similar style, then at least a congruence in thinking. This is demonstrated, for example, by comparing 'Behind the Locked Door', Evelyn's account of the experience of prison in the *Nation* in 1912, with the sentiments expressed in Henry's article 'Convict Souls' in the same paper some years later.[58]

They still read each other's work. Henry had never much enjoyed novels, let alone children's literature, and fairy tales were hardly in his line. *Nicolete* was his favourite of Evelyn's novels for juveniles probably because it focused less on children than most of her books. But they discussed whatever they were working on in the Edwardian years including Evelyn's draft stories and possible endings. When she was in prison Henry reviewed a batch of girls' books for her for the *Nation* without telling the paper that he had written the review. Although some of his poems and short stories contained veiled allusions to Nannie,[59] Evelyn does not seem to have featured in his fiction. In later years she helped Henry with the production of his non-fictional books, and some of their journalistic and other assignments overlapped, most notably in Germany.[60]

Henry always appreciated the sense of humour in Evelyn's stories. He told his old university friend Philip Webb that she possessed 'a peculiar humour, unexpected, stringent, keen without poison'. But he added, 'above all she is a supreme rebel against injustice'.[61] Several pages of the chapter on women's suffrage in his memoirs are devoted to her contribution to the movement. Here he praises the 'very gallant and wise' band of women who worked and suffered for the cause but, he declares, 'Evelyn Sharp will always be counted among the highest of that band' (one reviewer of her suffrage stories even dubbed her 'the war correspondent of militant suffragism').[62] It was women's suffrage that really brought Evelyn and Henry closer together. When, as Evelyn put it, 'that destructive campaign crashed into my life' its effect was profound and lasting.[63]

4

Words in Deed: women's suffrage

A successful woman artist who had been an opponent of votes for women realises that they are needed after all. She asks another artist, a friend now working for the suffragettes, how this conversion will affect her: 'Shall I feel glad soon, Hebe?' In response Hebe tears up papers savagely and flings the bits at a waste paper basket. 'Glad?' she echoes, 'It's going to drag you in two and tear you to pieces and break up your happiness in little pieces.'[1]

In this short story of 1913 Evelyn suggested something of the effect that women's suffrage had on her own life and her work. On 25 October 1906 she had taken a train to Tunbridge Wells. Her task was to report for the *Manchester Guardian* on the annual conference of the National Union of Women Workers (which became the National Council of Women). Mrs Millicent Fawcett, leader of the largest British women's suffrage organisation, the National Union of Women's Suffrage Societies (NUWSS) was its vice-president. That conference was to change Evelyn's life.[2]

The scene had been set in London. When the Prime Minister, Campbell-Bannerman, had refused to pledge the Liberal government to introduce Votes for Women in the new Parliament, a group of women protested in the lobby. Eleven were arrested, including a friend of Evelyn's, Mrs Cobden-Sanderson. They were charged with obstruction. The novelist and former actress Elizabeth Robins wanted to attend their court hearing but this was not permitted. She was then shocked to discover at the Tunbridge Wells conference that the audience of rather genteel ladies, Evelyn included, accepted the 'flagrantly untrue' accounts in the morning newspapers which had described the women as 'wild and hysterical'. Elizabeth Robins was a recent convert to the cause and sufficiently outraged to step on to the stage and make an unscripted intervention on behalf of these 'struggling sisters'. It was her first suffrage speech but this intelligent and beautiful actress was well practised in appealing to audiences. Evelyn had long admired Miss Robins's interpretations of Ibsen. She later recounted how

> The impression she made was profound, even on an audience predisposed to be hostile; and on me it was disastrous. From that moment I was not to know again for twelve years, if indeed ever again, what it meant to cease from mental strife; and I soon came to see with a horrible clarity why I had always hitherto shunned causes.[3]

Evelyn joined the moderate NUWSS whose supporters were known as suffragists. But within a few months, her recognition of the urgent need to effect change meant that she joined instead the Pankhursts' Women's Social and Political Union (WSPU). Despite a title that did not mention suffrage, these suffragettes became increasingly committed to militancy, thereby attracting most contemporary and historical attention. Their slogan was 'Deeds not Words'. Recognising none the less the essential and 'magnificent preparatory work' of the moderate constitutionalists, Evelyn neatly summed up the difference between suffragists and suffragettes. Suffragists had waited and worked for so long that they felt they could wait a little longer. Suffragettes who had become 'suddenly aware of an imperative need, could not wait another minute'.[4]

Evelyn's natural inclination was to support her father's party, the Liberal Party. She had canvassed for them and saw women's suffrage as part of the battle against injustice and intrinsic to 'the basic principles of Liberalism'.[5] Yet she and many others were alienated by the party's prevarication. This was compounded by the evident hostility of the Liberal leader, H. H. Asquith, who became prime minister in 1908. Evelyn now described herself as a 'some-time Liberal woman who is anxious to work again for her party as soon as it gives her the power to do so effectually'.[6]

Evelyn had delivered her maiden speech for the WSPU at Fulham Town Hall in January 1907. The tables were turned and Elizabeth Robins was in the audience. Robins's praise was appreciated, not least because many attending supported the left-wing Social Democratic Federation, more sympathetic to the extension of the vote to adults over twenty-one than to women on the same limited terms as men (the WSPU policy). Evelyn's task was made especially difficult since her speech followed one by Christabel Pankhurst who made no concession to the left-wingers' predilections and effectively drove her audience 'to a frenzy'.[7] Evelyn's approach was different. Although terrified by public speaking – her autobiography refers to 'that cold feeling at the pit of the stomach'[8] – she used humour to disarm her audiences in the many talks she gave across Britain.

Hugh Brown of Paisley wrote to tell her that she upset his preconceived notions of an aggressive, manly suffragette. Just five feet three inches tall, her 'Italian Madonna' face and 'half-girl-half-womanly voice' confused Brown. But it was her sparkling wit that unnerved him. He could not work out whether she was a 'meek little lamb' or, describing what sounded like one of her fictional Wymps, 'a demure little imp of mischief who made the teasing of poor old cabinet ministers a fine art and hugely enjoyed the rows'.[9]

It took immense courage for women brought up in Victorian Britain to speak out in public. Evelyn admitted in a letter to Elizabeth Robins that she continually battled with 'a natural indecision and a natural desire to evade public action of any kind'.[10] At rowdy outdoor meetings she was heckled and bombarded with missiles, from live mice to chestnuts and rotten eggs, though she found the frozen hostility of polite drawing rooms just as unsettling. Reflecting on the challenges some years later, Evelyn suggested that one of the women's greatest feats was acquiring agility in clothes 'designed for the feminine avocations of the idler on the pedestal'.[11] Hobbled skirts and hats did not aid the rapid exit. With some difficulty given their own upbringings, these women effectively challenged traditions of womanliness that deplored a dishevelled appearance.

Evelyn became a leading figure in her local branch of the WSPU based in Kensington Church Street. When Louise Eates moved abroad in 1910, Evelyn replaced her as its secretary, retaining the position until the summer of 1913. The Kensington branch was already one of the largest and strongest London branches.[12] Several of its committee members were imprisoned, including Mary Postlethwaite, known as 'Possy', and the surgeon Louisa Garrett Anderson. Both became close friends of Evelyn's.

Her involvement in the Edwardian suffrage campaign was intense and varied. Henry's daily and wonderfully informative diary permits a glimpse of its demands and the toll it exacted. Evelyn addressed many meetings across Britain, from Falmouth to Dover, Cardiff to Glasgow. Henry noted, time and again, the powerful effect she had on an audience. He was hardly an impartial listener yet he was a highly experienced journalist, familiar with the best speakers in campaigns across the world. Moreover, although his diary shows him quite critical at times of Evelyn's fiction, he had nothing but praise for her suffrage speeches and invariably stressed that she was a far more accomplished speaker than himself. Mrs Pankhurst believed her to be one of the best WSPU speakers.

At a Kensington WSPU meeting in March 1907 at the studio of Georgina Brackenbury, one of a trio of Brackenbury suffrage activists, Henry noted that Evelyn was 'supreme', displaying 'every sort of wit & eloquence & surprise & insight'. Like her Paisley critic, he was struck by the apparent contradiction between her appearance and words: 'A strange humorous pathos too, as when standing there so small and beautiful & exquisitely refined she said "It is no pleasure to me to fight with mounted policemen". The whole audience drew in their breath.' He added that 'everyone was overcome with delight & persuasion'. When she was a last-minute replacement at a Queens Hall meeting, 'a sniggering young army man' sitting next to Henry was (for the moment, at least) 'overcome & admired & believed'.

So what did Evelyn tell these audiences and why was she so successful? Like other suffrage speakers, she adapted her words to the particular social composition and location of her audience as well as the exact political situation of the moment. A Women Writers' Suffrage League (WWSL) reception required a style and focus that would not be appropriate for an audience at London's Albert Hall or outdoor crowds in Poplar or Eastbourne. The message for the King's Lynn by-election demanded a tone unlike that needed for a select At Home. Evelyn found the Men's Political Union for Women's Enfranchisement at the Creamery Café in Oxford (chaired by Henry) a very different proposition from Bedales School, the inaugural meeting of the Actresses Franchise League or addressing audiences in South Wales, Wolverhampton, Scarborough, Liverpool, Brixton or Bath. But she knew how to use her story-telling skills.

Like a number of speakers, she used history. She spoke about 'The Womanly Woman of Yesterday and Today'. She appealed to men to help women, as the latter had come to their aid in earlier struggles for the vote, and she cited many examples of this. She also maintained that if boys were taught more history in school and knew, for example, about the Norse and Celtic women who had fought with men, they might not be so keen to oppose equal rights.[13] She stressed the need for impatience and appealed to women not to stand aside because they were indispensable at home or afraid of wearing themselves out. She spoke about wages, and prostitution, and explained how women were driven to extremes by inequality. She drew on her sense of humour and on what Henry called her 'penetrating sincerity'.[14] His description of her speech to a crowd composed largely of 'sumptuous low-necked' titled people at Warwick House, London, in 1911, helps us see how she performed when faced with ladies like the Countess de la Warr. The progressive police magistrate Cecil Chapman talked about women's service to the state. Granville Barker followed, reading from notes, then Evelyn

> Swept in like cavalry – very swift, no notes, no hesitation, but modest, hardly moving, hands behind back. Began on the poor & rose steadily to speak of women's present exasperation: how reason alone was no good & all resolutions were carried by something more; how no ridicule or evil treatment can stop it now: how it is easier to do something wrong than something ill-mannered, & yet they go on. There was an intensity of moral earnestness about her that swept the whole audience. Even the antis ceased to snigger. The effect was supreme.[15]

When Danish suffragists[16] asked the WSPU for a speaker, the latter chose Evelyn. She spent a fortnight lecturing in Denmark in January 1909, struck by the absence of extremes of wealth and poverty. She also appreciated the lack of male gallantry so that a woman was never made to feel 'that she belonged to a different sphere' and could eat alone in a restaurant late at night if she so chose without attracting unwelcome attention.[17] Already predisposed towards a country that had produced the creator of 'The Ugly Duckling', she enjoyed staying with families and visiting schools in this 'land of the child'. A grand reception was held for her in Copenhagen where her talk prompted a national newspaper to comment that 'She is not at all like a wild cat'. Speeches were made to her throughout the meal, so Evelyn barely had a chance to enjoy the food.[18] Danish women had gained the municipal vote the previous year. By 1910 this small country with a female population of less than one and a half million had established over three hundred branches of its two main suffrage organisations.[19]

Given Evelyn's association with children's literature, it was appropriate that she became a patron of the Young Purple, White and Green Club, an organisation for those between the ages of eight and twenty-one who supported the WSPU. The club's name reflected the colours sported by the latter: purple, the royal colour representing freedom and dignity, white evoking purity and green for hope, the emblem of spring. Suffragettes were superb and inventive publicists. Evelyn helped devise the card game 'Suffragette'. She sewed banners and red caps of liberty in Sylvia Pankhurst's Bayswater studio, and was a founding member and vice-president of the WWSL. Elizabeth Robins was its president.

Evelyn's suffrage experiences were used in her short stories. *Rebel Women* was published in 1910. It brought together in fourteen revealing vignettes the mundane, yet extraordinary, lives of suffragettes.[20] Evelyn tells tales of the unexpected. We see a working-class mother and lady writer making common cause and a little rebel who seizes the moment to join the boys in her own version of cricket. The stories warn us never to jump to conclusions or judge people by appearance. At political meetings the ones to watch are not necessarily those dressed in purple, white and green but the quiet ones in black and grey (Evelyn often wore a grey dress edged with pink), carefully waiting for their opportunities. In 'Shaking Hands with the Middle Ages' it is the unassuming woman in black, ignored by the stewards, who interrupts the ministerial oration: 'The woman who had never been to a political meeting till she went to be thrown out of one.'

In a study of feminism, modernism and the Edwardian novel called *Rebel Women*, Jane Eldridge Miller suggests that by writing in the third person Evelyn dilutes the full effect of militant tactics.[21] Yet her method succeeds in demonstrating that the suffragette could be anyone. Not naming her actors universalises them. Evelyn's book opens with 'The Women at the Gate'. It eavesdrops (as had one of her *Yellow Book* stories) on a conversation aboard a London omnibus. We look down on the crowds in Parliament Square as suffragettes are arrested after trying to enter the House of Commons, a scene brought closer as the woman on the omnibus (from Clapham?) descends to take her place in this symbolic act that drew on earlier radical protests.[22]

Evelyn had participated in the 'Rush' of October 1908 when vast numbers – possibly sixty thousand – responded to the WSPU invitation to join a deputation to the Houses of Parliament. Prolonged scuffles in Parliament Square ensued (about five thousand policemen were present) and there were a few dozen arrests as groups of suffragettes tried to get to what Evelyn called 'the locked door of liberty'. She ducked under a policeman's elbow. Henry is represented in her story as a bystander who speaks so eloquently and knowingly of war and its lack of glory, and declares that the enemy can never kill the idea. Henry had found Evelyn the next day 'bruised & bleeding' and worn out with 'excitement & rage'.[23] Evelyn's *Rebel Women* stories shift the spotlight from the famous names associated with the movement. She recognised, as modern historians such as Jill Liddington and Krista Cowman have done, the need to celebrate ordinary campaigners and the vital organisers.[24] Evelyn was concerned with the fear and fortitude of those committing themselves for the first time, like 'The woman on the sugar-box, who had never stood on a sugar-box before'. Such figures invite a response closer to empathy than sympathy. One of the 'naturally timorous ladies' (who wears sandwich boards in wind, drizzle and mud) explains in 'Patrolling the Gutter' that 'the last fear that rebel women ever learn to overcome is the fear of being thought afraid'.

Eldridge Miller also argues that personal relationships disappear as a result of Evelyn's focus on the political and the public and that she fails to tell us how these women feel about one another or what being part of a group means to them. Yet this was not the purpose of these stories. Some had anyway been written to inform the readers of papers such as the *Daily Chronicle*. Evelyn wanted to explain how suffrage intersected with daily life, to convey ordinary conversations and the way that people worked for suffrage on a daily basis. 'Filling the War Chest' began as a story in the *Manchester Guardian*. A suffragette spends a week collecting money outside a London Tube station. We see the reactions of street hawkers and the gulf between the passers-by and 'those who are passed by'.[25] A review of the book compared her clear-sightedness and handling of society's ills to Galsworthy's writing and argued that 'it is only with Miss Evelyn Sharp that we see the [women's suffrage] movement on its human and personal side'.[26]

Evelyn may have been a well-known writer but she participated in the often unrewarding, undignified yet vital work required by any crusading campaign. Henry's diary refers to her collecting money outside the Tube station. It was necessary to stand in the road to avoid being arrested for obstructing the pavement. She sold *Votes for Women* in Kensington High Street (satchels in purple, white and green held four dozen copies) like the woman in another story who once a week sells the paper and endures the local cranks for the sake of the Cause. Evelyn's tales show how women learned to appropriate public space and gain self-confidence. One tells of the trials and tribulations of opening a shop and offices. A photograph from 1910

6. Evelyn outside the Votes for Women shop

shows Evelyn standing outside the WSPU shop in Kensington Church Street wearing a WSPU sash. This was the first shop opened by a local branch. In the same year she and the actress Fanny Brough opened the Woman's Press shop and offices at 156 Charing Cross Road. The shop was a 'blaze of purple, white and green' and sold many items, including motoring scarves, 'The Emmeline' and 'The Christabel' bags and 'The Pethick' tobacco pouch.[27] Evelyn's experiences validated her fiction whilst their focus marks them out from the drama of other suffrage stories.

Yet Evelyn also participated in the great set pieces that fuelled the theatre of suffrage. In 1908 she was one of the 'horses' pulling suffragettes released from Holloway to their banquet breakfast in 1908 and she and Cicely Hamilton carried the WWSL banner at the National Union's huge procession that June. She interrupted public meetings held by government ministers and was unceremoniously thrown out of them. In her autobiography she explained that so agonising was the suspense prior to the pre-arranged intervention that being evicted was almost a relief.[28]

Evelyn was ejected from the Albert Hall when Lloyd George, Chancellor of the Exchequer, addressed Liberal women at the end of

1908. She felt from the outset that there was an 'electric atmosphere' there.[29] Suffragettes in the front seats removed their overcoats revealing prison costume just before he began his speech. Each put on a white cap. They 'menaced Lloyd George with unwavering gaze and unbroken silence' like 'Banquo's ghost at a feast'. Henry vehemently denounced the chancellor's attitudes towards suffrage protesters and the *man*handling by stewards before he too was thrown out. After Evelyn was ejected from a Battersea meeting Henry wrote that she 'felt a peculiar horror of man, as though she had been violated'. When she defended militancy in the *Manchester Guardian*, anonymous personal correspondence denounced her as a whore deserving a sound flogging.

Evelyn wrote to hostile papers such as the *Daily Mail* correcting inaccuracies and misrepresentation. When one correspondent described a suffragette's interruption of a politician's speech as the 'screams of Votes for Women', Evelyn pointed out that such interjections by men were described very differently.[30] As a professional journalist she was well aware of her privileged access to publicity and she made the most of disseminating her ideas in the Liberal press. Editors of these papers, however, trod warily. In 1907 Evelyn supplied the *Daily Chronicle* with suffrage notes. But in November the editor decided to drop them since they alienated 'Antis' and might be interpreted by some readers as provoking disturbances at public meetings.

Three years later she sought, unsuccessfully, to question the prime minister outside the House of Commons. In exasperation one of the women with her broke the back window of Asquith's motor car. When the *Manchester Guardian* described such incidents as 'unwomanly', Evelyn was scathing. The last five years, she argued, had forced women to adjust their behaviour:

> Denied the right, freely exercised by men, of putting questions at a political meeting, denied the power of petition which we had thought was ours by the Bill of Rights, denied the passage into law, while there was time, opportunity, and a favourable majority in the House, of the measure that would have given us our just liberties, we cannot any longer be expected to remember our manners and forget our wrongs when a Prime Minister, guarded by police walks past us in the street.[31]

When the suffragettes Gladys Evans and Mary Leigh were sentenced to five years in prison for their arson attack on Dublin's Royal

Theatre in 1912, C. P. Scott described them in the *Manchester Guardian* as 'morally insane' and 'fooled and misled' by their leaders. Evelyn was quick to respond. Militancy, she stressed, was now 'an inextinguishable flame' and only militancy could convince the obdurate government that although rebels might be imprisoned, rebellion would persist until its cause was removed. Her emotive language generated many letters in the paper over the following ten days. They included support from her old friend Laurence Housman – Evelyn had helped to convince him of the importance of the women's struggle – and the young firebrand Hugh Franklin. Evelyn had drawn comparisons with the struggle for Parliamentary reform in 1831–32, a cause held dear by the paper's readers, and many letters focused on this. They were interspersed with comments from Evelyn herself and editorial remarks distancing the newspaper from the views of its regular contributor but stressing that she was none the less 'much the ablest of the promoters and apologists for militancy'.[32]

Evelyn was, though, now committed to deeds as well as words. She argued that it was 'absurd and disproportionate to set a few shop windows and a little damage against the damage that was being done to all the sweated and oppressed women in the country'. Women just broke what was breakable but the government sought to break what could not be broken: 'the spirit of the women in this movement'.[33]

Her spirit had already been tested. In 1911 she became prisoner number 11528 at Holloway Gaol. The government's announcement of its intention to introduce a Manhood Suffrage Bill on 7 November 1911 threatened to scupper women's chances of limited enfranchisement through the existing Conciliation Bill. The WSPU resumed militant tactics and many women responded. Evelyn was selected to break windows in government buildings. On the 11th she took action. She placed stones in a cloth bag with tapes enabling it to be used as a sling then smashed panes at the War Office – a suitable symbol for the woman who became a committed pacifist. The early training provided by her athletic brothers stood her in good stead: four out of five stones reached their target. Evelyn was marched off by 'a kind young constable' to Cannon Row police station. Holloway was already overcrowded so the 223 suffragettes were remanded for several days before sentencing until there was room in cells. Their numbers included actresses and musicians and they passed the time putting on variety acts.

Evelyn sent a four-page handwritten missive to C. P. Scott. In it she attacked his most recent leader. This had supported Lloyd George and the Manhood Suffrage Bill. When Evelyn appeared in court she admitted that she had committed her offence with 'a deep sense of the seriousness' of her action. It was, she explained, done 'for women who could not stand up for themselves . . . I quite anticipated I might have to suffer for what I was doing, but although you may imprison me you cannot not imprison the cause that made me do it.'[34] She was sentenced to a fine of 10s and 35s damages or fourteen days in gaol. She went to Holloway.

Imprisoned suffragettes were not recognised as political offenders.[35] 'Justice is for men and privileges are for women' was how Evelyn saw the treatment. But suffrage hunger strikers had helped to force some concessions so Evelyn was permitted to wear her own clothes, walk with others during the exercise period, receive food hampers and 'enjoy' some other comforts. Letters and visits were restricted to one each per fortnight. Henry sent an open letter in which he told 'Miss Sharp' that 'No one can say how we all miss you. Day and night we long for Saturday to come.'[36] She was allowed needlework but not paper and pen. Henry tried, unsuccessfully, to persuade the Home Secretary to let him supply writing materials. To Evelyn's amusement, a copy of *The Home Beautiful* was placed in all cells along with the Bible. In a letter to Henry, smuggled out by a prisoner who had just been released, Evelyn told how it was

> rather weary work sitting in semi-darkness [lights were extinguished between 8pm and 6am] with cold feet & a stuffy head, trying to read, while an endless noise of clanging keys goes on outside, & at any moment a wardress may look through a hole in the door, or fling the door open & say 'Doctor!' or 'Chaplain!'[37]

Later, in an article called 'Behind the Locked Door', commissioned by the progressive weekly paper the *Nation*, she complained that solitary confinement was a misnomer. The authorities never really left you alone. Endless regulations and the 'perpetual yielding up of personality' were annoying, though not as bad as the 'horror of the locked door'.[38]

Holloway also affected Evelyn in another way. It developed her compassion for those who were not political prisoners. Her story 'To Prison while the Sun Shines', set in the police court, compares these resigned and sad people with the spirited militants on remand.

As Evelyn put it, 'It may be a perilous business to hunt down the colour of life for other people; but it is a less hopeless kind of job than hunting it down for yourself.'[39] In the prison chapel she saw these other prisoners clad in russet-brown or blue serge. On the 'condemned pew' behind a screen sat a 'wretched woman who is not going to be hanged but is told that she will be', while 'others sing of the mercy of God'.[40] In her letter to Henry she admitted that she had wept throughout the service. The wardress was kind, thinking she was overcome with her own troubles but, Evelyn added, 'It makes me flame within to see those girls where but for the grace of God I should be'. Most were there for petty theft or soliciting but, she stressed in 'Behind the Locked Door', it took 'courage to rob those responsible for one's misery'.

So prison sharpened Evelyn's social conscience. In 'The Adventure' (1915) a former suffragette prisoner puts a do-gooder in her place by spelling out the economic need that had led a young woman called Flossie Talbot to become a prostitute. Mrs Arbuthnot, the meddling lady, explains that her family and her husband had always hidden everything real from her. Her excuse is that 'I was never taught anything but manners'.[41]

In 'Cynthia's Torn Blouse' (published in *Votes for Women*), Evelyn focused on a middle-class London family.[42] Here and in other stories she suggests that the family is a shell that camouflages a range of values and its members' ignorance about each other. It is Sunday evening and the parents, their sons and daughter are, as usual, gathered round the fire after supper. Cynthia begins sewing. But this is not fine needlework. She is mending a torn muslin blouse. As they begin discussing the speech given by the Home Secretary at the opening of a new training college for working mothers in the East End (reported in the father's newspaper), it becomes evident that Cynthia has been far from the fireside. Having done 'good works' in Bow, the smug speech she then heard at the opening of the college infuriated her. She caused uproar by interrupting and denouncing the horrors of motherhood. For this she was ejected. Her father (called James, like Evelyn's own father) is so shocked and angry when Cynthia admits that she was the subject of the incident reported in his paper that he can barely say the word 'Suffragette'. He can only see his daughter as a child. One brother badly wants to show solidarity 'but the words wouldn't come; so she never knew'. Evelyn adds 'It is like that in families'. But it is the mother's reaction that is most unexpected and interesting. For twenty-seven years she had supported her husband. Yet now she declares that they should be proud of a daughter prepared to speak out. This story, published a year after Evelyn went to prison, should be read in the context of her reconciliation with her own mother.

Mrs Sharp had been 'very unhappy' that her youngest daughter had chosen to earn her own living. When, some years later, she discovered that she had become a suffragette, Evelyn softened the blow by promising that she would not run the risk of being imprisoned. She had kept her promise until, in the spring of 1911, her mother relieved her of this commitment. Mrs Sharp, now in her eighties, had come to appreciate the burden she had placed on Evelyn. The letters she sent her are remarkable. Nearly a hundred years later they read as a poignant and selfless testimony to the love of this old lady for her daughter. Imagine, therefore, their effect on Evelyn.

This correspondence had been triggered by Evelyn complaining to her mother in 1909 that she had never approved of her actions. If this were how she thought, replied Jane Sharp, then it was all the more wonderful that she had such a 'devoted unselfish' daughter. Jane Sharp felt she had 'utterly failed' as a mother. Acknowledging her pride in Evelyn's success, she added that she would 'never get over how you have worked so unselfishly for *every one*! You will never never know how much I have appreciated all your loving kindness to me altho I so little deserved it.'

Jane Sharp was writing in June, the day after the Women's Parliament (the WSPU gathering at Caxton Hall close to the Houses of Parliament) sent its 'Bill of Rights' deputation to the Commons, watched by huge crowds. Their rejection prompted the smashing of government windows, resulting in over a hundred arrests. Evelyn had been present. Jane Sharp was relieved that Evelyn's name had not been included in the list of arrested suffragettes but appreciated the 'deep regret' her daughter would have felt at holding back. She added that Evelyn's father and great-aunt Mary Anne Angell would have approved of her actions. Seeking to be fair, she referred to Evelyn's 'splendid actions' and maintained that every one should do what they think is right and not attribute blame. Yet at this juncture, she could not condone arrest. She therefore ended by stating that now, in 'all you do – except being arrested – I am with you entirely'.[43]

Then Mrs Sharp wrote a letter, which Evelyn would cherish, freeing her daughter from her obligation:[44]

83 Brook Green W
Mar 25th

My dearest Evie – I am writing to exonerate you from the promise you made me – as regards being arrested – altho I hope you will never go to prison, still I feel I cannot any longer be so prejudiced & must really leave it to your own better judgment. So brave so enthusiastic as you have been for so long – I have really been very unhappy about it & feel I have no right to thwart you – much as I should regret feeling that you were undergoing those terrible hardships which so many noble & brave women have & are doing still – dear I hope you will understand all I feel – & altho it has caused you as much pain as it has me – I feel I can no longer think only of my own feelings, instead of yours so much more noble than mine! I have been through [thinking?] so much about you. I feel sure what a grief it has been that you could not accompany your friends: I cannot write more but you will be happy now, won't you? Believe me yr. dear old mother

Jane Sharp

When Evelyn was awaiting trial, Henry bluffed his way in to Bow Street and from there went to Brook Green to report to 'old Mrs Sharp' who received him with 'much gratitude'.[45] Friends sympathised with her over the disgrace of a convict daughter but she now 'reduced them to stupefaction by her brazen championship of the delinquent and of the cause that sent her there'.[46] The rebel daughter had gained a rebel mother. In Evelyn's story 'The Illiterate Voter', a suffragette's mother becomes supportive after her daughter is imprisoned, and eagerly converts her friends.[47]

Support also came from sister Bertha (who had been secretary for the Kensington contingent at the huge Hyde Park demonstration organised by the WSPU in June 1908),[48] and a letter from Evelyn was smuggled out to her. Nurse Brown, who had told Evelyn that it would almost break her heart to see her treated unkindly, remained loyal. She had heard Evelyn speak and believed that women's suffrage 'will be a grand thing for the labouring class' adding that 'the opposite sex get [*sic*] a little too much their own way'.[49]

When, after the longest two weeks she had known, Evelyn was released early in the morning, she was met by Henry who ran up to her, dodging a policeman. Elizabeth Robins, Louisa Garrett Anderson, Possy and a Kensington parson were also there. She was, Henry wrote, 'happy & beautiful but thin'.[50] They had breakfast in Harley Street with Louisa then took a taxi to Evelyn's flat which had been bedecked with flowers. Evelyn was sick all night and felt very weak the

7. Evelyn writes to her sister Bertha from prison

following day. The day after that, however, she was back addressing suffragettes. Small, motionless, with 'only the great eyes burning', she spoke about prison.[51]

From Holloway Evelyn had written that:

> just by sitting here with cold feet, & being given suet pudding (without treacle) for dinner, and going without a bath, and being treated like rather a dangerous child – one is doing more for the cause than all the eloquence of the last five years.[52]

But soon she began work outside gaol which was both demanding and debilitating.

The ensuing months saw more militant action by suffragettes. At 9.30 on the evening on 5 March 1912, detectives arrived at the WSPU headquarters at Clements Inn, London, to arrest Christabel Pankhurst along with Emmeline and Frederick Pethick-Lawrence, three of the movement's most important figures. It was the Pethick-Lawrences who edited and financed the union's newspaper *Votes for Women*. In his autobiography Frederick Pethick-Lawrence explains how, providentially, Evelyn appeared just before they were marched off to Bow Street to be charged with conspiracy.[53] He believed that Evelyn was the one person with the requisite technical experience and political acumen to take over the paper as assistant editor – it was just twenty-four hours away from going to press – and this she agreed to do.

Christabel was, however, not to be found at Clements Inn. It was Evelyn who was indirectly responsible for her dramatic flight since she went straight from the WSPU offices to Christabel's flat to warn her.[54] She got Christabel to sign a cheque transferring WSPU funds so that they could not be confiscated by court order. Early the next morning she delivered this to the physicist and suffragette Hertha Ayrton. The money was paid into Mrs Ayrton's account then transferred abroad. Christabel meanwhile was disguised in a nurse's uniform supplied by a suffragette nursing home in Pembridge Villas. The following day she fled to France. She was to stay in Paris, from where she directed WSPU affairs, until war broke out in 1914. As Pethick-Lawrence noted, it was curious that the police did not follow Evelyn. Had they done so, the next phase of the suffragette story might have been different.

The WSPU's official newspaper had first appeared in October 1907 as a monthly newspaper. It soon expanded and became a popular penny weekly. At its height between forty and fifty thousand copies were sold weekly though it was read by many more. Evelyn had contributed to the paper since its early days. Pethick-Lawrence commented how her articles 'had a pungency all her own without a trace of malice'.[55]

Now she was the salaried editor with responsibility for the paper's production. Volunteers helped prepare the newspaper's layout as well as pack and despatch. Contributors were not paid. Evelyn was keen to get people who did not usually write for the paper, including authors, politicians and ordinary supporters, to offer something. It was her task to persuade them and as a well-known writer she knew many people. As Elizabeth Robins put it, the paper now had an acting editor of 'distinguished ability and rare devotion'.[56] In August 1912, anticipating the release of four members of the Irish Women's Franchise League imprisoned after breaking government windows in Dublin, Evelyn wrote to Francis Sheehy Skeffington, asking whether he could write about any demonstration that might take place when the women (who included his wife, Hanna) were released. If Hanna felt up to it, perhaps she might write about her experience: 'You are always so good in sending us news for our paper, that this must be my excuse for troubling you again. Our readers, I know, would like nothing better than another of your impressions on the subject.'[57]

The paper's first issue after Mrs Pankhurst, Mrs Tuke and the Pethick-Lawrences were arrested and charged with conspiracy had, in place of its usual leader, the words 'A Challenge' followed by a provocatively blank space and Christabel's signature. There were many other blank paragraphs in this issue, signifying the 'suppression by the printers of articles, comments and historical facts considered by them to be inflammatory matter'.[58] It was also a challenging start for Evelyn.

This was a volatile period. There was a miners' strike and, in Parliament, the compromise Conciliation Bill[59] was defeated. Evelyn arranged a meeting at the Albert Hall. Louisa Garrett Anderson told her mother that this came at 'an extraordinarily opportune moment'.[60] Evelyn, Henry and Elizabeth Robins all spoke. Within a few minutes £10,000 was raised for the Fighting Fund.

Yet the time and energy this work demanded, along with Evelyn's own suffrage journalism, left little space for writing books, a vital source of enjoyment and income. She was able to publish only one new book between 1910 and 1915: *The Victories of Olivia*.[61] The suffrage work took its toll on her health. Even before assuming her editorial position she had been exhausted and depressed. She suffered periodically from neuritis and high blood pressure. Good-natured and conscientious, she was easily persuaded to take on extra speaking arrangements on top of working long hours in the office.[62] Henry's diary now uses words like 'querulous', 'worn' and 'downcast' to describe her. When possible, they escaped to the countryside but there were inevitably tensions.

Henry had experience of editing the paper run by the Men's League for Women's Suffrage and contributed behind the scenes to *Votes for Women*, inventing cartoons, arranging the transfer to new printers and writing part of the 'Wanderer' column in addition to supplying signed pieces. Yet men were not allowed to be members of the WSPU and Evelyn was sensitive to the society's needs. Henry noted in early April 1912 that she seemed 'quite determined to keep me out of the paper'.[63] Meanwhile, according to the Pethick-Lawrences, Christabel (who sent weekly instructions from Paris) was interfering unduly with Evelyn's editorial control.[64]

These were troubled months for Evelyn in other ways. In addition to financial and other worries caused by her two irresponsible younger brothers, sister Bertha died in August.[65] A few days later Evelyn was knocked over and bruised after a car mounted a crowded Notting Hill pavement to avoid hitting a baby. And more filthy letters came in response to her printed letters. There was also Henry's final, secret rupture with Nannie – in early September he was writing that he was 'too unhappy to think or live'.[66] The doctor advised total bed rest for Evelyn but she carried on with 'pitiless overwork of herself, allowing no help'.[67] When the 'Peth–Pank' split occurred in October and the Pethick-Lawrences were ejected from the WSPU by the Pankhursts, Henry was covering the first Balkan War in Bulgaria. On his return, at a meeting in the Steinway Hall, Mrs Pankhurst's name raised, for once, hardly a cheer. But then Evelyn spoke. Henry wrote that 'the whole temperature changed' as she stressed how important was impatience. The audience 'was roused as in the old times & transformed'.[68]

Evelyn continued to edit the paper for the Pethick-Lawrences but it soon had a Pankhurst rival called the *Suffragette*. The split caused Evelyn some soul-searching. In mid-October she told Elizabeth Robins 'I am in a terrible position. All my sympathies are with the Lawrences, but I cannot be sure that I think him [Frederick Pethick-Lawrence] right in his view of militancy.'[69] On this slippery subject he had told Evelyn that isolated acts of militancy (in his view) 'calculated to take human life' were both inexpedient and wrong. The paper was to remain 'as militant as ever' but 'would not incite to violence'.

Evelyn remained influential with the Pankhursts though her naturally modest manner marked her out from the confident, stylish Emmeline and her determined daughter Christabel. Nevertheless Evelyn persuaded Mrs Pankhurst to desist from endorsing militancy in January 1913 in order to enable amendments to the Manhood Suffrage Bill [70] to be heard (though the Speaker ruled them out of order). Evelyn remained dedicated to the cause so she continued with

Votes for Women. 'This is' she told Elizabeth Robins, 'a queer crisis for a dreamer like myself to come up against, isn't it?' Robins understood the tension between the desire to write fiction and the pull of suffrage.

Eight months later, on the point of defending free speech in Trafalgar Square and Hyde Park, Evelyn wrote wistfully: 'Who am I to be doing all these ugly things when I only long for solitude and a fairy tale to write. I don't know, I don't know. I only know I shall go on till I drop, and so will hundreds of others whose names will never be known.'[71]

She briefly received some solitude in the summer of 1913 when she returned to prison. Indeed, she was given John Masefield's 'Multitude and Solitude' to read. Evelyn had attended, on 24 July, as a representative of the WWSL, a Caxton Hall conference of women's organisations to protest against the new Prisoners' (Temporary Discharge for Ill-Health) Act, known as the Cat and Mouse Act. This permitted dangerously ill hunger strikers to be released on licence and rearrested without further trial. A resolution was to be taken to the prime minister. Henry and Evelyn were part of the deputation which was headed by Sir Edward Busk of London University. Asquith was away and the home secretary would agree to meet only Busk and not until the following day. Evelyn and Emmeline Pethick-Lawrence tried to address some MPs as they waited in the outer lobby of the House of Commons. All the members of the deputation were forcibly ejected from the House of Commons. When Evelyn, Emmeline Pethick-Lawrence and Lady Sybil Smith refused to leave they were arrested. After Henry had been 'flung out down the steps', he saw Evelyn being led off 'deadly white with indignation'.[72] A photograph shows the tiny offender, smartly dressed, being taken away by the police.

After a night of 'blind terror', Henry heard Evelyn sentenced to another fourteen days in prison after refusing bail. Evelyn's night had been worse. Refusing to comply with the conditions required by the Inspector, she had the dubious honour of being the only suffragette to spend the night in the police cells. As a result of pressure, prison conditions for suffragettes had improved since 1911 but this was not the case in police station cells. On being transferred to Holloway Evelyn found the atmosphere had changed there. With so many at advanced stages of hunger strikes, she wrote, 'you felt that something terrible was going on there, directly Black Maria dropped you at the gates'.[73] The three new prisoners went on hunger strike. Although Mabel Sharp had, according to Henry, appeared at Bow Street denouncing Evelyn's actions and behaving in an 'utterly stupid & harmful'

MORE SUFFRAGETTES ARRESTED AT THE HOUSES¹⁽

.e police marching Miss Evelyn Sharp off to Cannon-row Police Station after the scuffle which took place in St. Stephen's Hall yesterday. Inset—Lady Sybil Smith, also arrested

8. Evelyn is arrested again

manner, Mrs Sharp declared her support.[74] Signing herself 'your darling old mother', she wrote on 27 July to tell Evelyn that 'no one will ever realize, how much I admire your courage in going thro all this suffering for acting up to your strong conscience & principles which as you know I fully share'. But she was worried about the dangers of hunger striking and admitted that 'every mouth full I eat seems as *poison* to me'.[75] Meanwhile, wardresses tried in vain to tempt her increasingly giddy and nauseous daughter to take food.

The prisoners were suddenly released unconditionally after four days. Lady Sybil Smith was the daughter of the Countess of Antrim and mother of seven children. The authorities needed to tread carefully. Determined to stop preferential treatment, Lady Constance Lytton had entered prison in disguise, gone on hunger strike and been force fed with disastrous results for her health. The government could not afford further adverse publicity.[76] Henry rushed to meet Evelyn, armed with red roses and Muscat. 'Then perfect happiness again' he wrote in his diary.[77]

Compared to most of the incarcerated suffragettes, Evelyn got off lightly. She was not in prison for long and never forcibly fed. Moreover, she had support from a group of extremely loyal women friends as well as Henry. In contrast Lady Sybil Smith's husband was so 'cut up' about his wife's situation that she sadly remarked to Evelyn: 'we do not speak of suffrage matters'. In court he had tried to get her to accept the payment of sureties but she had not been prepared to commit herself to a year's good behaviour. Lady Sybil Smith also explained that her greatest friends were 'ominously silent' while her mother took the 'high-principled lunatic line'. She was deluged by phrases such as 'not your job', 'injuring the children', 'not fair to your husband'. And, she added, 'the notoriety scorches me'.[78]

On her release Evelyn, weighing less than seven stone, was taken to 41 Norfolk Square, Paddington, where Hertha Ayrton's house had become one of the nursing homes for 'mice', the released suffrage prisoners. Mrs Pankhurst was one of those who arrived there by stretcher under cover of darkness. Detectives and reporters were posted close to the house. Mrs Ayrton and her daughter Barbara had both been WSPU members since 1906. Evelyn spent a couple of days in bed tended by Louisa Garrett Anderson. Both she and Barbara had been in Holloway the previous year. Then Evelyn ('thin & feeble but happy' in Henry's estimation)[79] travelled to the pretty village of Chinnor in Oxfordshire with Barbara. Evelyn resumed the holiday she had been enjoying there before the recent drama. Barbara was married to the poet and writer Gerald Gould, also a suffrage supporter. In these suffrage years a lasting friendship developed between the two women. Evelyn later wrote her mother's biography. Barbara became Evelyn's executrix. Henry and Gerald Gould joined the women a few days later.

Evelyn visited Chinnor whenever possible, staying at Chiltern View, a porticoed two-storey house looking across to the Chilterns and lovely walks along Bledlow Ridge. Its owner, Mrs Emilie Levermore, had been shocked to see her lodger's name in the paper but Evelyn found that villagers behaved charmingly considering they believed 'we might at any moment blow their village sky high'.[80] On a later visit, though, when a telegram was sent to Sylvia Pankhurst, the village policeman was posted at the railway station. Suffrage militancy was at its height and so too was public anxiety.

After a week's convalescence Evelyn was still ailing. And there were fresh anxieties. In September 1913 her mother had a stroke. Evelyn's brother-in-law Malcolm McCall (Ethel's husband) was dying of cancer and there were renewed worries about her brother's drink problems. Personal concerns were compounded by troubles in the WSPU. Evelyn was now being discouraged from public speaking. Barbara visited Christabel in Paris and, attributing the sidelining of Evelyn to jealousy and distrust, had a 'furious quarrel' with Christabel.[81] When Christabel had first arrived in France, she had expressed her gratitude for Evelyn's knock on her door that had allowed her to escape: 'You were the first link in the chain of dear people that got me here. What memories we shall enjoy together when we have entered into the promised land!'[82] And she had thanked Evelyn for the way she gave so generously to the cause – 'you just pour it out with both hands'.

Christabel was not, however, finding it easy residing so far from home.[83] Henry maintained that she understood that, unlike some activists, Evelyn had a political brain. He thought her envious of Evelyn's position at home at the centre of affairs. So concerned had he become about the direction in which the WSPU was moving, and Christabel's views in particular, that his diary reflected the hyperbole he attributed to her. Worried about her isolation in Paris and bids to retain power, he wrote that there was

> a kind of spy-mania, a terror & blindness . . . She has actually thought we were plotting to extradite her! It is all the nearest thing to insanity I've known in the movement . . . it is like the French Terror, but that power is lacking to behead us all. And here are we ready literally to die rather than let her be harmed or wronged.[84]

The solution for Henry and Evelyn came in the form of a new suffrage organisation. Although Henry still favoured delay and offered to see Emmeline Pankhurst to discuss coming to terms, Evelyn, the Goulds and another pro-suffrage couple, Joseph and Margaret Clayton, believed that further prevarication was pointless and that a new mixed-sex society was the way forward. During December Evelyn and Henry joined in frequent discussions about the new society. On 9 January 1914, with Henry in the chair, the United Suffragists discussed a manifesto. Barbara became its first secretary and the committee, which included Evelyn, had equal numbers of men and women. The society gave a further twist to the many meanings of militancy, shying away from extremism but deliberately choosing not to blame those who opted for such actions. Priding themselves on their inclusiveness and openness (they were non-party but opposed to any government not supporting suffrage), their slogan was 'Join US' and they sought, though did not always find, harmony.

Evelyn became in time the United Suffragists' most energetic member.[85] Yet such changes had been unsettling. There was something of a rift with Louisa Garrett Anderson who had been very supportive and helpful when Evelyn was imprisoned, even visiting Evelyn's mother. Louie, as she signed herself, had written passionate letters to Evelyn, praising her 'courage & single heartedness & clear sight'.[86] It is more difficult to discern Evelyn's feelings for her. She was clearly deeply attached to Louisa and later wrote of her 'considerable personal charm' and 'gracious and beautiful appearance' allied with her strength of character.[87] Evelyn and Louisa had spent summer holidays in 1910 and 1911 at Alde House, Newtonmore, Highland holiday home of Louisa's elderly mother, the pioneer doctor Dr Elizabeth Garrett Anderson (Louisa's aunt Millicent Fawcett and Emmeline Pankhurst also visited, so suffrage came too). Louisa was initially wary of joining the United Suffragists and this disappointed Evelyn but she changed her mind and became one of its many distinguished vice-presidents.

Henry's diary suggests that it was Louisa's close friendship with Dr Flora Murray (with whom she had founded the Women's Hospital for Children) that Evelyn could not tolerate. He even refers to Dr Murray's 'bullying absorption' of Louisa.[88] Many years later, in the 1930s, Louisa visited Evelyn and Henry, and after Henry's death the two elderly women met occasionally in Kensington. Evelyn acknowledged in her diary that Flora Murray had come between them in the past. Her words, written when she knew that Louisa was dying of cancer, affirm her feelings. In turn it seems that Louisa had cared deeply, even passionately, for Evelyn.[89]

But in the spring of 1914 Evelyn was distressed by such 'neglect by friends'. This, along with 'grinding work, divorce fr natural expression of self & disagreement with the paper', prompted Henry to advise her to give up the paper.[90] Evelyn would not contemplate this though she moved from Kensington to a small flat at 38 Doughty Street where she hoped to have a little more privacy. It marked the start of many years in Bloomsbury. Doughty Street boasted literary connections: Sydney Smith and Dickens had lived there as would Vera Brittain and Winifred Holtby. But the new home did not solve personal and public pressure. Evelyn doubted whether the United Suffragists were sufficiently militant and wondered whether she was in the wrong organisation. Henry noted that she was frequently short-tempered with him though never with others. Family problems and illness continued to wear her down. Mrs Sharp was diagnosed with cancer in July and Evelyn was 'really ill & worn out & suffering internally'.[91] After initial hesitation, the Pethick-Lawrences joined the United Suffragists and in the summer handed *Votes for Women* to the society. Evelyn continued to edit it. But the circumstances in which she did this were about to change dramatically.

5

Working with war

In 1914 Evelyn's birthday fell on Bank Holiday Monday. This day, 4 August, was also the day Britain declared war on Germany. Inevitably, the war years had a profound impact on her way of life. Evelyn's fundamental beliefs about war and peace were also transformed. But her active commitment to women's suffrage remained unchanged. It was, though, now channelled through the United Suffragists. Formed in peacetime, they were most effective during war.

Acounts of women's suffrage used to imply misleadingly that the movement was more or less synonymous with the views and influence of Emmeline and Christabel Pankhurst, with militancy giving way to militarism once war broke out.[1] The actions of the United Suffragists show that the chronology of suffrage must also embrace the war years. Just as Evelyn had been a key figure in holding the suffragettes together once Christabel went abroad, so now her editorial, organisational and speaking skills helped the new society to triumph.

The United Suffragists, sporting colours of purple, gold and white, announced their presence in *Votes for Women* on 6 February 1914. Coincidentally, it was on the same day four years later that the women's suffrage bill became law. During those four years Evelyn and Henry were members of the society's committee. In addition to regularly addressing audiences in the big London halls and other venues in and around London, Evelyn spoke in many other places such as Ashford, Bolton and Stroud. Her influence was evident too in the society's distinctive publicity which marked it out from earlier suffrage organisations. Members were asked to keep in mind 'the important truth that a merry heart goes all the way, and that a spirit of comradeship, good temper, and a sense of humour has always characterised the women's fight for freedom'.[2]

It was not always easy to maintain that sense of humour. Evelyn remained at the helm of the newspaper, writing leaders and taking responsibility for the production of a professional weekly until March 1916 when it became a monthly. As acting editor, she had earned a salary but was too busy to continue writing regularly for the *Manchester Guardian*. When the United Suffragists took over *Votes for Women* in the summer of 1914 she no longer received payment, had little time at her disposal yet still needed to earn a living. She wrote to the paper's editor C. P. Scott to see if she could resume writing her regular back page column. The timing was not propitious. War had reduced the space available and rates were decreased from three guineas an article to two and a half. But Scott valued her writing and she continued writing her articles, albeit not as frequently as before.

Votes for Women proclaimed itself 'The War Paper for Women'. Yet it took a very different approach from Mrs Pankhurst's jingoistic press. Indeed, the society lost some members because of its equivocal attitude towards war work. The writer Beatrice Harraden objected to the unpatriotic tone of some of the paper's articles. Laurence Housman, a United Suffragist vice-president, later recalled the 'devoted service of Evelyn Sharp', adding that most who remained active in the cause were pacifists 'or of pacifist tendency, and were suspect to the rest'.[3] Evelyn was anxious to challenge the notion that women had no right to a voice in questions of war and peace because they did not actively participate in war. In the columns of the paper and in her own stories she demonstrated the insidious impact of war on women's lives.

Evelyn and the United Suffragists were concerned about the ending of separation allowances. Soldiers' and sailors' wives were paid 12s 6d weekly with an extra 2s for each child, many receiving rather more money than their prewar housekeeping allowance had provided. Heightened fears about the greater freedom of working-class women and their increased frequenting of public houses in the early days of the war led to calls for surveillance.[4] In October 1914 the War Office and Home Office issued a memorandum on stopping allowances to the 'Unworthy', requesting that the police check whether recipients were guilty of drunkenness or consorting with men. 'Policing' was not restricted to the police. In Cardiff, for example, a nonconformist minister counted local women purchasing flagons of beer.[5] In November Evelyn chaired a Caxton Hall meeting at which Henry, Sylvia Pankhurst and two soldiers' wives protested against the monitoring of separation allowances.

In Evelyn's one-act play *At the Bricklayers Arms*, a social reformer collects statistics outside a London pub.[6] Mrs Pendlebury is convinced that the allowance is too large and that it provides a great temptation to the women. As her more progressive daughter observes, she is oblivious to the drunkenness of men. One poor woman who is rather the worse for drink tries to offer Mrs Pendlebury money for a drop of gin. Ironically, it is a temperance lecturer who shows some understanding of the circumstances. She criticises those who 'set out to reform the world without having lived in the world'. She explains that the woman has just lost her son, and that her husband and brother were killed in the South African War. Warfare is the problem. This was turned into a short story in Evelyn's collection *A Communion of Sinners*.[7] Here the daughter is called Dora. It was the Defence of the Realm Act known as DORA that enabled the extraordinary wartime powers.

A number of the sketches in Evelyn's book were first aired in Lansbury's paper, the *Herald*, for three guineas per story. Evelyn could be relied upon to look at matters differently from the official eye. In 'The Choice' she shows a wife whose separation allowance enables her to eat enough for the first time in her life.[8] Evelyn could see from the window of her flat how local children were being clothed decently now that mothers were really controlling the household purse. Jobs were more plentiful for women too. Yet she refused to write about war as a boon. Rather it made her think about 'How we waste peace'.[9] In another collection, entitled *The War of All the Ages* (1915), a wife hears that her cruel husband – who used to beat her and their child – has been killed in the war. Will she go to his funeral? She does but she wears a blue hat with a magenta feather. And it turns out that the War Office has made a 'bloomin mistake' and he is a prisoner. She let the service go ahead because she knew how much he needed others to pray for him.

War is seen from the perspectives of mothers. The self-important husband who has just been made a special constable and keeps proclaiming that war is 'a man's business' makes a fuss about adjusting to night duty. He acts as though women have no experience of interrupted nights. A disabled patriot and an old countrywoman converse on a tram (another example of conversations between strangers on public transport) and the old woman shocks her fellow travellers by declaring that, English or German, 'they be all lads to me, the poor babes'. The charwoman is scornful of a sentimental war poem about love of country. She questions whether love can really have much to do with it if women from both sides are patriotically surrendering their sons to be killed.

Boys play war in the street, telling a girl that she knows 'nuffink about war'. But she understands that there is a real casualty in their home: the baby who has died because there is a war. Her father is out of work and the pawnshop has closed. Children taunt a girl whose father is German and has been taken away but 'they were not really cruel – no more so, probably, than the grown-up people who place Providence in an awkward position by praying for the slaughter of their enemies'.[10] We see children walking five miles to queue for bread at reduced prices. War disjoints daily life for all. Retrenchment in middle-class homes reduces the number of jobs in domestic service. Consequently some children start working younger.

Evelyn was concerned to show that two wars were being waged: 'one in the trenches and a much older one in the garrets at home.' Gone now are her literary depictions of the squirearchy. In their place are somewhat sentimental depictions of impoverished London families. Evelyn's sketches focus on the desperately poor, largely ignoring the less dramatic lower middle class and respectable working class.[11]

She has, though, interesting observations about how war can both emasculate and strengthen men. In 'Making a Man of Him' a war hero is given the Victoria Cross but his angry wife questions the price paid as she finds that war has reduced her husband to a child. 'Though One Rose from the Dead' brings the gentle Peter Campion back home from the trenches to face celebrations in his village. Shocked by the difference between people's perception of war and the horrors he had faced, he is unable to tell them the truth. He knows they would not believe him even if he could break his silence. He leaves after only forty-eight hours. In another story Jenny refuses to marry Bert when he is strong and well but does want him when he loses an arm and half his foot in the war. She insists that this is not from pity but because his views have changed. He used to believe that since men had muscles they must be superior to women.

The effect of war on gender relations unites Evelyn's sketches. Suffragettes are never far away. When a soldier suggests that destruction is for a good cause, Nell, who had gone to prison for a vote, reminds him that this is what militant suffragists have long argued. A city clerk wants the world to see that war is wrong. His sister tells him for the first time that she has been to prison and forcibly fed. She can admit this now since he has been forced to understand causes. They have something in common.

In 'The University Set' a Belgian refugee professor is to address a dinner held by the citizens of Milchester. It seems as though the rights of small nations might unite two factions: before the war Molly Egerton and the university set advocated the vote while the Colonel's wife and her family and friends believed that suffragettes 'had no *savoir faire*'.[12] Yet Molly's feminism is not a passing fad and when she discovers that the Colonel's order forbidding the sale of intoxicating drinks to women between 7pm and 8am is extended to the female guests at the banquet, she threatens to boycott the event. The Colonel has to brave her committee. It proposes gender equality, both in the application of the order and at the dinner by banning all drink. How could they pose as the champions of minorities if they trampled on the rights of their own countrywomen? Outwitted, the Colonel decides they will do without the intellectuals. But his wife, the epitome of femininity, informs him as they sip lemonade that she and her friends refuse to be under police supervision. They would rather become suffragettes than attend. Evelyn enjoyed showing how a little solidarity between women inspired confidence and how small but significant gestures emanated from those least expected to rebel.

Readers would have been aware of the debates surrounding the application of DORA which permitted all inhabitants of an area to be kept indoors at night. In Cardiff Colonel East, Commander of the Severn Defences, used these extraordinary powers to target prostitutes. 'Women of a certain character' were banned from public houses between 7pm and 6am and a curfew was imposed on them between the hours of 7pm and 8am with the threat of a court martial. A group of women were tried, court martialled and sentenced to two months in prison in what many saw as discrimination and an attack on civil liberties. Evelyn travelled to Cardiff to speak against their detention and she, Barbara Ayrton Gould, Lady Mackworth and George Lansbury formed part of a deputation to Colonel East. His Order was lifted.

'The Adventure' is about this curfew. A lady secretly visits the home of the prostitute Flossie Talbot and explains 'with a graciousness that was a trifle overdone' that she approves of the Order, though not the poverty it produces. But her visit does not go quite as planned. Flossie's friend, speaking slowly and deliberately, remarks how kind she had been to explain why she must be kept off the streets after dark: 'I shan't mind starving nearly so much, of course, now.'[13] She adds that if the law really were enacted for their protection, it might have been simpler to keep the troops at home.

Evelyn's sketch describing the United Suffragists' club begins with the words 'We made it as unlike an institution as possible'.[14] She was concerned not to appear patronising. It was started in November 1914 at Borough Road in Southwark (about thirty women and babies came to the opening) and was aimed at working-class mothers whose husbands were in the forces. It did not preach religion or turn away those who had been to the pub though the organisers hoped to replace drinking with activities deemed more wholesome, such as music and illustrated talks. The club provided copy for some of Evelyn's sketches. Her amused tone and assumed demotic language to describe members' reactions suggest that, although 'Our Club' differed from many others in having weekly suffrage meetings, its recipients would not have found it that distinctive. Yet Evelyn was keen to distinguish it from her fictional Britannia Club. This was run by Mrs Puckleberry, 'one of those naturally mild old ladies whose souls suddenly become khaki-coloured when their country goes to war'.[15] Mrs Pankhurst, now fervently patriotic, had renamed the *Suffragette* newspaper *Britannia*.

In 1915 the United Suffragists reprinted *Rebel Women* with a new introduction by Elizabeth Robins. It included 'The Women at the Gate' in which the Henry Nevinson figure, familiar with war and observing suffrage militancy, declares 'There is never any glory in war – at least, not where the war is'.[16] The story had a new relevance. And according to her memoirs, Evelyn became more and more of a pacifist as the war progressed.[17] She was, though, asked by Scott to modify the pacifist tone of one of her stories for the *Manchester Guardian* as early as 1914.[18]

Evelyn did not lose any of her immediate family through war though Lewin died from tuberculosis in October 1914. Her elderly mother died four months later. Algie was the only brother called up and he did not see active service. But her godson Christopher Dearmer was killed in the Dardanelles and his artist mother (Evelyn's friend Mabel) lost her life in Serbia where she had been nursing. Lewin's two sons came close to death and Charlie (Cecil's only son), who was in the Grenadiers, was badly wounded. The nephews survived but in November 1916, two months after Charlie's near escape, Henry noted that Evelyn felt she 'must take up peace'. She had been deeply affected by seeing Charlie.[19] Before the war the cause of peace had mattered to Evelyn and other women involved in suffrage and concerned about social justice. But it was war that propelled it into a priority.[20] In July 1918 the government forbade a Women's Peace by Negotiation meeting in Hyde Park. Henry noted that Evelyn 'boiled with rage' and was now 'willing to take any risk to end the war'.[21]

Evelyn spent one summer holiday helping in Sussex hayfields. She also worked for a couple of weeks on a Sussex fruit farm and briefly assisted a gardener in Cheltenham. The closest she got to the fighting was a weekend at the British hospital run by Louisa Garrett Anderson and Flora Murray (under the Royal Army Medical corps) at Wimereux near Boulogne. Since Henry went there in late November 1914, Evelyn probably visited the hospital with him. Earlier that month she had obtained a passport. [22]

Evelyn wanted to cross the Channel in April 1915 for the Women's International Congress being held at The Hague. It had been initiated by a small group of women in the Netherlands involved in women's suffrage and appalled by the outbreak of war. An informal conference in Amsterdam was followed by the famous Hague meeting over which the American Jane Addams[23] presided. Its hugely ambitious aims were designed to bring together delegates from both sides of the war for the future settlement of international disputes by other means than warfare and for women to have a voice in the affairs of nations. It thus brought together two movements felt to be 'vitally connected': the women's movement and the pacifist movement.[24] Evelyn was one of 156 women on the Congress's British Committee (Mrs Fawcett did not endorse the Congress so there were notable resignations from the National Union) and one of the 180 British women requesting Exit Permits to attend the Congress in neutral Holland.

In mid-April the women learned that the government had refused the permits. Evelyn discovered that about ten of them would probably be allowed though they might all be stopped 'for naval considerations'.[25] With Reginald McKenna (the man who had been responsible for the infamous Cat and Mouse Act) still Home Secretary, former militants stood no chance. C. P. Scott sent an 'excellent testimonial'[26] on Evelyn's behalf but to no avail. A dossier on each applicant did select a couple of dozen women but at the last moment an Admiralty Order closed the North Sea to shipping so they were stranded at Tilbury. Only three British women were able to attend this historic event which brought together close to fifteen hundred women from twelve countries. Two (Chrystal Macmillan and Kathleen Courtney) were already in the Netherlands. Emmeline Pethick-Lawrence had been in New York and accompanied Jane Addams and the American delegation.

This major transnational gathering, the first since the start of the war, created the basis for the modern international women's peace movement.[27] The decision was taken to send women envoys to both belligerent and neutral governments to ask them to declare their war aims and set up a permanent conference for conciliation. A tuppenny newssheet called *Towards Permanent Peace* was published in 1915, providing a record of the proceedings and resolutions agreed at The Hague between 28 April and 1 May. It included an article by Evelyn about the way the press reported the Congress.[28] Although she praised some newspapers[29] and stressed that journalists were not so much to blame as the current system of newspaper proprietorship, Evelyn derided the 'abusive impudence', the 'wilful inaccuracy, and the underlying note of fear' that characterised much of the reporting. She complained that adjectives such as 'misguided' and 'hysterical' were freely bandied about. One paper disparagingly referred to the 'spring jaunt' to Holland. Another called the venture 'Folly in Petticoats'. The Congress was inevitably a fiasco in the eyes of the *Irish Times*. Why, therefore, Evelyn asked, did they devote a whole column to it? Behind many of the attacks was the belief that these women were being disloyal 'Pro-Hun Peacettes'. The *Sunday Pictorial* suggested that 'The ladies who would sit with German women for the purpose of theoretical discussion' – hardly a 'spring jaunt' – displayed a 'strange want of imagination and of public decency, and a ridiculous sense of unreality'. An incandescent Evelyn asked when they should sit down together. Perhaps it was only when husbands, sons and brothers had all been killed and it was too late.

The formal instigation of the Women's International League (WIL), part of the International Committee of Women for Permanent Peace, was in October 1915.[30] Within a couple of years WIL had over 3,500 British members. Evelyn was involved from the start. She spoke at their meetings and at a conference on the problem of prostitution (focusing on women as administrators of law) and gave a talk entitled 'Is there a Woman's Point of View?'[31] For three years from February 1922 Evelyn sat on WIL's Council. This period of increased activity (also reflected in her giving extra financial donations) coincided, as we shall see, with her greater involvement in Quaker famine relief in Europe.[32]

The Hague Conference was not Evelyn's only brush with the authorities in 1915. She refused to pay income tax on her earnings.

To do so, she argued, amounted to 'taxation without representation', thereby contravening an old constitutional right long upheld by radicals as a basic principle of British freedom. Withholding taxation was one of a number of forms of passive resistance adopted by suffrage supporters, particularly members of the Women's Freedom League, to draw attention to the denial of their full citizenship. In 1911 Evelyn had been one of many who had refused to complete her Census form. She had skated into the small hours with Henry and others, ensuring that they were away from their homes when the enumerators came round.

There was a tradition of 'No Vote. No Tax!' Back in the 1870s the Priestman sisters had refused to pay. In 1906 Dora Montefiore had been besieged in her Hammersmith home (christened Fort Montefiore by the press) after refusing to pay her taxes. Bailiffs spent weeks attempting to distrain her furniture.[33] A Women's Tax Resistance League was founded in 1909, with Henry's wife Margaret chairing its inaugural meeting. But with the outbreak of war, most suffrage tax resisters paid their arrears. A handful of women still refused to pay up. Evelyn was the last one to hold out. She believed that war sharpened the significance of the ancient right of people to refuse to be taxed without their consent.

In March 1915 she moved from her tiny Doughty Street home to a larger flat down the road at 16 John Street. Its back windows looked out over London rooftops. The five-storeyed house had once been the home of another journalist, the playwright and translator John Oxenford who, in the 1840s, was theatre critic for *The Times*. To make a little income Evelyn sublet her largest room to a war worker. In May a bailiff arrived at Evelyn's rooms. He came daily for six weeks. Others carted off her furniture. Her carpets, curtains, chairs, books, papers and precious typewriter all went. By July her rooms had been stripped bare. Even her wash-stand had been removed and only her clothes and bed remained. Henry noted that 'She feels the petty insults very bitterly'.[34] She was concerned about how her landlady might react. Heating, lighting and telephone were cut off, though friends' guarantees ensured that her gas and electricity were restored. In one of Evelyn's short stories an old rebel leader explains that there are more ways than one of dying for a cause: 'I died, when they threw my books into the lake and robbed me of everything that made life beautiful and gracious.'[35]

Meanwhile her correspondence was intercepted so she asked friends to send her mail to Barbara. All royalties were confiscated. By

1917 Evelyn owed six years' tax and the cost of judgements had risen to over £56. A petition was filed against her for this amount and she was declared bankrupt. There were three adjournments before she was publicly examined by the Receiver.

The *Christian Commonwealth* protested: 'While other women in a similar position are being left alone, Miss Sharp is being relentlessly pursued and the method adopted is a particularly mean and unchivalrous one.'[36] Evelyn told Lansbury in June 1917 that

> The Crown has placed me in an intolerable position by taking these proceedings against me just at a moment when it is impossible to put up a fight against it. Yet it is no more *right* to pay 6 years' arrears of income tax now than it was before . . . [But] we seem on the point of gaining a real victory, and the rest doesn't matter.[37]

Evelyn's treatment was harsh compared to that meted out to some of the deliberate fraudsters she encountered at the Bankruptcy court. It was due to her obduracy – she simply stated that the franchise was her reason for refusal – and also because, in addition to refusing to pay her tax, she would not reveal her sources of income[38] (she received £75 a year from the family Trust Fund set up by her father in 1891). Her furniture was sold at public auction. As had happened in other cases, suffrage friends rallied round, purchased items and lent them to her. Henry went to see the Receiver to argue that her books and typewriters were part of the tools of her trade and that tradesmen were not denied their means of work. He was told that Evelyn's money and goods would be confiscated until she died unless she came to terms with the authorities. He 'came away raging'. [39] Evelyn's typewriter was finally returned in mid-December 1917.

Several dozen friends provided moral support at court appearances and made representations to the Chancellor of the Exchequer. But it was not until 18 May 1918 that she was 'finally extricated from the briary bush' at the Bankruptcy court.[40]

This was some months after she was enfranchised. In September 1916 the National Council for Adult Suffrage had been formed. Recognising that manhood suffrage now seemed a real possibility, the United Suffragists decided to endorse it. Evelyn sat on its executive and Henry chaired it. The proposal for a Speakers' Conference with a Reform Bill that included women (as well as all adult men) came from the United Suffragists and laid the grounds for the bill that eventually became law. In December 1917, at the end of a tough year, exacerbated by fear of Zeppelin raids, Evelyn's Leader in *Votes for Women* was entitled 'In Sight of the Promised Land'.

When, on 10 January 1918, Evelyn and Henry heard that a majority in the House of Lords had voted for the Representation of the People Bill, they were so excited that a porter at the National Liberal Club, realising that something dramatic had happened, asked them if there had been an air raid. Two evenings later Henry hosted a dinner in honour of suffrage victory. Guests included Evelyn, the Goulds, Elizabeth Robins and J. A. Hobson. It was the first of many celebrations. A week later the United Suffragists decided to disband.[41] A suffrage dinner followed at the Lyceum Club where Evelyn's 'superb' speech displayed what Henry called 'a kind of humorous passion'.[42] But when the Royal Assent was finally announced in Parliament at about 8.45pm on 6 February, giving the vote to women over thirty who fulfilled residential qualifications, only three suffrage activists were there to hear the news: Bertha Brewster, who was the secretary of the United Suffragists, Henry and Evelyn. 'I think' wrote Evelyn, in her memoirs, that 'almost the happiest moment of my life was that in which I walked away up Whitehall' on the evening that a 'lost' cause triumphed.[43]

Henry bought Evelyn a new gown. The couple attended a Thanksgiving service at St Martin's in the Fields and another at City Temple where Maude Royden preached. Evelyn received lengthy applause for her speech at the WIL's celebrations. Elizabeth Robins, Henry Massingham and Lady Sybil Smith organised a dinner in April to honour Henry's 'many-sided public services' as a war correspondent, suffragist and man of letters. There were 187 guests at the Grafton Hall. Henry was presented with a silver casket and a cheque for £280.

But it was Evelyn who received the most accolades. She had first been honoured with a gift from an anonymous group of suffrage admirers in November 1916. They wrote that 'without your true courage and devotion, especially during these terrible times, when the attention of so many is directed to other interests, the cause of Woman Suffrage could hardly have been maintained as a living question'.[44] In the second volume of his autobiography, published in 1925, Henry devoted several pages to praising Evelyn's suffrage work. He emphasised out that it was the persistence of the United Suffragists that had made the triumph of 1918 possible. He added that all its members would admit that 'our success and our very existence through those four years from February 1914 to February 1918, were almost entirely due to the brilliant mind and dogged resolution of Evelyn Sharp, who inspired our members to maintain their enthusiasm'.[45]

Gertrude Baillie Weaver, who had shared many of the suffrage struggles with Evelyn, wrote to say: 'what a splendid possession you will have for ever – the knowledge of the ceaseless, brave, selfsacrificing [*sic*] fight you have put up'.[46] Barbara's long letter praised Evelyn as 'the *one* person who has never let *anything* come' between her and 'the Cause'.[47] She stressed that 'there is *no one* else in the whole movement who has gone straight ahead and never faltered or turned aside right through to the very end'. She was writing just after the final triumphant United Suffragist party in mid-March at which Evelyn was guest of honour and presented with a bouquet and a case containing a cheque for £324. Evelyn was, Henry wrote, so astonished and overwhelmed that she could barely speak. Many cried with emotion and 'even I had to assume a stern and martial aspect'.[48]

Louisa Garrett Anderson was there. She had come straight from the Albert Hall where she had apparently heard the Pankhursts 'clamouring for perpetual war & the slaughter of all Germans'. She compared Christabel, 'so fresh & vital still', with the 'overworked & exhausted' United Suffragists.[49] Evelyn's 'Comrades in the Long Fight' presented her with a book signed by 265 individuals, including 'Teddy the flower seller', the Pethick-Lawrences, sister Ethel, Charlotte Despard and Henry.[50] Suffrage groups contributed too. Bolton United Suffragists wrote: 'We love Miss Sharp, and her example and writings – nay her whole life-work is an inspiration to many of us.' One tribute suggested that 'if her spirit was more widely shared, we could soon pilot the world past war, and start building the new world for which we all long so'.

And helping to pilot the world past war was precisely what Evelyn now saw as her goal. The United Suffragists' motto had been 'Usque Ad Finem'. It was not the end as she well knew. Not until 1928 would all women get the right to vote. But the legislation marked the close of a vital and protracted stage. Evelyn would remain a believer in women's rights for the rest of her life but with the coming of peace she began to look beyond Britain and to devote herself to the tough, practical work of helping to rebuild the lives of those defeated in war and now paying the economic and social costs.

6

The relief of peace: in Weimar Germany

The year 1920 marked the start of Evelyn's international humanitarian work. She made the first of a number of visits to Germany. The signing of the Armistice in November 1918 had not been followed by the lifting of the Allied blockade. The following April Evelyn was one of the speakers protesting against the delay at a Trafalgar Square demonstration held by what was now called the Women's International League for Peace and Freedom (WILPF). She had an audience of ten thousand.[1] The speakers (who included Barbara Ayrton Gould and Emmeline Pethick-Lawrence) and the crowd then marched to Downing Street to deliver their resolution for the urgent raising of the blockade and the organisation of adequate feeding for the starving millions of Europe.

Evelyn also joined the committee of the Fight the Famine Council formed at the start of 1919 to secure the end of the blockade and disseminate genuine information about conditions in Central Europe. In March of this year she wrote a sombre piece in the *Manchester Guardian* on the physical and moral effects of the blockade on Germany's young people, drawing on a pamphlet starkly entitled 'Hunger'.[2] This had been written by a doctor in Chemnitz and a Berlin teacher. Evelyn's Fight the Famine Council work brought her into contact with the eminent Quaker Ruth Fry and she began to immerse herself in a new form of collective commitment: Quaker relief work. Before the end of the year she was addressing Wandsworth Friends on the uselessness of violence. But she now wanted to go further afield.

She decided to volunteer to delouse refugees in Poland. This was part of a Quaker effort to control the spread of typhus, one of several horrendous epidemics that now plagued Europe in the wake of the war. Henry, who had just joined the Council of the new Save the Children Fund and covered their conference in Geneva early in 1920, was alarmed at Evelyn's plans. Hearing in Switzerland of the dangers involved in Polish relief, he admitted to being 'overwhelmed with misery & terror'.[3] But although the Friends were happy to accept Evelyn and she was vaccinated (causing several weeks of illness), the British authorities kept refusing to issue a permit. Evelyn had already sublet her flat in anticipation of being abroad for a few months so had to stay with her sister Ethel in Elgin Avenue. Several months passed with no news. The editor of the *Nation*, Henry Massingham, commented in his paper on Evelyn's 'excellent qualities as a writer and her entirely disinterested and straightforward character'.[4] Now she was needed in Berlin rather than Warsaw but there were further delays by the Foreign Office. Massingham pointed out that her only wish was to relieve the distress in Europe. His paper was concerned about 'secret interference with the liberties of the people' and he urged the need to know who and what was preventing Evelyn from going abroad.

Evelyn had already written to Lord Curzon, the Foreign Secretary. C. P. Scott now privately contacted Sir Basil Thomson, who was in charge of passports, and the matter was raised in Parliament by Lord Robert Cecil. She was then granted an interview with Sir Basil. Since March 1919 she had been on the staff of the *Daily Herald* (with old friends Lansbury and Gould as editor and associate editor),[5] writing short stories and special features. The paper had reverted to its daily format after weekly production in wartime. It was an integral part of the labour movement, yet in post-Russian Revolution times some saw it as more subversive than it actually was. The explanation provided for the authorities' prevarication was that some of Evelyn's short stories were 'very extreme'. During the delay Evelyn worked (for a small salary) for the Friends' Appeal for Central European Students and Professors. She finally left England in early May 1920 and remained in Germany for three months.[6]

So what impelled Evelyn to work with the Quakers? The war had convinced her of the need to strive for peace and we have seen that she was active in the WIL(PF)[7] from its inception. [8] In July 1918 Evelyn and Henry attended a Quaker conference on the moral influences of war. Evelyn admired the Friends' courage and international work as well as the fact that they did not patronise women and believed in equality.

Evelyn's long involvement in women's suffrage had recently ended. Just as Henry was always chasing a new cause, so it might be said that Evelyn now needed a novel commitment. Both had joined the Labour

Party after the war and Evelyn electioneered for several Labour candidates, including Barbara Ayrton Gould.[9] But neither she nor Henry was really prepared to toe party lines despite both being asked (and refusing) to stand for Parliament. Suffrage had given Evelyn many friends and, for a woman who would list friendships as one of her hobbies in *Who's Who*, the Society of Friends offered real comradeship. But, what were her views about its most fundamental belief?

In her youth Evelyn had dutifully attended Church of England services at the twelfth-century church in Weston Turville, next to the Sharps' Manor House. At the turn of the century she was influenced by the Reverend Percy and Mabel Dearmer and called herself a Christian Socialist. She then became a lapsed Anglican, increasingly critical of most organised religion. War reactivated her faith. Here she differed from the educationist Mary Sheepshanks, secretary from 1913 of the International Women's Suffrage Alliance and editor of the monthly *Jus Suffragii*.[10] Both women edited their papers in wartime and were international humanitarians and committed pacifists. Yet the war turned Sheepshanks, daughter of an English bishop, into an atheist whereas for Evelyn 'the actual teaching of Christ suddenly seemed to shine out like a diamond from a dust-heap'. Now she believed that 'the Christian morality could not be surpassed'. The Quakers were the only people she knew who were 'honestly endeavouring to live the Christian life in a non-Christian society'.[11] These words were written in the early 1930s after some time working with them. But as early as 1919 Evelyn declared in print that the practical application of the teachings of Christ offered the only hope for civilisation in the future.[12]

She never became a member of the Society of Friends though she occasionally attended Quaker meetings for worship. In explanation she stressed that she was prejudiced against labels[13] despite the fact that she had proudly called herself a suffragette for many years. She also admitted that she was not sure that she could subscribe to all the tenets of the Quaker faith. Part of her uncertainty probably concerned her relationship with a married man. Henry was sympathetic to the principles of the Quakers and shared their platforms and interests in his anti-slavery work and wartime efforts with the Friends Ambulance Unit. Yet he always felt slightly uneasy in their presence, both because they were so worthy and as a result of his personal memories of an intense evangelical upbringing.[14] He may have shared their opposition to injustice but he lacked their quietude and subjugation of self, qualities Evelyn did possess. Yet she also retained a satirical, quizzical element in her thinking and writing that might have, in her own view at least, distanced her from the Friends.

Evelyn's deepening spirituality can be seen in her writings of this time, most notably in *Somewhere in Christendom* (1919). Evelyn's political fantasy set in the land of Ethuria includes a female prophet who envisages a world where 'all the nations are one human family; they all belong equally to God's chosen people, and none is greater or lesser than another'.[15] The opening story in her wartime collection *A Communion of Sinners* is about a young woman from a Tudor manor house who has allowed her conscience to dictate – suffrage is not mentioned by name – and has gone to prison for her beliefs. This story questions what is Christian about the forced attendance at chapel where prisoners are herded like sheep but suggests that prison may be 'the only place on God's earth where we are all equal'. It ends with reference to Galilee and Christ preaching 'the communion of saints because He believed in the communion of sinners'.[16] Entitled 'Number Seventeen's Christmas', this was one of a number of Christmas and Easter stories by Evelyn designed to make people think about the meaning of such celebrations.

In 'The Miracle in the Barn', tramps have a baby in a barn and the respectable people of the parish think it a scandal that the child was not born in the workhouse infirmary. There is the usual irony – the villagers were ashamed that they had 'allowed Christmas Day to trick them into strong feelings' – mingled with a Christian and Socialist message. Those who care for the new-born are 'the idlers and good-for-nothings'. The new Vicar is thought to be a Bolshevik and it is the little girl, ridiculed by her elders for confusing Christmas with some-body's birthday, who unwittingly thinks and does the right thing.[17]

Although Evelyn was most closely associated with writing for chil-dren, her main task during her first visit to Germany was assisting with the feeding of students in Berlin as part of the international relief effort organised by the Quakers. The first railway trucks of food to help starving mothers and babies had arrived in Berlin in April 1919 and a small number of British Friends and American Friends and WILPF representatives were permitted to visit the city in early July just after the signing of the Peace and a few days before the blockade was finally lifted. Two of the latter (Jane Addams and Dr Alice Hamilton) met Henry in London before leaving for Germany. He had spent several months investigating conditions in Cologne just after the war. Now he told the women a little of what they might find.

Yet they were going to a post-revolutionary Germany that had witnessed attempts from both the Left and the Right to overthrow the government. The country was experiencing a democratic experiment in the form of the Weimar Republic. German women over twenty had gained the vote though this was not something that Evelyn focused on in her writings. She was more concerned with the social and economic problems and their effects on everyday life.

The new welfare state faced a wellnigh impossible task. The circumstances and time at which it came into being meant that it could never really hope to meet its ideals and popular expectations.[18] However, for those living through its early days, not knowing what lay ahead, there seemed to be some hope. When the American delegation reached Berlin, a newspaper editor told them that, when he finally took home a bottle of milk, his little girl shouted to her mother that peace had come.[19] The food situation was now, according to the delegates, marginally better than it had been but the situation remained grave. In November the future president of the United States, Herbert Hoover, a Quaker and the International Ford Controller, arranged that the American Friends should administer the relief effort in Germany. By the end of June 1920 at least one million children in over fifteen hundred centres were receiving regular meals in feeding centres organised by Quakers.

In going to Germany Evelyn was signalling her unhappiness with the Versailles settlement and her distaste for retribution and the reparations demanded from the defeated Germans. In June 1919 she had spoken at a WILPF demonstration in Trafalgar Square that had protested against a 'Peace of Violence' and supported instead a Peace of Reconciliation based upon freedom, self-determination and economic justice.[20] Evelyn was also concerned about the freedom of the press. In Cologne Henry observed the effects of the influenza pandemic. This and the blockade, he felt, were hastening the demoralisation and disintegration of a nation he had once known well. He was told by the Bürgermeister that 'We are too exhausted even to hate'.[21] Henry spoke German fluently and was at pains to expose the situation in print, not least because he believed the Northcliffe press to be camouflaging the true situation.[22] Evelyn proudly wrote that he had been 'the first correspondent to break through the conspiracy of silence in the press'.[23] He produced excoriating accounts of his findings.[24]

In February 1920 Ruth Fry asked Henry if he could visit Germany again in order to publicise some of the problems facing the country. He was sympathetic but too busy to go. Within a few months he was in the United States where he attended his first Quaker meeting at Haverford College. Evelyn, however, finally left for Berlin on the evening of 6 May with Elizabeth Fox Howard (Ruth Fry's cousin), who later wrote that 'we experienced together the first impact of a whole people who for years had been physically and spiritually starved'.[25] The women arrived in Germany not long after the Kapp *putsch* in Berlin attempted to overthrow the Weimar Republic and reinstate militaristic rule. Instability, inflation and unemployment dominated everyday life. Some of the most wretched were the refugees. Fifty thousand people had come to Germany from the East since the war.[26]

Evelyn felt that the real evidence of ruin lay 'underneath, in the mental and moral deterioration'. She was struck by people's slowness of movement, understanding and taking action, all of which suggested how war and underfeeding affected the intellect: 'You see haunted faces and vacant faces and sad faces and grim set faces.'[27] In her hotel bedroom there was a sign warning against putting shoes outside the bedroom door and she saw this as an indication that 'one of the most honest peoples in the world' had changed owing to desperation. All except for the very rich seemed to be underfed though the worst hit were the unemployed, the unorganised workers on low wages and middle-class people on fixed incomes, the professionals and officials, many of whom were starving. Evelyn ate daily at a vegetarian restaurant and noted how little people ate there and how pale and emaciated they looked. The nation seemed to be living on substitutes with children's frocks and men's braces made from paper, soap composed of grit and grease and bicycles running on solid paper tyres.

Evelyn performed several tasks in Berlin. The relief workers were based at the Quaker headquarters overlooking the old imperial residence. They took it in turn to be on duty. Evelyn's first caller was grey with hunger. He asked for a glass of water and emptied a white powder into it. She feared that he was committing suicide but a Canadian helper calmly gave him a lump of sourdough bread and he went on his way. Evelyn had studied German in school but felt very inexperienced and, on more than one occasion, was tempted to resign. She soon learned what to do, dealing with numerous requests for food, clothing and much else. Many came for student dinner tickets to enable them to have a meal at the new student dining hall.

The American relief scheme had not included Germany's hundred thousand students, of whom there were about fourteen thousand (male and female) in Berlin alone. Many came from middle-class families now in dire financial straits, yet a university degree was essential for professional and official posts. With no proper halls of residence they lived at home or in lodgings where there were other hungry mouths to feed. So on 26 May 1920 the Quakers opened a *Speisehalle* at 6 Breitestrasse, Berlin, for 125 of the poorest students. Evelyn kept the register at this very cheap, subsidised student dining hall. The recipients liked the atmosphere, noting that the place did not look like a national kitchen.[28] For the first time many students were working as well as studying in order to survive, and what became known as the *Quaker-Speisung* was their only meal. So successful was this experiment that from June the city of Berlin provided free accommodation, cooking and service whilst Quakers supplied food for eight hundred students in two shifts. Before long almost all Germany's universities had a similar scheme, feeding more than fifteen thousand students.

Evelyn, a couple of American Friends and John Stephens (a Reader in English at Berlin University) also set up an evening club which was open until 10pm nightly at the Berlin *Speisehalle*. Evelyn particularly enjoyed the social gatherings there. The atmosphere was helped by flowers, tablecloths and reading lamps. Students read newspapers and practised their English with the helpers. This could be confusing for them since the latter included people from London, Yorkshire, Canada, America and Ireland. There were discussions on issues such as the cost of living and the ethics of killing. The students' stories of scavenging in the streets in the previous winter and, before that, conditions during the 'turnip winter' of 1916–17, so unknown to most British people, were humbling. Evelyn never forgot the comment of one young man. After remarking on how few babies were now to be seen in Berlin (many died for want of milk), he added, 'Myself, I am glad that they have died because they will not grow up to make a war of revenge'.[29]

She discovered that the socialist students tended not to come from industrial working-class families as she had presumed. She also encountered some student reactionaries, both militaristic and anti-Semitic. Evelyn, who always sought to see the best in people, was most upset by a Prussian ex-officer with kind eyes but a cruel mouth: 'you could see in him what four years of war and militarist upbringing could make of a naturally decent boy'. On one weekend excursion to the countryside he told her that he despaired of pacifists. In 1933 she recalled how he used to speak about 'when the time came'. She was only too well aware of where he was likely to stand in the new Germany.[30]

Most users of the club, though, were anti-militarist – hardly surprising in a Quaker-run organisation – and hopeful for a new Germany and international brotherhood. Owing to the war, many were old to be students. Innate pride and clean, neat appearances often camouflaged their situations. At the club they played guitars and Evelyn mended their clothes. She wrote that 'sometimes it seems hardly credible that I should be sitting here . . . between a man who had lost his leg, and another who had lost his arm in the war . . . calmly discussing how to avoid the next war'.[31]

Evelyn also visited sick children in a charity hospital, a workhouse, an Industrial School and a number of feeding centres. Even in one of the better-off districts, many went barefoot and those with neat clothes were still shockingly thin. In scenes reminiscent of *Oliver Twist*, long queues of children held up enamel bowls to teachers who ladled out bean soup. Each child wore round his or her neck an admission card from the Society of Friends declaring that they had, for 250 years, 'maintained the principle that only love and desire to help, and not war and force' could 'bring peace and happiness to mankind'.[32] Accompanying this soup (sometimes replaced by cocoa) were large white rolls that were nicknamed 'Quakers'.

The children were fed in the morning because until they had eaten they were too hungry to think. Many suffered from rickets or tuberculosis. Evelyn noted that children ate slowly and languidly. 'It is as though they had forgotten how to eat', commented one teacher.[33] They were not supposed to take food home, but many wanted to share the rolls with their mothers. And teachers (who could not eat any of this food) looked, if anything, more hungry than their pupils. Violet Bonham Carter visited Germany in 1923 and noted in her diary that no child over two years old received milk in urban Germany and that there was no state feeding in schools. She added that 'the Quaker Speise is really their only hope of growing up normal human beings'.[34]

During her first week in Berlin Evelyn had attended a peace meeting at Berlin University held by the German Students' Pacifist League. Many in the audience were wounded former soldiers now in the newly formed Peace League of Ex-Service Men. On two occasions she addressed the university's English seminar in a large lecture theatre. At the end of her first lecture she suggested that not until many years after a war could the winner really be determined. The nation that

9. Evelyn lecturing in Berlin University in 1920

won the spiritual issue and refused to take revenge was the true victor. Evelyn received thunderous applause, and so many attended her second lecture that the audience spilled out into the corridors.

June also saw Evelyn and her colleague Alexander Purdy speak at Leipzig University where they fielded a 'perfectly justifiable' attack from a professor questioning the Peace Treaty and Britain's treatment of a defeated country.[35] They helped establish a *Speisehalle* in Leipzig (five hundred students were soon being fed at this university) before moving on to Munich where Evelyn and Carolena Wood (an American Friend in charge of the Berlin Friends Mission in Joan Fry's absence) spoke at a public meeting of the Frieden und Freiheit Bund. Their words provoked 'hot discussion' about the ethics of the feeding scheme. Several people admitted that they were ashamed of this. One man declared that they need not be since the feeding was only to salve English consciences after imposing a blockade. Evelyn's notes state that at the end 'a nice International working man' in an old uniform got up to explain that he accepted the food as a gift of brotherhood and goodwill.[36]

Evelyn the writer turned this into the second half of a *Daily Herald* story called 'The Internationalists'.[37] A hungry-looking man declares at the end of a lecture that he too takes foreigners' food for his children but not 'in anger and contempt'. He stresses that food comes to Germans as a gesture of brotherhood and love 'as we should do to them if we had conquered and crushed them'. The story ends with one of the women on the stage relieved that this man is an Internationalist. But the relief worker smiles and says 'I prefer to call him a Christian'.

Evelyn returned home at the end of July. Within a few weeks the Germany Sub-committee of the Friends Emergency and War Victims' Relief Committee (FEWVRC) were considering whether she could be persuaded to replace a relief worker who was leaving Berlin. But Evelyn wanted to pick up the pieces of her life and writing career at home.[38] She recognised the value of newspaper articles about conditions in Germany and sought to counteract prejudice against the former enemy through stories showing how ordinary Germans were now suffering.[39] She gave talks on German distress to organisations such as the 1917 Club[40] and the Hampstead Quakers. In an article for the *Manchester Guardian* entitled 'The Little Enemy',[41] she adopted a technique that she later developed in her work on the London child. She told of childhood privation and Quaker feeding by personalising her story, citing here the case of a child she called little Johanna. This was reproduced as a Friends' pamphlet which also appealed for funds to undertake the feeding of children in Cologne. By the end of the year British Quakers were feeding twelve thousand children there.

When a Dutch committee that arranged hospitality for parties of underfed German children asked the English Friends for a speaker about German conditions, they approached Evelyn. Her initial reaction was to suggest that her time might be better spent in Germany collecting fresh information for publicity at home. But twenty-four Dutch towns requested lectures by Evelyn so she went ahead with the two-week tour, accompanied by Marion C. Fox to share the load. The Friends supplied lantern slides and a lecture on Germany that they hoped Evelyn would use.

She stayed in members' homes and was driven around the country to meetings. She featured as part of a variety bill in a theatre and feared that her speech was rather dull compared with the other acts, especially since the interpreter translated it sentence by sentence so that it sounded like a Litany. When she was thanked at Leiden for generously speaking on behalf of her enemies she explained that she was not conscious of having enemies, earning her the presentation of a bead bag.[42] But when she was asked to address the English-speaking club in Leeuwarden about 'England after the war', the British vice-consul walked out when she began talking about the Labour Party. Her stay with a Bürgermeister and his family of five children just before the festival of St Nicholas, and speaking in a remote Friesland village, provided Evelyn with material for a fairy tale, 'At the Back of the North Wind', in which the Bürgermeister's car becomes a reindeer sledge.[43] In the seaside town of Zandvoort she visited a children's home run by Yorkshire Quakers who nourished fifty-five starving German children for ten weeks at a time.

Evelyn's tour ended at The Hague where her lecture was attended by Prince Heinrich, the Queen of the Netherlands' German husband. He questioned her closely about her subject afterwards. She also met the German Ambassador Baron von Rosen and was invited to lunch at the German Embassy. On her return home Evelyn received a letter from Prince Heinrich telling her that 'We were greatly impressed' by the lecture and 'will do what we can to bring an immediate relief'. He asked for the lecture to be given to the League of Nations but Evelyn heard no more of this. She spoke to the FEWVRC about her fortnight in Holland and was thanked for her 'great services' for internationalism and goodwill.[44] The tour raised £87.

Early in 1923 Evelyn returned to Germany. This time she was accompanied by Henry. Both were there on press assignments.[45] Evelyn was to send 'Letters' to the *Daily Herald*, now edited by her old friend Hamilton Fyfe and owned by the Trades Union Congress and Labour Party. The paper prided itself on its international coverage. Henry's friend the correspondent Noel Brailsford had provided first-hand evidence from postwar Central Europe. Resident in Germany for the *Herald* was the experienced journalist Morgan Philips Price.

Evelyn's task in Germany marked a departure for her. This work was much more in Henry's line. He was investigating for the *Manchester Guardian* which had Frederick Voigt, of German parentage, based in Berlin as a resident correspondent. Now Evelyn briefly joined a tiny group of pioneer women foreign correspondents in postwar Germany.[46] British-born Elizabeth Wiskemann wrote for the *New Statesman* and other papers from 1928, and Sheila Grant Duff reported from the Saar in 1935.

The political and economic situation had deteriorated since Evelyn's last visit. The Treaty of Versailles had stipulated that Germany must pay the Allies compensation for war damage. France, which had suffered so directly during the war, chaired the Reparations Commission. In April 1921 it fixed the liability at a rate exceeding Germany's ability to repay. At the beginning of 1923, with the British representative abstaining, the Commission declared that Germany was in default over payments of coal to the Allies. On 11 January French and Belgian troops occupied the Ruhr and the heart of German industry became cut off from the rest of the country. Four days later twelve-year-old Käthe Bosse of Wittenberg effectively summed up the feelings of many Germans when she wrote in her diary:

> The French are doing more bad things. Their army has now marched into Essen, and they have taken other towns too. This means that they have broken the Peace Agreement, and it will surely do much harm to our industries . . . nobody knows what will happen. Some are talking of war.[47]

Germans now adopted a policy of passive resistance and most production was halted. Henry opened the first of his articles from Berlin with the question 'What is to be done when a whole country is falling into ruin?'[48] His brief was to cover conditions in Germany outside the Ruhr. Evelyn's articles were to examine the effect of the French occupation on German industry.[49]

Henry's memoirs, written in 1928 when Margaret was still alive, do not mention Evelyn being with him. Evelyn's were published the year after Margaret died. She casually refers to H. W. Nevinson 'covering much the same ground as myself', writing that that they were in the Chemnitz Valley at the same time. In fact, as the diary Evelyn kept during this trip makes plain, they spent more than two weeks together investigating the situation. Henry had last been in Berlin when war was declared. He now asked where in the world and its history could be found 'so complete a reversal of fortune and in so short a time'.[50]

Evelyn and Henry met the Quaker John Fletcher and went to the students' club where they helped to wash the dishes after supper and sang songs with the students. They ate with Socialists at the Reichstag

(German Parliament) and heard anger expressed at the way Britain and America were calmly looking on whilst a nation was destroyed. They interviewed an influential banker and trade unionists, and visited homes and a settlement, gauging opinions. In common with many British radicals, Evelyn and Henry deplored the French action. Evelyn's first article opened with a comment on German anger at French aggression and their boycotting of French goods such as wine.[51] She met the Rosens again, now in greatly reduced circumstances. She wrote that it 'was enough to make the angels weep' to see their reaction to the rare treat of a decent lunch.[52]

Evelyn was able to compare the current economic state of affairs with the situation three years earlier though the irony was that even a day could make a big difference. She observed that the earlier scarcity had been replaced by 'a normal plenty', but the 'rush downwards of the Mark, and the rush upwards of prices' were causing alarm. She noticed the increase in jewellery shops, a sign not of the city's wealth but of the desperation of those on fixed incomes in particular to sell all such luxuries. It was evidence too of the rapacity of foreign speculators.[53] As for those used to living on their savings, even necessities such as furniture were being sacrificed. When one woman was asked what she would do when it was all sold, she replied 'I suppose I shall turn on the gas, as others do'.

After three days in Berlin Evelyn compared coping with the 'madness of the mark' to trying to walk upstairs on a down escalator. On the day she wrote her second article unrationed bread had cost 606 Marks in the morning but 1,300 Marks by the evening. An average worker's wage was 25,000 Marks a week. At the beginning of February margarine was 4,000 Marks a pound though it was soon 6,000 Marks. By early March a German miner would have to work for a day and a half to earn a pound of margarine. And the wild fluctuation of the Mark produced some curious anomalies. A four-hour train journey to Dresden cost the same as a pound of margarine.

Always concerned to demonstrate the position for ordinary women, Evelyn ended her first article by commenting on the tragic discrepancy between the plenty she saw in shop windows and the paper Marks in the housewife's purse that decreased in value between the time she went to bed and went out to spend them the next morning.

In 'The Cheap Holiday', a story that could be applied to western attitudes towards parts of the world today, Evelyn shows her compatriots delighting in the bargains found on holiday in Germany (see Appendix

2). Aunt Joanna (a character who crops up in several stories), dismissed as eccentric by her family but actually perspicacious, sympathises with the plight of impoverished Berliners.

Evelyn and Henry noted that the Nationalists were becoming more influential. They also remarked on the widespread feeling that the country's ruin could be averted only by a return to arms, though 'mercifully there is no army to mobilise'. Well aware that British people's sympathies were not, in the main, with those who had so recently been the enemy, Evelyn's message was clear. Help was needed in a dire economic situation that was likely to have disastrous consequences. She ended one article by starkly asserting that 'Germany is doomed to die unless the rest of the world steps in to save her'. Although Britain's lack of opposition to France was frowned upon by those she talked to, Evelyn noted in her diary (after their visit to Leipzig University) that she had not encountered unfriendliness. Nevertheless, gone was the 'active friendliness' she had known as a Quaker worker three years earlier.

In order to gauge the effect of the Ruhr developments on industry in unoccupied Germany, Evelyn and Henry visited the Saxon textile and engineering district of Chemnitz. They found many refugees from the Ruhr. High prices and concern that the price of raw materials would become prohibitively expensive for purchasers fuelled fear of unemployment. Henry wrote that the slums he saw there represented 'Human misery about at its lowest' though Evelyn felt that conditions were no worse than homes she had visited in the East End of London. In the surrounding coal mining villages women embroidered stockings and made gloves. Evelyn and Henry watched these glove-workers working in overheated sheds in the village of Lugau.[54] Evelyn was impressed by Herr Steinert, the trade union official who showed them round the district, and agreed to help improve his English by correspondence.

A newspaper editor, Herr Hoeltermann, active in the Socialist youth movement, took Evelyn and Henry to a meeting in Magdeburg about the Ruhr situation (Hoeltermann later sought to counteract Hitler's influence there). They joined an audience of about two thousand, mostly workers, and heard Herr von Gerlach, leader of the German Pacifists, address the Ex-Soldiers' Federation. Both Evelyn and Henry commented on his somewhat 'violently pacific' behaviour when an elderly ex-General attacked France and Gerlach himself. Gerlach 'sprang up as at a challenge'. The audience shouted the speaker down and the chairman pushed him – to the back of the platform according to Henry's diary but off the platform in Evelyn's written account. In Henry's memoirs he was 'hustled from the building'. Keen to cover different angles, Evelyn also interviewed Herr Hechmann, a shipping magnate in Hamburg. She was not impressed by his 'big business mind' or his anger with the workers for earning decent wages.[55]

The effect of the French occupation on children was perceived as a topic suited to Evelyn rather than Henry, so, as a regular writer for the *Manchester Guardian*, she wrote about this subject. She had visited schools wherever possible, noting that children looked much younger than their actual age and how tuberculosis had increased. In her diary she remarked how she liked schoolteachers everywhere.[56] She also wrote an enthusiastic account of an experimental school in Hamburg in which children, parents and teachers worked together, formulating and organising their own study in the face of huge economic disadvantages. She appreciated that this sounded 'too wild to be possible' but was impressed by its results.[57] Unlike Henry, Evelyn tended to describe the effect of her visits on her own feelings, writing about one Magdeburg school: 'I think I shall never forget the starved looks of the sparsely clad boys'.[58]

Evelyn appealed to readers' emotions. Replying in the *Manchester Guardian* to a letter enquiring how Germans were starving when there was full employment, she explained that unemployment and short-time working were returning. She stressed the collapse of the Mark and the inexorable rise in prices against the background of an invading force on an unarmed population. She added that she was no economist. Yet in her direct and disarmingly guileless manner, unlike the approach of most newspaper journalists, she explained that she knew since she had witnessed the situation.[59]

Meanwhile Henry was at his most ironical in an article in the *New Leader*, suggesting that Poincaré, the French premier since early 1922, must be rejoicing: 'Few have so successfully combined the joys of destroying a helpless enemy and swindling an honourable ally.' Poincaré also achieved what has been called 'full-dress villain status' in the *Herald*.[60] Yet neither Henry nor Evelyn exculpated their own nation, arguing that a policy of so-called benevolent neutrality was problematic. Poincaré was completing the process of putting the enemy down 'while we benevolently look the other way'.[61]

In a story Evelyn wrote for the *Daily Herald* on her return, a character called Miss Trotter berates striking English dockers for not honouring an agreement. Her dressmaker compares this to the promises made by the Allies to Germany at the Armistice. 'Dear me, Miss Prim', replies her employer, 'How you do mix up things! A promise made to a beaten enemy is not binding in the same way – that is the law of war, you know. But a contract between Englishmen – '.[62]

Evelyn and Henry spent a few days in Thuringia during their visit. Henry had visited Weimar in 1880 and was devoted to German literature. His first book had been about Herder. Now he and Evelyn wandered round Weimar in search of literary associations. Henry and Margaret had spent a year in Jena after marrying in 1884 and their daughter Philippa was born there. He was studying at the university. Now, nearly forty years later, Henry showed Evelyn his old haunts. He was delighted to address the University of Jena's English Seminar, a group of about fifteen young men and women. But such associations also underscored for Evelyn and Henry the contrast between the richness of German culture and the impoverishment of the daily lives and prospects for its postwar citizens. Evelyn talked to Herr Winters, a communist newspaper editor who welcomed the crisis since he saw it as hastening the revolution. She wrote 'I liked him without agreeing with everything he said' and was more impressed by the co-partnership principles successfully implemented at the vast Zeiss optical works (years earlier Henry had given private English tuition to the Zeiss family).

Back home that spring Evelyn gave several talks about the scenes she had witnessed in Germany.[63] A couple of weeks earlier French troops had fired on a crowd of Krupp's workers in the Ruhr, killing fourteen and wounding many more. In May, Violet Bonham Carter, who had recently visited the Ruhr, moved a resolution at the National Liberal Federation conference in Buxton, condemning the French occupation. Evelyn heartily concurred with her sentiments. Bonham Carter asked what was the good of disarming Germany 'when you are making an arsenal of every German heart – when you are forging in hatreds, weapons more bitter and more deadly than steel?'[64]

The severe shortage in raw materials from the Ruhr had knock-on effects on employment elsewhere. Less than 30 per cent of the entire German workforce was now fully employed. In late September the new Chancellor Stresemann called off passive resistance. A state of emergency was declared which lasted until the following February. A commission, led by the American financial expert General Dawes, investigated the country's ability to pay reparations. The Dawes Plan proposed a two-year moratorium on payments, the return of the Ruhr to Germany and a foreign loan in return for a German undertaking to resume payment in increasing annuities. It was accepted by the German government in the spring of 1924. But before this Evelyn witnessed the dire economic and political conditions for herself. In October 1923 her contract with the *Daily Herald* ended and she was worried about the loss of a regular income. The paper did, however, send her to the Ruhr in that month as a special correspondent. Once more there were problems in getting official permission for travel. She was told that no women were being issued the special visa required for entering the occupied territory. But she persisted and was able to leave London on 30 October, coincidentally (for once) on the same day as Henry was sent out again for the *Manchester Guardian*.

They travelled together from Victoria station. He had been booked into the Dom, the grand Cologne hotel where he had been based just after the war ended. She was in the modest Quaker guesthouse nearby but moved to the Dom after two days, spending her time with the 'exceedingly nice crowd' of distinguished male correspondents gathered there.[65] They included the *Daily Express* journalist W. Beach Thomas, who greeted Evelyn as 'Becky' after many years and remarked that he would never have known her. He could, she thought, have been more tactful. Many of the great correspondents were now gathered there. Henry's autobiography somewhat disingenuously mentions Evelyn 'as a new and welcome figure among us correspondents . . . with all her passionate understanding of the "human side" of war'.[66]

As Evelyn put it, if her previous stay in Germany had seemed like an uneasy dream, this was more like a nightmare.[67] The Separatist Movement (Sonderbündler) for the forcible creation of a Rhineland Republic was being encouraged and financed by the French. On 1 November Evelyn, Henry, the *Manchester Guardian* correspondent Cecil Sprigge ('a charming and precocious youth exactly like his name') and Colonel Kennard of the American *Christian Science Monitor* (who became a friend – he was at Evelyn's party in London that Christmas) travelled by car to the French territory. Evelyn told her readers that the division of the beautiful Rhine area into zones made the traveller feel like Alice in *Through the Looking-Glass*, journeying from one square to another on a gigantic chess-board.[68]

In the small town of Düren they had a scoop: finding the new Rhineland Republic 'in full swing'. The small band of Separatists who had suddenly occupied the town a few days earlier looked like 'degenerates and cutthroats' to Evelyn, reminding her of Borstal failures. Henry compared them to Falstaff's scarecrows in burlesque with French, Moroccan and Belgian soldiers armed with rifles, tanks, guns and armoured cars to support them.[69] They interviewed the ringleaders, visited the besieged home of the Bürgermeister and saw Separatists in Aachen protected by Belgians with machine guns.

The Separatist tactic, as Evelyn saw it, was to descend on a Rhineland town like a horde of barbarians and demand the town's keys, documents and funds which would be taken by force if not immediately surrendered. The green, white and red flag of the Rhineland Republic would be flown and these 'scallywags' (as both Evelyn and Henry called them) would live 'an uneasy life among an outraged population'.[70] She conceded that many wanted autonomy for the Rhineland but within the Reich, and she knew of no citizen supportive of 'this ludicrous travesty of a Rhineland Republic'.[71]

The following day Evelyn and Henry made a long and circuitous train journey to Essen via Düsseldorf as they had been denied permits to travel to the Ruhr by car. The French had dismissed experienced German railwaymen (though a small number had returned with the cessation of passive resistance) and travelling by train was difficult. Evelyn told her readers how she saw an Englishman being commanded by a French officer to open his luggage in the waiting room at Düsseldorf station. She did not admit that this was actually Henry Nevinson. He took no notice of the instructions. Concerned German passengers then explained that the gentleman was English. Henry also chose to ignore the officer's sudden abject apologies and grovelling. But kind-hearted Evelyn who knew that these young Frenchmen were indoctrinated into hating the Germans (her diary commented that French barracks were plastered with 'hate' posters reminding the French of German atrocities) began to feel sorry for the young man.[72]

Evelyn and Henry stayed at the private hotel owned by Krupp since other hotels had been commandeered. They visited the works, now operating at roughly half capacity, two thousand workers having been discharged. In place of guns, all kinds of other machines were being made. Since employers could no longer print banknotes they had difficulty getting enough paper money to pay employees. After a couple of days Henry 'left ES pursuing a released workman' (Herr Müller was a Christian Socialist who had just spent six months in prison) and returned to Cologne. Here he sent both his and Evelyn's articles by the new method of airmail – he called it 'air-post' – before travelling on with fellow correspondents in search of Separatists.[73] Meanwhile, Müller and Evelyn spoke at a meeting of Christian trade unionists. Evelyn's German had improved but she was nervous, addressing her audience 'with shaking knees'.[74]

She spent a week staying at the Huyssen Stiftung, a hospital run by deaconesses, paying for board and lodging with much appreciated sterling. Evelyn's behaviour was unlike that of most of her contemporary correspondents. She chose to live on the same meagre diet as the staff and to see personally all the tragic cases brought to the hospital. When Henry met the superintendent Schwester Johanna a few weeks later, he wrote that she 'overflowed with praise of ES'.[75] Ruth Fry was now visiting the Essen Quaker house and Evelyn accompanied her and the Quaker Alfred Lowry to Gelsenkirchen, 'an industrial town which has ceased to function'.[76] Here were enormous coal deposits yet the population had no coal in their homes (95 per cent of mines lay idle in the Ruhr coalfield) whilst the streets of Bochum were crowded with unemployed workers. The looting of shops by Separatists in Duisberg had provoked a riot in which three civilians were killed. Two Separatist leaders gave Evelyn a hollow assurance that all was going splendidly.

Her fellow correspondent, the Marxist Morgan Philips Price (who had made his last tour of the Ruhr in late September), told *Daily Herald* readers that 'The condition of Germany now literally beggars description'. He had witnessed the Russian Revolution yet believed the Germans to be suffering a greater economic catastrophe, with 'scarcely a ray of light on the horizon'.[77]

Evelyn and Lowry attended the French military court. She wrote a full page for the *New Leader* on militarism in the Ruhr, begging British workers to collaborate with their French equivalents to try to get civilian political prisoners released.[78] At the same time there was an attempted *putsch* by Hitler and Ludendorff in Munich. Ludendorff gave himself up and Hitler was soon caught but the beleaguered Weimar Republic seemed to be battered from all sides. In January 1924 Price commented: 'It can truly be said that the only thing which has been stabilised up to now in Germany is poverty.'[79]

Before leaving, Evelyn secured an interview with General Jacquemot at the French headquarters. She compared this meeting to a sea-shanty since practically all her questions about the occupation produced the same response: that the French were there to collect Reparations. She was told to assure her paper that all was going well and that reports to the contrary were untrue. She also spent a day with Henry in the medieval town of Andernach. It was now under the Separatist flag. They watched unemployed workers cutting trees in woods. Then Evelyn returned home alone. Her diary mentions a nasty incident on the train when French officials mistook her for a German. But she did not elaborate, merely adding that all was well once she left the occupied territory.[80]

Evelyn did not return to Germany until 1931. The previous year had seen the Allies complete the evacuation of the Rhineland and the Nazis increase almost tenfold the number of seats in the Reichstag. Evelyn's memoirs state that she was on a mission of investigation for the Germany Committee of the Friends Council for International Service, but the British government was also interested in what she discovered. She left Liverpool on 6 March. Evelyn was a bad sailor, the weather was bitterly cold and it was a rough crossing. Henry had seen her off, disappointed not to be accompanying her, but Margaret was seriously ill and he had a deadline for his Goethe biography. Evelyn went to Magdeburg, to stay in the Wetzlers' flat. She knew Ernst Wetzler, headmaster of a large boys' school, through his work for Teubner's of Leipzig who wanted to publish some of her fiction. His twelve-year-old son was, Evelyn noted, 'a Nazi of course'.[81]

She spent the next few days visiting schools in the district. Since she was seen as an expert in writing about the English child, [82] she was especially interested in the educational provision and welfare of their German equivalents. She was impressed by a co-educational experimental school that had been lent money by the state. A former fort, it had been converted by parents who were out of work into a largely open-air school in which fee-paying pupils defrayed the fees of the majority of the children. Evelyn felt that children were generally faring better than they were in 1923, though in a big secular socialist school she discovered that 60 per cent of the children in one class had parents who were unemployed. All teachers' salaries had recently been reduced. Her notes include information on class sizes (increased from thirty to fifty in elementary schools) and the reduction of resources. When she cited the Magdeburg experiment in her journalism as a way of arguing against reducing education budgets at home, Sir Michael Sadler wrote to thank her: 'You will make many people think of it in a new light.'[83]

Moving on to Dresden, Evelyn went to the Quaker depot where food parcels and daily meals were distributed to the indigent. She met Joan Fry and interviewed educationalists, newspaper editors and anyone else willing to talk. She wrote in her diary that the working class 'Hitlerites' and Communists now in evidence had not previously taken any interest in politics. At supper one evening she heard 'Hitler boys' parading and singing through the streets. Hotel guests went nervously to the window. Evelyn thought the youths looked like a lot of schoolboys going to camp. Writing her memoirs nearly two years later, they seemed much more sinister and she called them 'storm-troops'.

Evelyn remarked that people looked better fed than they had been eight years earlier – the currency had been stabilised in 1924 – but she was aware that conditions were rapidly deteriorating again. Salaries of government officials had been cut in February. Evelyn was, however, most troubled by what she called the spiritual change. She believed that postwar distress had been primarily physical. German youth had sought spiritual outlets, both religious and cultural. Early in 1923 she had been struck by the way that many Germans were prepared to argue that the French had been duped by their own government rather than admitting anti-French sentiments and a narrow nationalism. The German people at that stage retained faith in their unions and in passive resistance. Evelyn had reported back to the Friends Relief Committee in London in February 1923. She had explained that people in unoccupied Germany were 'taking a stand definitely against force and violence'.[84] Nevertheless, she had cautioned that there was 'a general feeling that if things get worse the position will be extremely serious', and her experiences later that year in the occupied territories confirmed her sense of their deprivation and humiliation.

By 1931 the pacifist youths Evelyn had known in 1920 had been replaced by those who had undergone severe privation as postwar schoolchildren. They had 'revolvers instead of guitars in their hands and political invective instead of folk songs on their lips'.[85] They formed part of a 'warlike movement that waved Hitler or Communist banners, breathed hatred and class war'.[86] Nevertheless, Evelyn believed organised workers to be less bitter and desperate than those from the middle and upper classes. She argued that the mass of mature Socialists still believed in what the Revolution had stood for and retained faith in internationalism. In Stettin she attended a meeting of the National Socialists and heard Stöler (formerly vice-president of the Reichstag) speak for two hours. She deplored the sale of 'horrible' anti-Semitic poems and the Nazi salutes. It all 'seemed childish when it wasn't dull' but, she added, 'these things can be sometimes more dangerous for that'. She noted how Hitler was making a big bid for student support: large numbers of students were graduating with no prospect of work.[87]

Evelyn, though, was an optimist. Like Henry, she appreciated German literature and music. She was heartened by a crowded performance of *The Magic Flute* in Halle, particularly since the university was appealing to citizens to demonstrate their support for such cultural activities. She was also impressed by the pacifist head of the women's employment department. It had seen a huge upsurge in the number of wives of unemployed workers seeking jobs. Only in Essen did she experience anti-English sentiment and a note of helplessness and resentment that Germany had been abandoned. From here she wrote to the prime minister, her old friend Ramsay MacDonald, telling him about what she had seen.[88]

After three gruelling weeks Evelyn returned home with a hacking cough. She was in her sixty-second year and not only tired from her travels but also worried about shrinking opportunities for earning her living. Henry had recently lent her £50 to cover insurance bills. But she soon rallied and in mid-April, keen to inform those in power about what she had seen in Germany, she dined with her old friend Frederick Pethick-Lawrence, now a Labour MP. Two days later she had lunch with the prime minister, to give what Henry enigmatically called 'valuable information'.[89] At the beginning of May the *New Statesman and Nation* published her article on 'The Threat to German Culture'. Written in sombre tones, it ends with a warning:

> There is accumulating below the surface a dull resentment and sense of injustice that is poisoning the springs of a culture which the world can ill afford to lose. If German culture is worth saving it is time that the causes of Germany's discontent were examined.[90]

In the autumn Evelyn went to Germany on holiday with Henry and their friends Charles and Lillian Robertson.[91] Although they visited beautiful places in the Black Forest, it was, she wrote, 'difficult to take a holiday with a free mind when there is a political and economic – and – every-other – kind of crisis going on in England'. But for once it was the economic situation at home rather than in Germany that affected travel plans. Reading a German newspaper one morning, the travellers discovered that Britain had come off the Gold Standard. They made a brief visit to Heidelberg followed by a nostalgic return to Cologne's Dom Hotel, but after ten days the financial crisis forced them to cut their holiday short. Before the end of the decade they would see their country at war again with Germany.

7

Irish Rebels

When Evelyn encountered the tactics of the Separatists in the Rhineland towns in 1923 she was reminded of the excesses of the Black-and-Tans in Ireland. During these years her journalism and humanitarian work not only covered Weimar Germany but also involved her in observing and writing about the struggle for Irish freedom.

She had made her first visit to Ireland in 1903, spending a month on holiday at a hotel in Donegal with Stephen and May Gwynn and their young children.[1] Returning sixteen years later, she again stayed with the Gwynns though they now lived outside Dublin in Terenure, next to their daughter Sheila, a market gardener. Stephen Gwynn later recalled Evelyn wearing her old Land Suit (from her spell of farm work during the war) and 'plucking gooseberries and currants against time' in Sheila's garden.[2] Henry's erstwhile lover Nannie Dryhurst also had a home in Terenure. Henry had long immersed himself in Irish cultural and political matters, inspired by Nannie. Now he accompanied Evelyn across the water. They spent much of the time together but neither acknowledged it in print. When, for example, Henry quoted from his diary (for July 1919) in his autobiography, he carefully changed the use of the word 'us' in the original to the singular.[3]

Evelyn and Henry had supported Irish Home Rule. Henry was committed to the self-determination of small nations. He admired the Irish socialist James Connolly. Evelyn's support for the underdog and experience at the heart of 'another rebel movement' (women's suffrage), helped to fuel her opposition to British government policy.[4] Evelyn and Henry deplored the treatment of the rebels in the wake of the Easter Rising of 1916 and were especially outraged by the treatment given to the unarmed non-combatant, Francis Sheehy Skeffington. He was seized and allowed no legal representation. His execution by a firing party took place without even confirmation of his sentence by the commander-in-chief (the officer responsible was later court-martialled). Evelyn had known the gentle 'Skeffy'. His wife Hanna was never officially notified of her husband's fate or allowed to see or remove his body. Evelyn told her 'how outraged I feel at his tragic fate and how deeply sympathetic with you'.[5] She added that his death was a loss to women's suffrage (he had been a keen supporter), to Ireland and to humanity.

Evelyn met a number of Irish political figures during the summer visit of 1919. They included the Quaker Anna Haslam who, with her husband Thomas, had formed the Dublin Women's Suffrage Association in 1876, and Louie Bennett, a founder of the umbrella group, the Irishwomen's Suffrage Federation. She had also attended the 1915 Hague Conference and set up the Irish WILPF. Thanks to the Gwynns and Henry (who had been visiting Ireland since the late 1890s), Evelyn had tea with the famed rebel Maud Gonne and visited the nationalist historian Alice Stopford Green. She toured the Drogheda area with Henry, Constantine Curran (Dublin correspondent for the *Nation*) and James MacNeill, future governor-general of the Irish Free State.

Evelyn was aware of a pervasive fear and insecurity in Ireland. At the end of 1918, after great success in the parliamentary election, Sinn Féin MPs had refused to take their seats at Westminster. Instead in January 1919 they formed the Dáil Eireann (Parliament of the Irish Republic) and issued a Declaration of Independence. Eamon de Valera became president of the provisional government. The same month the Irish War of Independence began. The Irish Republican Army (IRA) saw itself as the legal army of the Republic established at Easter 1916 and engaged in a guerrilla war with the British. With British rule being effectively challenged, efforts were being made to restore order via both legal measures and enforcement on the ground. In the autumn after Evelyn's visit the Dáil was declared illegal and all nationalist organisations (except for the Gaelic League) outlawed. In May 1920 Dublin's beautiful eighteenth-century Customs House was burnt down, effectively symbolising the fate of British civil administration. The Restoration of Order in Ireland Act was implemented from September, and soon military courts of inquiry replaced coroners' inquests. Martial Law was imposed with curfews, frequent night raids and arrests.

Ex-service men had been sent to Ireland in the spring of 1919 to aid the Royal Irish Constabulary. The first company went to Limerick where the khaki and black of their uniform earned them the name of a famous pack of local hounds, the Black-and-Tans. But it was the subsequent auxiliary division of ex-officers, recruited at double the pay to tackle the effective IRA system of flying columns in the countryside, who were most dreaded. The Auxiliaries were disparagingly labelled 'ex-gentlemen' by Henry. Evelyn met some imaginative and moderate Sinn Féiners in 1919, such as the Quaker James Douglas, trustee and treasurer of the Irish White Cross which distributed relief irrespective of class, creed or politics. But she was convinced that the reprisals ensured that moderate proposals for a settlement were heeded less than extremist voices.[6]

Evelyn was sickened by the intensification of violence. She demonstrated her support for an Irish republican hunger striker. Terence MacSwiney, Lord Mayor of Cork, had been arrested, charged with possessing a secret cipher to decode police messages and republican propaganda. He was gaoled in Brixton and denied the status of a political prisoner so went on hunger strike. Evelyn (standing in a coal cart), Henry and Professor Stockley (Professor of English at Cork University) spoke outside Brixton Gaol. Evelyn's speech about the hunger strike as a tactic was, in Henry's opinion, 'v. excellent'.[7] When, on 19 October 1920, it was asked in the House of Commons whether it was true that MacSwiney had been without food for sixty-eight days, there was laughter. On the same day Evelyn and Henry took part in a procession against reprisals in Whitehall where they encountered some hostile onlookers. King George V sent a telegram from Balmoral stating that it would be deplorable if MacSwiney were allowed to die in prison. He advocated clemency but the prime minister (Lloyd George) was holidaying in Switzerland and unaware of the King's plea. MacSwiney died on 25 October.

On the same day, the non-party Peace with Ireland Committee was formed in London by a group of influential figures including Basil Williams, Sir Horace Plunkett and George Bernard Shaw. It opposed reprisals and wanted the 'undisciplined forces' withdrawn. Evelyn and Henry were on its list of principal speakers. WILPF, the Society of Friends and the Labour Party sent delegates to Ireland to investigate alleged outrages. The Labour Commission to Ireland produced a report on the violence, held a special conference at the end of the year and instigated a campaign of mass meetings across the country to demand peace with Ireland. Evelyn was to be one of the speakers.

Wishing to be personally acquainted with the situation before such an undertaking, Evelyn went to Ireland on 5 January 1920. Less than six weeks earlier, on 21 November, British policemen and intelligence officers had been assassinated in their Dublin homes in the morning, and in retaliation the Black-and-Tans had opened fire on an unarmed crowd at an Irish football match. The day became known as 'Bloody Sunday'. Henry, who was already in Ireland, had been reminded of conflicts he had witnessed in South Africa, Macedonia and Russia.[8] On 3 January 1921 the British government officially sanctioned military reprisals. Two days later Evelyn was packing for a fortnight in Ireland. 'The credit of England', she wrote later, 'can scarcely ever have sunk lower'.[9]

She used the words 'travelling to see Ireland' when signing hotel registers. She was anxious not to stay with those she knew lest she placed them in danger. She deliberately kept no diary or notes, not the easiest of situations for a journalist on a fact-finding mission. Essential names and addresses for information were hidden in her shoes. Evelyn was recovering from a chill after a long train journey when she was visited in her hotel bedroom by Maud Gonne. The effect on a previously indifferent hotel staff was immediate. They were now anxious to help her. When she dined with friends, her waiter slipped her a note, warning that government supporters were eating at the next table.

Aware that women could blend more easily into surroundings than men, Evelyn carried a shopping bag to evade suspicion. Another ruse 'in one or two tight corners' was to assume the air of an Englishwoman on holiday and ask the nearest policeman the way to the cathedral. But it was a lonely and, at times, terrifying experience. When a lorry full of the Black-and-Tans swung into town it took great control not to run away. Evelyn was aware that those who did that were presumed guilty and might be pursued and shot. Her fellow speaker at Brixton, Professor Stockley, was on the run though innocent of treason. Evelyn met him secretly for a few hours in a safe house. Cork's centre had been burnt and sacked three weeks earlier. The Labour Party had published a document called 'Who Burnt Cork City?' In that city there was now a popular saying that 'Every cat and dog knows who burnt Cork'. Auxiliaries took to wearing burned corks on their hats.

Evelyn wrote a series of articles in the *Daily Herald* (on page 4 where she usually wrote fiction). She cited examples of unprovoked attacks on ordinary people. They were graphic but lost some of their force as they were necessarily imprecise. She could not supply names and in many instances events were relayed to her rather than witnessed and verified directly. She was at pains to point out that the 'Black-and-Tan Terror' (the title of a chapter of her memoirs), with its raids, looting and burning, failed to terrorise or break its targets. It made some all the more defiant. She recounted how a young woman had explained that she couldn't get married because her fiancé was on the run. When Evelyn had expressed sympathy, the response was 'And do you think I'd be engaged to a man who was *not* on the run?' Women, she found, did not inform on their countrymen whilst some men and women were even persuaded by the violence of the alien forces to support Sinn Féin for the first time. She was told about a Unionist farmer whose farm was looted and damaged by the Black-and-Tans. Soon after complaining to the Colonel the farmer's life was threatened and he too went into hiding.

In one town Evelyn saw the ruins of five small houses including a general store razed to the ground as a reprisal for a Sinn Féin ambush. This shop belonged, so far as she could tell, to ordinary people quite unconnected with Sinn Féin activities. The Black-and-Tans arrived at night drunk, emptied the shop and set fire to the buildings. They forced the women and girls to dance round the fire with them. Evelyn was especially angry when a little girl was shot in a Dublin street after Black-and-Tans chased four young men, recently demobbed, who had been playing cards on the ground. Nobody in Ireland, she declared, was free from the threat of being robbed or shot by mistake. She asked her readers what they thought of that. She explained that any civilian out after curfew might be shot. She described raids and looting of shops by Auxiliaries and Black-and-Tans too intoxicated to walk straight. Accounts were given greater veracity by Evelyn's descriptions of personally watching the streets of Limerick from behind closed curtains.

She tried to demonstrate that peace was not being restored. Instead Ireland's law and order, along with its economy, was being paralysed. Henry had introduced her to George Russell, known as Æ, whose intellect and integrity he had long admired. He was the leading spirit behind what had been a great success: Irish Creameries and Cooperative stores. But they were now being attacked and burnt (over fifty were destroyed even though they were non-political). Evelyn met Æ to discuss the situation. He believed that a deliberate attempt was being made to ruin the trade and prosperity of Ireland. Evelyn was in Mallow just after its stores and Creamery met this fate.

In the *Herald* she warned that such disasters would have wider repercussions. The costly failure would be reflected in taxation. Reprisals inevitably affected production and sent prices soaring. Trade with mainland Britain was suffering since Irish shopkeepers were so afraid of goods being looted that they kept only very limited stock. Evelyn expressed concern that England[10] was fast losing an important market and that the situation was likely to have a deleterious effect on employment at home (she was writing on the eve of a Labour Party conference on unemployment). Clearly partisan, she wanted to engage readers, so appealed to them by showing how they too could be disadvantaged by events in Ireland.

She described the Black-and-Tans as men who had been taught by four years of war to hold life and property cheap. Fed hostile propaganda before being sent to an alien and unwelcoming environment, it was perhaps not surprising that they ran amok. It was too much of a coincidence, Evelyn declared, that the shops raided (ostensibly for finding where men might be hiding) were so often sweet, tobacco or wine stores whose goods the raiders could then devour. And she could not resist adding that 'you could not, perhaps, expect boys of the bulldog breed to look for rebels in a bookshop'.

But if she sought to explain how these ex-soldiers had become coarsened, Evelyn was not prepared to make allowances for the officer class who comprised the Auxiliaries. She depicted the worst of them as public school bullies with dubious definitions of what constituted fair game, manliness and having a lark.[11] Evelyn suggested that it was the Auxiliaries' 'contemptuous insolence' that made them so deeply detested. She even went so far as to suggest to *Herald* readers that they could be used in future against rebellious workers at home (though she conceded that this was not the best reason for advocating justice in Ireland).

Evelyn arrived back in London in mid-January 1921. The next day she left for the first talk for the Labour Party campaign for peace in Ireland, travelling all the way to Glasgow where she was given just fifteen minutes to speak. She had a punishing schedule over the following few weeks, addressing audiences in Ilford, Guildford, Southampton, Portsmouth, Bradford, Newport, Barrow-in-Furness and Wigan. At the Bedford Corn Exchange Evelyn and Henry spoke from the same platform. The campaign mustered over five hundred meetings across the country and must have reminded Evelyn of suffrage days.

At the vast meeting Evelyn and Henry attended in the Albert Hall on 15 February, exactly a month after her return from Ireland, an IRA anthem was sung. So exhausted was she by this point that Henry replaced her at a five-hundred-strong meeting in Bournemouth. On returning from speaking in a Norfolk village she learned that her beloved nurse had died aged ninety-three. Tired and depressed, Evelyn carried on, travelling to Glamorgan, Cornwall and Derbyshire in early March, still writing weekly for the *Herald* and *Manchester Guardian*.

By the beginning of June she was badly in need of a break. 'Driven by the pain of mankind wherever I look',[12] and 'in search of sunshine and rest', she escaped to Blenheim Cottage, Chinnor, where she stayed for a month. Writing from there to Hanna Sheehy Skeffington she explained:

> I broke down . . . I think it is the cumulative shame of being an Englishwoman, with Ireland in its present condition, that has smashed me up more than the overwork of the past few years – But I am very strong, & as soon as I can be of any use again you may rest assured that I shall be working once more for your country's freedom which, in my mind is the cause that all English people should put first at this time.[13]

She took long walks, ate wild strawberries, re-read *Cranford* (one of her favourite novels) and relaxed in sunshine. Mrs Gaskell's writing helped to revive her sense of humour, never far from the surface, as she settled into her surroundings. Another visitor, a 'rather a racy old lady' called Mrs Macnamara was a minor canon's daughter and enjoyed her whiskey though the very religious landlady hid the bottle on Sundays. Mrs Macnamara told Evelyn that 'Dissent is distressingly strong in the village', adding 'It's *almost* a religion with them'.

Evelyn was mildly annoyed by the tirades against organised labour and striking miners in particular – the local pub was the only other subscriber to the *Daily Herald* – but she enjoyed the lack of urgency and 'how much time there is for everything in the country'. The vicar preached the same sermon as on her previous visit two years earlier. But Evelyn was unconcerned and a little ambivalent about the value of change in English villages. After a conversation in Chinnor with Miss Taylor (daughter of the former owner of the *Manchester Guardian*) Evelyn wrote that she hoped Chinnor was not about to become like Surrey 'with any more splendid women living in artistic cottages' whilst 'the real villagers are jammed into overcrowded huts or asked to pay high rents for new ones with impossible conditions attached to them'. Yet she may well have been perceived by others as another example of a 'splendid' woman, and Henry, who visited several times, was lionised by his hosts.

On 27 June Evelyn cycled to Ilmer with its thirteenth-century church and brass plaque to the four men it had lost in the war. She was shown round by a woman whose own son had been wounded and was missing. That very day his medals had been returned to her. This mother said, almost mechanically, 'You don't seem to get over it so easily when it's your only one'. It was, Evelyn wrote, 'one of the most moving experiences I ever had'. She cycled home, 'raging' against those who 'rush on & on making more wars while sad crushed parents' were left to cope. The incident was turned into a story called 'The Little Lane' (the village was given the fictional name Elmswick).[14]

After a few weeks Evelyn felt 'almost placid' and 'near to forgetting altogether that there is a world of pain outside'. She took another holiday in July with her sister in Littlehampton and, just a few days after returning to London, departed for Ireland once more. But, 'What a contrast' she wrote in her holiday diary, from her last visit 'when one went in fear of one's life'.[15] There was, nevertheless, a 'tedious' examination of luggage at Holyhead for bombs 'with which we were supposed to go holiday-making'. Evelyn added, 'I wonder when we shall learn that war would cease to exist in a week if the people everywhere took the trouble to express their instinctive feeling about it'.

There was a truce as peace terms were being discussed between Lloyd George, de Valera and Sir James Craig, head of the Unionist government. The terms proposed were for Dominion Status which would bestow the wide powers of self-government possessed by Dominions such as Canada. But although the Irish would have full control of home affairs, allegiance to the Crown, membership of the British Empire and recognition of Northern Ireland signified for many the continuation of an untenable dependency.

Henry had come over too for the 'Day of the Dáil', reporting for the *Herald*. On 16 August, for the first time since the Rebellion, the newly elected Dáil met. Evelyn went with May Gwynn to the opening ceremony at the Rotunda of the Mansion House. Nannie was there too, sitting at a distance from Henry and only deigning to give him a cursory nod. Evelyn was warned by a young IRA man at the press table not to be nervous when flashlight photography was used. She thought it especially thrilling watching men with prison records, and others who had escaped to America after 1916, being sworn in and seeing Mrs O'Callaghan and Mrs Pearse, widows of murdered rebels, come forward to take the oath to defend the Irish Republic and its government. Yet neither Evelyn nor Henry seems to have been alive to the importance and significance of the use of the Irish language in the proceedings. De Valera declared that the verdict of the nation at the polls was for Ireland's total independence. Evelyn was not alone in thinking that there remained little chance of the terms being accepted.

Evelyn and Henry were invited to a reception at the Speaker's house near Blackrock. This was attended by de Valera and many other politicians. Ten days later, after the Dáil had deliberated privately, Evelyn was present for the declaration of the result. The proposed peace terms were read out and categorically rejected 'amid dangerous applause'.[16] The following day Evelyn, Henry and their friend Linnet Howell (widow of an army general whom Henry had known in the war) took the boat home.

Evelyn's direct involvement with Irish politics had ended. There would be, though, further twists. In December the terms were accepted and Evelyn was 'full of joy'.[17] Yet what followed was bitter civil war. Evelyn remained deeply ashamed of her country's behaviour in recent years but felt that there was at least now one saving grace: even though the ensuing bloodshed was a consequence of centuries of oppression of Ireland, this conflict, unlike the events of 1920–21, was Ireland's own affair.

8

Somewhere in Russia: fiction and famine

The setting is a club in London's West End. Celia (nicknamed Bolshevik though she is not particularly interested in politics) is regaling members with the story of her summer holiday. She had wanted to visit Russia but had never actually got there since she was held up by a small nation 'overlooked at the Peace settlement'. The natives of this country simply wish to till their fields and write poetry but they have to endure a foreign army and police spies. People are imprisoned on the slightest pretext. The gaols are crowded and the capital has a machine gun pointing at the trade union headquarters. Celia's companions mutter how terrible this is and proudly remark that the British Empire, where such things never happen, is busy wiping out the wicked Bolsheviks who persecute innocent peoples. They wonder what might be the name of the country that is so harassed. 'In English' replied Celia, 'we call it Ireland'.

This *Daily Herald* short story appeared in the summer of 1919. It tells us something of Evelyn's view of Ireland and its treatment.[1] But it also formed part of her concerted effort to expose people's preconceptions about post-revolutionary Russia and use of the term Bolshevik. In November 1917 Evelyn had been 'thrilled at the news of the Russian Revolution'.[2] At this stage she had envisaged the Bolsheviks' seizure of power from the 'Provisional Government' which had, earlier that year, overthrown the tsar, as marking an end to tyranny. She had welcomed Lenin as architect of the new regime. Before the war she had been so absorbed in women's suffrage that there had been little free time to become actively involved in other political activity. She then became a founder member of the new 1917 Club in Gerrard Street, Soho. Its first debate was in January 1918. The club brought together a range of progressive intellectuals including radical Liberals and Labour Party members as well as Communists. They initially welcomed what Henry (in an enthusiastic article in the *Contemporary Review*) called 'The Dayspring in Russia'.[3] Ramsay MacDonald was the club's first president, followed by figures such as E. M. Forster and J. A. Hobson. It provided an opportunity to discuss ideas without contravening DORA. Evelyn and Henry (who was the club's president in 1924) attended regularly.

In 1919 Evelyn wrote an article entitled 'The Arrival of Bolshevism' for the *Nation*. It is a remarkable piece, expressing a certainty and optimism that in retrospect seem naive. Evelyn believed that Bolshevism represented not a vague menace that required opposing but a new order of society 'in which no one shall starve, and no able-bodied person shall be idle'. She equated Communism – 'the most magnificent ideal of life ever conceived'[4] – with the basic teachings of Christianity. Communism, she thought, was 'bound to come' to Great Britain. If both the rich (who stood to lose a lot) and the poor (with more to forgive) were prepared to make the necessary mutual sacrifices, then what would otherwise be a Reign of Terror could be converted into 'a new era of mankind'.

Yet Evelyn did not join the Communist Party of Great Britain on its formation in 1920. Her pacifism prevailed. Despite having been a militant suffragette, she was not prepared to commit herself to a party that could countenance armed force, even as a possibility. She also came, in time, to argue that dictatorship, even of the proletariat, was an alien and therefore unwelcome concept for the British worker. An undiluted Marxist programme from Moscow, she believed, could be received in Britain only with the customary suspicion reserved for ideas that were not indigenous. But in the five years after 1917 she devoted time and energy to the principles and practice behind the Russian Revolution.

Evelyn's most ambitious and experimental exploration of political, personal and religious creeds was what she called 'A Revolutionary Fantasia':[5] *Somewhere in Christendom*. She also turned it into a play called *But Why Not?* or *Revolution without Tears*. Published when she was fifty, the first part of the book is simply called 'The Revolution'. It opens with King Michael looking out on his kingdom Ethuria which has been ravaged by the opposing armies of Christendom in the Nine Years' War. It is a small country with no resources envied by other nations. But it has the misfortune to be encircled by Great Powers constantly spoiling for a fight with each other so that it has become a casualty of their greed and aggression. And now it faces internal problems as revolution and civil war wreak havoc. Aware that the days of royalty are numbered, the king has sent for a prophet, hoping that 'the worship of an Idea' can save his people. What he gets is a woman prophet. With her words 'a strange inaction' seizes the revolutionaries. The prophet is dressed as a poor peasant but even Peter the Ploughman, extremist revolutionary leader, understands that he is in the presence of 'some one inspired by a living faith'. The prophet talks of peaceful Ethuria in the future, announcing that the new era of universal friendship will be born in the heart of a child. She appeals to the people to lay down their arms and treat all babies with equal care and protection since they cannot yet know who will be the chosen child.

Ten months later Ethuria is at peace and famine has been averted. The former king and queen survive but are now part of a society where all earn the same wages and respect. The former palace is a day nursery. A thousand babies have been born and are treated with reverence in the hope that one will be the future leader of the world. Consequently parenthood is taken very seriously. State socialism flourishes in the next quarter of a century but the aggression of neighbouring Tritonia and Hygeia[6] at loggerheads with each other means that, even as the small Ethurian nation rejects war, its strategic position makes it a convenient battleground for its neighbours. The ex-monarch's son Mike has married Helen, daughter of their erstwhile faithful retainer, but she is murdered and seen as the female messiah who has died for the sins of the world. And ultimately, after the Five Hours' War, Tritonia and Hygeia are converted to the creed of Ethurianism.

Henry believed this to be Evelyn's greatest book. He had a few reservations on first reading it: the notion of one thousand babies collected in one hall was, he joked, 'too much for the masculine mind' and he found it a little sentimental in parts.[7] But he enjoyed its satire, comparing Evelyn's 'ironic story of the times' to Swift's *Gulliver's Travels* and Samuel Butler's *Erewhon* (an anagram of 'nowhere'), and told the American *Christian Science Monitor* that its combination of fun and 'blazing indignation' was, to his mind, unexampled in literature.[8]

It was published by Allen & Unwin in December 1919 with a print run of 2,800 after Macmillan had rejected it.[9] Just eight hundred copies were sold in the first four months, the majority in the cheap edition retailing at 6s 6d. These were disappointing figures for Evelyn, way below the sales of her last novel, *Nicolete*. But that had been in 1907. In the intervening period she had devoted her literary energies to journalism and books of short stories. And that was part of the problem: Evelyn was now much more skilled at producing witty sketches, especially stories tailored for the working-class politicised readers of the *Daily Herald*. That elusive animal the General Reader was less certain how to interpret her fiction, teasing and amusing one minute and sardonic and angry the next. The play ends with air machines taking off for the stars. So was this science fiction by a contemporary of H. G. Wells? Or was it a lesson in ethics and a politics that many found unpalatable?

The reader's report by Bernard Miall for Allen & Unwin had reflected this uneasiness.[10] Miall's somewhat facetious summary of the plot included comments such as 'The two armies invade but both go Bolshevik – I mean Ethurian'. In his opinion 'Miss Sharp is usually amusing even when she is trying to be serious'. Summing up, he declared it 'a trifle amateurish, with flashes of real cleverness' but suggested that if her work was usually marketable then 'it should be a safe investment'. In fact the firm had done quite well from Evelyn's collection of stories *A Communion of Sinners*, and there was the added advantage that Stanley Unwin was a personal friend. Unwin added a positive note to the report, emphasising that Evelyn enjoyed 'a pretty good following'.

Evelyn was writing at a time when peace was a novelty yet before the economic problems that soon defined interwar Britain. Post-revolutionary Ethuria seems to have represented her ideal society. Ethuria condemns killing of any sort, nobody is overworked and there is full employment. There are no armed forces or prisons and the police are merely helpful guides. Since no one will be a butcher by profession, those who want to eat meat have first to kill animals themselves, so vegetarianism prevails. Ethurians treat foreigners as themselves. There are no churches or professional clergy. Evelyn remained critical of organised religion. Universal fellowship forms the core of beliefs. Like her *Daily Herald* editor and friend George Lansbury, she believed that 'Religion is not a matter of churches or of words, it is a matter of deeds'. [11]

Yet this is not a straightforward utopian novel. Hygeian society is a warning: here all imagination is under state control. Hygeia has become 'a breeding-machine for docile, card-indexed materialists'. And one of the greatest dangers emanates from the Cosmos Press. This is the largest power in the world. Lord Cosmos owns all the world's presses except Ethuria's and 'sits like a spider in a wireless web'. Attacking the newspaper barons of her day, Harmsworth and Hearst,

Evelyn derides the 'spin' of the monopolistic press which produces a uniformity of opinion and foments both news and war.[12]

The book brings together many subjects dear to Evelyn. Elements of her fairy stories can be seen here, not least in the naming of 'baddies' such as President Blinkingtoff and Comrade Dumps. Some of the adventures and bizarre situations facing characters such as the ex-Queen Anna have echoes of those encountered by Lewis Carroll's Alice. However, this is a book written by a former suffragette. Anna is Matron-of-State for Embryonic Citizenship (the play deploys the somewhat prescient title of 'Children's Minister'). The loyal retainer John is an under-housemaid whose favourite form of recreation is polishing silver. Helen works in a day nursery and is writing a thesis. Her future husband declares that if she is better at spreading the cause of Ethurianism than he is, then he will stay at home and look after their family. Evelyn's vision, written a year after she was enfranchised, shows women enjoying an equal role in society.

Yet Ethuria is not a matriarchy and in this respect it differs from Charlotte Perkins Gilman's feminist utopia, the eponymous all-female *Herland* (1915). Romance, marriage, monogamy and motherhood matter in Evelyn's society. Indeed, the shift in her thinking from a single-minded focus on women's suffrage to a wider humanitarian impulse is summed up in the statement that 'Universal comradeship had long made feminism meaningless in Ethuria'. But, crucially, this perspective is possible because the state has already changed its laws and attitudes. These changes are an essential prerequisite to the realisation of comradeship.

Since Evelyn was a popular writer of children's stories, it is not surprising that the child is presented as the key to the future. The wariness she would later voice about the psychology of childhood[13] is signalled in her description of the conference held in the Tritonic capital by the All-Christendom League for the Standardization of the Hours of Sleep for Schoolchildren. But her overriding interest is now the importance of an anti-war message. It is Ethuria's refusal to believe in revenge and bellicosity that ultimately discredits war and heralds peace. The book includes a discussion about the wisdom of women's military service. Anna argues that, if Ethuria has to go to war, then women should be conscripted since, as mothers of the race, the safety of the home and maintenance of economic stability matters more to them than to men. Anna stresses that women are better suited than men to face the perils and pain of war because they are already familiar with the danger and demands of childbirth. Yet the Military Service (Women's) bill does not secure a reading and is ordered to be read again fifty years thence. Pacifism has become paramount for Evelyn.

Evelyn's book shares some characteristics with *Moving the Mountain*, serialised eight years earlier in the United States by Charlotte Perkins Gilman. The American writer was then best known for her study *Women and Economics* but is today chiefly remembered for the story 'The Yellow Wallpaper'.[14] *Moving the Mountain* has a male narrator who returns to America in 1940, thirty years after he disappeared in Tibet. In his absence women have acquired a new social consciousness which has fundamentally transformed society. This new world is revealed through his bemused eyes. Gilman described her book as 'a short distance Utopia, a baby Utopia'. It challenges individualism, replacing warfare and aggression with a new religion of 'Living and Life'.[15] This has nothing to do with organised religion and there is no mention of God but social service is religion. Women and men now live together in harmony in a world that has shifted from being 'masculinist' to 'humanist', in which the profit motive has been eliminated, a married women is as free as a married man and being a child-culturalist (rearing children) is one job amongst many. Caring for children is, however, only undertaken by those with aptitude for it. Women are primarily seen as human rather than female beings in an egalitarian society, echoing Evelyn's sentiments. Yet although we are told there is 'no labor problem – no color problem – no sex problem – almost no disease', Gilman's focus is on how people's thinking has changed and so altered the structure of society.[16] Unlike Evelyn, she does not consider international relations.

Late Victorian socialist utopian writing had also influenced Evelyn. Her title nods to William Morris's *News from Nowhere* of 1890.[17] The ideas of the sexual radical, socialist and author Edward Carpenter would also have influenced her thinking. Carpenter was a close friend of both Evelyn and Henry. He held, and put into practice in his own life, progressive ideas about the transformation of social and gender relations, underpinned by a commitment to spiritual freedom and belief in people enjoying closer harmony with their inner nature and nature itself.

At the same time Evelyn drew on biblical and medieval literary imagery. The name of the revolutionary Peter the Ploughman, for example, evokes William Langland's great allegorical poem *Piers Plowman* with its Christian theme and social satire. But it was the specific context of contemporary war and revolution that gave her utopian novel its particular focus and force.

Yet, when Evelyn gave a two-hour reading of the play *But Why Not?* in October 1923 to a group of friends, including the journalist S. K. Ratcliffe, Joan Fry and writer Ella D'Arcy, Henry noted in his diary that it was 'too pacifist & ideal' for a British audience.[18] Harold Laski, one of Britain's leading intellectuals, was more positive, despite reinforcing gender stereotypes. He told Evelyn that her novel

> makes me feel the sterility of political science for you go straight to the heart of human nature while people like myself go floundering on discovering with pain and sweat what you seem to know by intuition.

Humour is never far away in Evelyn's fiction, even when concerned as here with serious subjects close to her heart.[19] *Somewhere in Christendom* even contains the occasional mischievous private joke. Friends would surely have recognised the female prophet with her

> wide humorous mouth, a low, well-shaped forehead, great deep eyes, and a nose too large for her face. She walked without gesture, straight, lissome, with a spring in her step and a laugh in her eyes that would have arrested attention anywhere.

Here was a perfect description of Evelyn.

However, critics felt that this insistent humour diluted the effectiveness of the book's theme: abstract weighty concepts tended to be equated with solemnity (and male writers). *Punch* suggested that the theme of a great book was spoilt by being handled in a trivial manner.[20] At the same time, for those who valued Evelyn's customary quirkiness and wit, the underlying message from a writer who was deeply concerned about the future of the world made rather less comfortable reading than her earlier fantasies. Writing just after the end of one devastating world war, Evelyn's stage directions for the play version set it 'Immediately after the Next War'. This fantasy was intended to disturb as well as entertain. Evelyn's brave and unusual 'mixed mode' of writing, born out of and reflecting her varied experiences over the previous two decades, helped ensure that its reception was equally mixed, never really receiving the serious attention it deserved.

Ignorance and unease about Communist life in the new Russian Soviet Federated Socialist Republic[21] would not have helped book sales. The privations faced by Russians could not be fully appreciated by westerners. Journalists were not permitted to be based in Moscow and were largely dependent on reports from Riga culled from White Russians and other hostile sources. But by the summer of 1921 it was becoming evident that millions were starving in the Volga region. Evelyn decided to go there.

She was one of a number of left-minded British visitors to Russia in these years. These 'fellow travellers' included Evelyn's friend Charles Roden Buxton,[22] Noel Brailsford, eminent journalist and friend of Henry's who was a foreign correspondent for the *Daily Herald* in these years, and the paper's editor Lansbury who had undertaken a nine-week tour in early 1920 and met Lenin. He provided the first eye-witness account of Soviet Russia published in Britain.[23]

Russians were exhausted from the huge losses of life and demands of war with Germany which had ended with the surrender of much territory in the March 1918 Treaty of Brest-Litovsk. Tsarist admirals and generals (the 'White Guards') who were supporters of the old regime, aided by foreign armies, sought to put the revolution down. Russia was convulsed by the invading forces of foreign powers and a civil war which lasted for three years. By 1919 vast areas had fallen to the Whites and the Red Army was racked with disease and hunger. Not part of his original plan for transforming Russia, Lenin's War Communism sought to meet this emergency situation and sustain the army through seizing not only the wealth of the propertied classes but also whatever the workers and peasants possessed.

Nevertheless, the Bolsheviks triumphed against the Whites who finally withdrew in October 1920. The civil war ended though the banditry of former soldiers and violent peasant uprisings helped spur Lenin's decision in the spring of 1921 to replace collectivisation with his New Economic Policy. This abandoned the requisition of peasants' surplus grain for a tax in kind, based on a percentage of the crops harvested. But it was too late to save harvests in 1921 and early 1922. The exceptional drought of 1921 led to one of the worst famines known. Millions perished in the Volga region and Ukraine.[24]

The Volga region had been one of the richest in the country. But the crops had totally failed and between twenty-five and thirty million people were now without food. In the summer of 1921 the *Chicago Tribune* called this famine 'The greatest story in the world' and was keen for exclusive eye-witness reportage from a non-Soviet source. Its correspondent Floyd Gibbons took up the challenge. After bribing an official in Riga where he had been arrested for not having a visa, he accompanied Litvinov, Soviet Ambassador to Latvia, to Moscow by train. From there he made the long journey to Samara where the stench and danger of disease was so great that he worked with his face covered by a towel soaked in disinfectant. He saw a boy of twelve 'with a face of sixty' carrying a six-month-old baby. The boy placed the infant under a railway carriage, chewed ravenously on some dried fish-heads then transferred the half-masticated food from his mouth to the baby's 'as a mother bird feeds her young'.[25]

Evelyn saw equally harrowing sights. Her Russian journey was undertaken with the Quakers.[26] The Friends had British and American workers in Russia in 1917 but found it difficult to sustain their work, not least because Russian doctors returning from the front resumed responsibility for medical relief. Quakers began concentrating on the surroundings and town of Buzuluk in the Samara province (about 530 miles east and slightly south of Moscow). But they had to return home in the summer of 1919. Over the next year or so they inched their way back. Early in 1920, with infant mortality standing at 30 per cent, the British War Office permitted the export of goods to Russian children's hospitals and supplies began arriving (via Finland). Later that year the engineer Arthur Watts and the American Quaker Anna Haines (who had worked with the Quaker mission in the Buzuluk district during the war) negotiated agreements with the People's Commissariat of Food Production and the Central Association of Russian Cooperatives enabling them to organise their own distribution scheme and that of the British Save the Children Fund. Friends were soon supplementing the rations of about fifteen thousand Moscow children.

After news in July 1921 of the failure of the harvest for the fourth year in succession, Anna Haines returned to the Buzuluk district with the first consignment of foreign relief and reported on its famine. Meanwhile her compatriot the left-wing journalist Anna Louise Strong began the feeding of children in and around Samara. The Soviets now agreed to provide personnel, office and warehouse space, free lodging for relief workers, free travel and free transportation of goods as well as telegraphic and telephonic communication. Ruth Fry stressed that the Soviets provided much of the relief. She knew that rumours circulated at home that they intercepted supplies to feed the Red Army. Yet food was being transported safely for hundreds of miles by starving people. Fry noted that more goods were stolen from trains at home than pilfered from Russian trains.

Some effort was, however, now being made within Britain to pub-licise the plight of starving Russians. Brailsford was instrumental in getting the Russian Famine Relief Fund going. This organisation, the Friends and the Save the Children Fund then joined forces in an All-British Appeal. There was a government grant of £200,000 for food as well as £50,000 worth of meat from Australia, with further money raised through publicity. After a conference in Geneva held by the International Red Cross, the Norwegian diplomat and Arctic explorer Dr Nansen became the Commissioner for Russian Relief and negotiated on behalf of the European relief agencies with the Soviet government. But the League of Nations rejected his appeal for inter-national effort lest it bolster the Bolsheviks. Nevertheless, groups of people in fifteen countries now sent food to the Russian people. The American Relief Administration provided most of the foreign aid. Around Buzuluk a small group of American Friends concentrated on the eastern area whilst British Friends took responsibility for Buzuluk town and its hinterland to the north. Having extended their control, the Quakers were now responsible for an area as large as Belgium. It was, recalled Ruth Fry, one of the worst affected famine areas, 'a land where death seemed more real than life'.[27] And it was here that Evelyn arrived in January 1922.

The Friends Relief Committee in London had decided that eye-witness accounts would help raise funds, so asked Ruth Fry as Honorary Secretary and Evelyn Sharp with her 'literary ability' to visit 'to prove to the sceptics here' that they were actually feeding starving Russians.[28] Evelyn, dressed 'like an arctic explorer', Ruth Fry and Fred Brennan of the Workers' Educational Association left London on New Year's Day, travelling first to Berlin then on to Poland.[29] At each stage of their 2,780-mile journey they were met by Friends. In Warsaw they dined with the men of the mission who resided in a former palace. Evelyn's diary described sitting at a long, candlelit table with gold spoons and elegant glasses: 'It seems a long way from John Street.' It was even further removed from what she was about to encounter.

Major George Perry (who spoke fluent Russian and had formerly been attached to the British Embassy in St Petersburg) joined Evelyn and they took the weekly diplomatic train for the Russian border. The Friends had helped obtain Evelyn's passport: 'I think only the Quakers could have convinced them [the British authorities] that I was going to Russia on an unpolitical mission and not to plot the downfall of the British constitution.'[30] When they reached the frontier at Stolpce, they and their luggage were moved to a waiting train. But there was no engine. They had cabbage soup, walked in the slippery snow and rigged up candles in the train, then, wrapped in rugs, they attempted to sleep. The engine, 'the sort of thing you see in an illustrated History of the Steam Engine', arrived the next day. It was stoked with wood. They soon ran into a blizzard. It took frequent rests and the journey lasted three days but Evelyn enjoyed a landscape where 'birch trees looked like lace against the sky'. And after this adventure, not unlike one of her children's stories, they finally reached Moscow. It was 5am on the Russian Christmas Day and, as they squeezed into tiny sledges, the bells were ringing.

Evelyn thought Moscow beautiful. She stayed at a flat occupied by the Friends Moscow Unit. There were now five men and six women there, including Anna Louise Strong who was recovering from typhus contracted in the Volga 'Hunger Land'. Evelyn wrote to tell Henry about the city (he was in America for four months covering a disarmament conference).[31] The Moscow that Evelyn saw was very different from the city Henry had known just after the 1905 Revolution and also unlike the images of Soviet Russia at home. Evelyn found the cathedral packed with Christmas worshippers, private trading had been restored (though she thought the Soviet stores were the best shops) and the ballet and opera flourished. She saw a performance of *Don Quixote* from a diplomatic box at the opera house and attended a wrestling match, surprising Ruth Fry with her knowledge of a sport where men wore 'the least respectable form of bathing costume'. Thanks to their interpreter, Evelyn witnessed the funeral of a high-ranking official who had died of typhus, an experience that would provide a dramatic contrast to the scenes she would soon witness of the disposal of the dead in Buzuluk. At the funeral she met Kalenin who chaired the central executive committee of the Soviets, and Kamenev and Zinoviev, both members of the Politburo. When she asked if one mourner who arrived by sleigh was someone important, she was firmly told 'Nobody is important here'. Yet when she visited the Kremlin a Rolls Royce drew up alongside them. Inside was Trotsky.

Evelyn and Ruth had a meeting with Lunacharsky, the People's Commissar for Education. Evelyn called him 'A very charming intellectual'; Fry was also impressed by this 'delightfully human, tender man, obviously most keen for the children's welfare'.[32] The women visited institutions where the Quakers provided condensed milk. When a toddler rushed to embrace her at one orphanage, Evelyn was 'smugly flattered' until told that the last Quaker relief worker to visit had given chocolate to the children.[33] At one day nursery for brewery workers' children, their crimson velvet coats and caps were made from curtains that formerly hung in the director's house.

Evelyn was especially impressed by the forty-six Forest Schools on a former merchant's estate just outside Moscow. They lay between pine trees, 'just like a fairytale forest'. Pupils helped build the wooden huts they lived in and drew up their own time-tables. Four were nature study schools (educational reforms currently advocated the study of labour, nature and society rather than traditional subjects). She also visited a school for recovering tubercular children where they were enjoying a Christmas party. Echoing Lunacharsky's words, she told Henry that there was 'a passion for education and culture' and that comparing the healthy-looking children skiing in the forest, with 'those I left behind at Wapping, I just boil'.[34]

Later she spent a night at the School of the October Revolution, 'a sort of farm colony' for 225 boys and girls. Farming and gardening were part of their education. They performed traditional Russian dances, sang old songs and presented the visitors with an exercise book of dried flowers, verses and photographs. Evelyn was especially pleased that the school had a woman principal and a male head of housekeeping. Yet, despite being predisposed to champion Soviet education – and Evelyn was impressed by the way teachers and pupils interacted – she was wary of assuming too much from formal visits and conscious of the problems of feeding these children adequately.[35]

After five days in Moscow (their train had been held up by a snow-storm) the four travellers finally boarded the Tashkent Express. It did not live up to its name. They took four days to reach their destination. Much of the line was a single track. After crossing the River Volga, Evelyn saw, for the first time, a caravan of camels. The travellers had to wait two days at Samara where they enjoyed the luxury of warm water. Workers tunnelled through snow further down the line though the delay was also because numbers entering the famine district were limited. Underfed workers had to tackle gigantic snowdrifts. Sixty per cent of railway employees now had typhus.

At last, in painfully cold weather, they reached the provincial town of Buzuluk on 16 January and were driven to a wooden house at the Quaker headquarters. No other foreign relief organisation operating in Russia currently permitted women workers. The Buzuluk Quakers included Violet Tillard, who, like Evelyn, had been imprisoned for the suffrage cause. The mission was headed by Arthur Watts. Evelyn wrote in her diary: 'You could tell from the faces of the workers what horrors they had all looked upon.'

On her first morning in Buzuluk Evelyn passed a corpse lying face down in the snow. 'Before the day was out', she wrote in her diary, 'I came to think he was the happiest thing I had seen that day'. She visited the warehouse from which camels transported stores, then she went to her first feeding centre. Here nine hundred children were fed daily. By the spring of 1922 there were nine hundred feeding points in 280 villages in the Buzuluk area alone. In these villages about three-quarters of the people were being fed by the Friends, the Soviet government covering the rest.

But it was the afternoon's encounter that gave Evelyn the greatest shock. She was taken to a receiving station or *pre-emnyk* where abandoned children were temporarily housed before being sent to a home or evacuated by a Red Cross 'sanitary train' to another part of Russia. Yet so infrequent were these trains that instead of spending just twenty-four hours there, children remained in these overcrowded places. This one, reckoned to be the best, currently held four hundred, more than double its recommended number. Dysentery was rife and eighty children had been admitted to hospital that morning.

Eight children had died in the last six days in the next home. Yet many of its inhabitants managed to beam and mutter thanks when the supervisor said they were from the Quakers. 'You have never seen a child's smile till you have seen it on the face of a child who is near death's door from hunger' wrote Evelyn in her diary. In a couple of crowded rooms, she saw children with twisted spines and protruding stomachs and heard moans and wails. Many crouched motionless in rows, as close to the wall as possible since the stove warmed it. They stared blankly with 'little, old, dead faces'. She watched a boy whose arms were outstretched. He had the face of a skull and vacant eyes that slowly closed. It was, she told *Manchester Guardian* readers, as if he were 'being crucified for the apathy of mankind'.[36] After visiting a hospital, she wrote, 'the shortage of *everything* made wards almost into torture chambers'.[37] Gertrude Ostler, who had recently visited Buzuluk, had reported that in one hospital there were four fevered children to each bed.[38]

Evelyn's tour ended in the cemetery, close to the foothills of the Ural Mountains, by a little white church with a brilliant dome. Here she saw heaps of tangled corpses, four hundred bodies awaiting burial, since it was impossible to cover more than a hundred daily in the pit hacked out in the frozen ground. Many were half naked. One American Friend had recently become insane after witnessing this scene. Evelyn found it terrible and revolting yet wrote in her diary that these poor bodies discarded 'like rats on a refuse heap' had on their faces 'a strange dignity'.

Ruth Fry left, accompanying a deputation from the British Famine Fund and the International Red Cross headed by Sir Benjamin Robertson (a former chief commissioner in India and expert on famines). Robertson had, as Evelyn tersely put it, 'come out to see if there really was a famine – he found there was'.[39] The visitors had declared that, with the exception of Saratoff where they had visited a refugee camp, this was the worst famine area they had seen. Friends now fervently hoped that more supplies would be directed to the region.

Several other workers, including Violet Tillard, also moved on. Evelyn was now the sole woman relief worker in the Buzuluk mission though there were ten men, including Russian sleigh drivers. She was expected to be 'mother' and 'look after their meals and cut hands' (but there was a young Russian maid and an elderly cook). When she heard of yet another formal visit, this time from a Dutch delegation and the Imperial War Fund, she worried about the budget, swept out rooms, planned meals, looked after a sick sledge driver, put together a medical package for an outpost and then went to market.

Most of the time, accompanied by Astoria, a German-speaking interpreter, she inspected children's homes and receiving stations, dressed in a leather coat sporting the red and black Quaker star. She checked that children were receiving their proper rations. Over four thousand were being fed by the Friends in homes throughout the district, and in Buzuluk itself two thousand children now received food outside residential homes. This latter development was seen as the way forward. There were other promising signs. Although Evelyn still found many 'deserted mites' and handed them in to homes, far fewer children – about twenty rather than two hundred a day – were now dumped in town since many more were receiving food in their own country areas.

Nevertheless, between 25 December and 20 January, 2,200 people had died of starvation or disease in the town; 237 had been found dead in the streets. Evelyn's diary was punctuated with references to abandoned frozen bodies in the snow, their sheepskin coats invariably missing. In just three and a half days three hundred new corpses were added to the piles in the cemetery. Writing to Henry, Evelyn admitted that

> This is the most awful experience I have ever had. As I sit here, I can see through the window three corpses lying in the snow outside. Every morning there are corpses in the street waiting to be picked up.[40]

She was well aware that the Friends could not have saved them and that, had they dragged the dying inside, they would have been surrounded by many other pathetic moribund figures. But the notion of acceptance was problematic:

> I am not sure that it consoles me to hear that in time you get used to seeing people drop dead: it is that fatal propensity to 'get used' to things no one should see unmoved that causes most of the cruelty in the world to go on.

Yet she knew that those who were living – just – were in the worst position and to sit down to eat with the sound of a starving woman crying outside in exceptionally cold weather (−24°F) was 'almost intolerable'.[41] When they visited the local Soviet headquarters they were followed by 'screaming starving people' who kept catching hold of them. Evelyn told the *Manchester Guardian* that the children's crying was unlike anything she was used to: they uttered cries of anguish or moaned in a high-pitched key which, if you were not careful, would remain in your head even when no children were present.[42] She admitted in a letter to Henry that the smell of the children's homes was never out of her nostrils. Their wailing rang in her ears.[43]

When Evelyn first arrived, relief was for children. The only adults in the district to receive food were some nursing mothers and personnel at the feeding stations. From 20 January, however, working with the local Soviets, the Quakers extended their feeding in the district to encompass large numbers of adults. They now considered it vital to take care of parents in order to reduce the number of orphaned children. Four days later the Red Cross train evacuated about five hundred boys and girls to more prosperous parts of the country and the following day twenty-eight wagons brought food from England, enabling the feeding of thirty thousand adults and seventy thousand children up to the end of February.

After ten days three relief workers arrived from England. Arthur Watts now sent Evelyn, Harry Wiltshire and a French-speaking Russian interpreter called Mademoiselle Papoff to visit Alexievky, the worst famine spot in Samara province. They missed by minutes a train that was already three weeks late but at midnight two days later set off for the outpost. Early the next morning they found that their train had been uncoupled and left in a siding close to Pavlovka, but the local Soviet arranged for two camels, drivers and wooden freight sleighs (crudely constructed with wooden runners raised just above the ground) to convey them and their luggage. The sleighs swayed from side to side and moved very slowly. Evelyn sat on a sack containing dried camel grass, narrowly avoiding being pitched off her sleigh whenever a camel tried to grab a mouthful of the fodder.

Camels were in demand since, unlike horses that required expensive hay, they could live off straw and carry heavy loads. Henry had needed patience in Angola some years earlier when he had spent weeks inching his way through its untamed interior in a wagon drawn by oxen. Now Evelyn was at the whim of a complaining camel who crawled across the undulating steppe, tipped his rider into a snowdrift and then sat down, refusing to budge, in the loneliest part of the route after the drivers had lost the track. But, of course, this also provided her with a story and a moral, readers at home learning how the humanitarians valiantly resisted the drivers' plea to strike the camel on the nose in order to make the creature move. The camel moved when the camel felt like it and fortunately force was once more shown to be redundant.[44]

The drivers regaled them with tales (relayed by the interpreter) of man-eating wolves and of bandits. At the village of Zuevka they were greeted by the local Soviet and slept at a priest's home. Here they learned that the population of 3,500 had been reduced by a third in a community where there had once been many reasonably comfortable peasant proprietors. Their hospital had no medicine or equipment, just an unqualified medical assistant. Yet the villagers were finally receiving the help they desperately needed, the Friends Relief Mission and the Russian government together providing bread, soup and cocoa in a spotless *stolovia* or kitchen.

The last part of the journey to Alexievky was in horse-drawn sledges. It was just as well since they encountered blizzards and drifting snow on the steppe. They passed hamlets – one completely deserted – with their 'skeleton snowbound houses' falling into ruin. Many inhabitants had fled to Ukraine in a search for grain. Those who remained were dying from starvation brought on by war, counter-revolution and the consequences of drought. In one hamlet the baker

10. Evelyn on the Russian steppe, 1922

pounded dried camel grass in a wooden mortar, put it through a sieve then mixed it with a little water and linseed. As she did this she regaled the visitors with tales of cannibalism. Yet this was preferable to the 'bread' made from grass and the ground bones of dogs, cats and horses. Evelyn began to understand why so many children contracted dysentery.

They eventually reached the Friends Mission at Alexievky. Marjorie Rackstraw, its head, had not seen visitors since the previous October. Now that all local children were being fed, Evelyn saw, for a change, boys and girls laughing and playing in the streets. She helped supervise the distribution of the Quaker food portion in some of the *stolovia* (the Quakers covered twenty-four communities scattered across the steppe), often from peasants' small cottages where scales for weighing bread were suspended from ceiling beams. When the visitors promised clothes to a destitute girl of thirteen who looked thirty, their feet were kissed. To Evelyn's embarrassment, this form of thanks accompanied by blessings was repeated by many.

Quakers supplied twenty-seven kitchens in Alexievky and the Soviets fifteen. The town had already lost five thousand of its eight thousand inhabitants. Evelyn attended a meeting of the local famine committee and the Mission in the Co-operative Store.[45] The first thing she saw was a bust of the pioneer Welsh co-operator, Robert Owen.

She was upset by what followed. As they left the meeting villagers fell on their knees imploring them to feed them too. They wore eastern garments and headdresses (they were now close to Asia) and Evelyn was reminded of biblical scenes. It was necessary to explain that dividing the meagre amounts even further would help nobody. Yet, typically Evelyn's thoughts were not for herself but for the terrible choices that had to be faced by those who were not just helping out for a few weeks.

Wrapped in a sheepskin coat, fur helmet and felt boots, Evelyn and Tom Copeman (who had been at Buzuluk when Evelyn first arrived there) now had to endure the long journey back across the steppe in a driving blizzard, the wind whipping their faces with frozen snow particles. Reaching a village just before dark, they went with the young drivers to the priest's house. Evelyn simply said the word 'Quakery' and they were given a warm welcome.[46] The next day was especially bleak and desolate with that special silence that comes from travelling across virgin snow. The edited version of Evelyn's diary tells how:

> Now and then we passed the gallows-like structure of a disused well, and once there was a wooden cross over the grave of some unknown traveller; but for these not very encouraging features there was nothing to show that anybody had ever travelled that way in a sledge, or ever would again.[47]

Eventually, the two travellers, stiff and extremely cold, reached Pavlovka. Three of the relief workers there were recovering from typhus. Violet Tillard, who had been nursing them, had already left but soon afterwards she died of the disease. Before Evelyn and Tom sat down to supper, news came that a Quaker wagon could be attached to a goods train that night so they left immediately for the station.

At the junction for the Siberian railway Evelyn concocted a meal of bully beef, bread, marmalade, honey and coffee that seemed like a feast. But they were soon stranded in a siding. Eventually they were transferred to a slow passenger train, but it took nine days to reach Moscow (with a food supply for forty-eight hours). Evelyn composed a long letter to Henry, wrote a couple of newspaper articles, learned a little Russian and played chess with Tom. They read the Bible and *Northanger Abbey* to each other but found Jane Austen 'too out of touch with this situation'. On reaching Moscow Evelyn luxuriated in what she called 'the greatest bath of my life'. She had not slept in a bed with sheets and a pillow since her previous visit to Moscow. A few days later they started on the final leg of their journey, arriving in London on 23 February.

Evelyn now publicised her findings to raise funds for further relief. She admitted in her memoirs of 1933 that it was necessary to tone down some of her impressions of the new order in Russia so that she was believed in drawing room and other gatherings.[48] She gave talks on the famine in many venues, such as a church hall in Hither Green, south-east London, where she delivered an 'excellent, straight-forward narrative'.[49] In March she joined Catherine Marshall (for WILPF), Eleanor Rathbone (National Union of Societies for Equal Citizenship) and E. M. White (Federation of Women Civil Servants) in a deputation to Downing Street. They met Austen Chamberlain and handed in a petition requesting a government grant for Nansen's Russian appeal. The following month both Evelyn and Henry participated in WILPF's Easter Vacation School in the Lake District. Evelyn spoke about Russia and international understanding.

She also contributed short stories based on her experiences to the *Daily Herald*. One entitled 'Brothers' was reprinted as a pamphlet by the Friends Relief Committee.[50] The first half is about Ivan and based on one of the fifteen-year-olds who had driven Evelyn and Tom across the steppe in a blizzard. The boy is offered a chunk of real bread instead of the terrible substitutes he has endured for months. He shares it with a starving old man. The second half concerns John, a young Englishman who has just won fifteen shillings. He goes to a lecture and sees lantern slides about a starving foreign child who gives his bread to an old man. The child's name means John and the young man finds himself giving up his winnings when a plate comes round. Not yet reconciled to charity, he tells a friend that he has given his money to a brother.

The *Manchester Guardian* played an important part in raising funds for Russian famine relief. Evelyn had been delighted to see vital sacks of rye arriving in Buzuluk stamped *Manchester Guardian*. Both Evelyn and Ruth Fry wrote letters to the press appealing for funds and Evelyn contributed articles about the Friends' work, often personalising accounts by naming children and following individual fates. Having praised those who were helping 'in far off Manchester', she was prepared to shame readers into contributing more. After describing how they had to turn away some desperate peasants, she stated that they could not give them food because:

enough kind people in our own country – I am sure they are all kind – had not the imagination to visualise what it means to sit all day in a little bare wooden house, with nothing in the cupboard except a compound of earth and grass, just dying in sharp agonies of pain, day by day, till the blessed sleep comes that ends in death.

Evelyn continued to use fiction to deplore the ignorance and suspicion that circulated in the wake of the revolution and periodically flourished during 'red scares'. Although in 1920 a 'Hands off Russia' campaign (with the *Daily Herald* and Lansbury playing a crucial role) saw trade unions and the Labour Party successfully resist the possibility of British military intervention against the Soviet regime, attitudes subsequently hardened. The *Herald* paid a price: the government attempted to discredit its Soviet links and question how it was funded.

After Lloyd George resigned in October 1922, Evelyn used the approaching general election to expose in a series of *Daily Herald* stories the assumptions prompted by political and economic uncertainties. In 'The Woman Voter Sees It Through' (a pun on the title of H. G. Wells's wartime novel about Mr Britling), the newly enfranchised Laura Brunton says she will vote Labour so long as they are not all Bolsheviks, that is, people who want to change everything in a minute.[51] A Liberal canvasser on the doorstep assures a family that if the Bolsheviks get into power they will rob honest folk like themselves of all their hard-earned savings. Once he sees inside their house, however, he witnesses their abject poverty. Saving was a concept alien to this family.[52]

Percy Comfort MP is pulled from the wheels of a lorry in another story. But the working man who rescues him recoils from being called a hero. He had been labelled thus in 1918. In the 1922 election he was called an honest working man. Then he was branded a Bolshevik.[53] In 'Recognising Russia!' Mrs Pettigrew believes anything printed that demonises Bolsheviks. She sees them as breaking up family life, 'snatching innocent children from their homes and shutting them up in communist schools, where they learn all kinds of wickedness'. Here Evelyn uses the tactic adopted in the story that began this chapter: Mrs Pettigrew discovers that the state institution her son describes, which she readily disparages, is actually a school in Stoke-on-Trent.[54]

Throughout her time in Russia, Evelyn had kept a diary. Extracts from the two volumes were published by the Friends Relief Committee in a sixpenny twenty-four-page pamphlet entitled 'In the Volga Valley'. It is not exactly the same as the handwritten volumes and it includes a number of emotive headings such as 'The Smile of a Starving Child' and 'The Staff of Death'. But it would be misleading to suggest that this was simply the polished version. The original was compiled in full knowledge that this was the first stage of what would become a public document and was somewhat stylised. This is especially evident in the final entries. They were quite dramatic and were carefully composed. The diaries were, after all, written by a woman who wrote for a living. Evelyn's letters to Henry from Russia, written in pencil, were more frank and personal than the diaries. A letter from Buzuluk, written on 25 January, ends: 'I miss you every day & can hardly believe that some day we shall be together again.'

The letters and diaries demonstrate Evelyn's bravery and determination to be positive. She assured Henry that she was having 'a great experience and you know I always have a charmed life wherever I go because I am never afraid of catching anything'. In the two months in Russia she had been exposed on many occasions to deadly diseases. She took risks and was lucky. In a children's home in Alexievky she found a little boy with '*no* flesh on his bones, only skin drawn tightly over them'. The child was whimpering like a sick animal. Evelyn stroked his face and hands and this quietened him. Foolishly, she did not wash her hands afterwards. When Arthur Ransome visited the Volga region in 1921 he covered himself in turpentine which, he believed, saved him. Some of Evelyn's own comrades were not so fortunate.[55]

One of Evelyn's favourite sayings was Adelaide Procter's couplet:

Two women looked thro' prison bars.
The one saw fog; the other stars.[56]

Evelyn was determined to be positive. She even managed to extract some good features from the nightmare trip across the steppe during her nine-day journey back to Moscow. The 'blizzard effects', she wrote, were 'simply great' and Henry's son, the artist C. R. W. Nevinson, would make wonderful pictures from the snowy steppes.[57] Alex Sidney, who travelled from England to Buzuluk in the autumn of 1922, wrote of his destination, that 'the desolation appalled me, the snow, the bleakness & the misery seemed endless'.[58] Evelyn was equally shocked by the human misery but she also praised the beauty of the Russian landscape and Buzuluk's occasional stunning blue sky.

In 1926 the writer and former suffragette Beatrice Harraden published a novel called *Rachel*. One chapter set in Poland was dedicated to the Polish and other Relief Organisations. It included a panegyric to one 'gallant creature, full of enterprise and initiative, inspiriting, extraordinarily human and ardently devoted to the work of relief'. Later the author admitted that Evelyn was the model for this woman who was never patronising and always respected other people's pride and feelings.[59]

Evelyn had been in Buzuluk district when degradation had reached its nadir. By the spring of 1922 there were nine hundred feeding points in 280 villages in that region alone. Many of the crops sown in 1920 began to grow again. The Imperial War Relief Fund helped boost the aid for the Quakers. Evelyn sat on the general committee of the Friends Relief Committee in 1923 and attended meetings regularly[60] but the improving situation meant that in 1924 Quakers began gradually withdrawing from the area.

Evelyn nevertheless remained interested in Soviet politics. In her final days in Moscow she had met one of the new breed of Soviet figureheads, Shimovitch. He expressed his certainty that Russia was going forward but needed international union for this to succeed, adding that Christ was the first Communist. Evelyn's fervent hope was that no more bloodshed would follow. She wrote in her diary: 'I knew I was a pacifist & thought I was a communist.' Shimovitch she called 'a very great man' who appeared to offer 'a real germ of hope for the future everywhere'.

Evelyn's accounts of meeting Soviet officials suggest a credulity that seems more evident in retrospect than it would have done in the early 1920s. But Evelyn, like Lansbury, was an idealist who 'believed in the perfectability of people'.[61] Both were struck by the educational experiments and treatment of women and wanted to believe that the new system heralded a better future. Evelyn's prime purpose was to provide relief for the starving and later to help raise funds for further aid. In subsequent articles contrasting for example, Soviet (and German) education with state schools in London, her aim was to suggest novel ways of improving conditions at home.

Evelyn was prepared to defend the Soviet Union for rather longer than Henry was. His anger at the treatment of Georgia by the USSR, quite apart from his inherent opposition to the power of the state, soon made him a fierce critic. Indeed, it was one of the few subjects on which the couple disagreed. A few months after she returned, Henry described Evelyn as a 'champion of Lenin', and just after the infamous Zinoviev Letter and Labour's defeat in 1924 wrote that Evelyn 'cannot endure the smallest criticism agst the soviets'.[62] But she never joined the Communist Party and a decade later was critical of Soviet actions.[63]

Evelyn's experience in Russia in 1922 had, in another way, helped to seal her relationship with Henry. Unlike most British women and men, she could empathise with his love of travel and adventure. She grasped something of the devastation he had witnessed in war-torn places such as Macedonia and appreciated both the privations and pleasures involved in his mammoth journeys across the Russian Empire. Henry had met Tolstoy in 1905. Some years later Evelyn talked to Tolstoy's translator in Moscow (he was anti-Communist and 'Tried to make for a case for Tsardom', claiming that people had been freer and happier than they were now). Both Evelyn and Henry were familiar with the frustrations of not speaking the local language and endured a severe lack of comfort and adverse climates and terrain far from home. Both used the pen to convey experiences to a public that could never fully understand. Henry, himself an inveterate diarist, found Evelyn's Russian diary enthralling, both 'splendid & terrible'.[64] Evelyn would record her future adventures in diaries. But her journey to Russia remained, by her own admission, 'the outstanding adventure of my life'.[65]

9

Still rebelling: Women, writing and politics in the 1920s

In 1922, when Evelyn worked to alleviate the horrors of the Russian famine, Winifred Coombe Tennant, from South Wales, became a delegate to the third assembly of the League of Nations. She was a parliamentary candidate, member of the National Union of Societies for Equal Citizenship and patron of Welsh artists. Her League of Nations selection was commented upon in the press because she was Britain's first woman delegate. Evelyn added her voice but her *Daily Herald* column in early September took a different tack.

Evelyn appreciated that women were at last being seen fit to hold important public posts (Winifred Coombe Tennant was, like Margaret Wynne Nevinson, one of the pioneer postwar female Justices of the Peace). But although she applauded the Sex Disqualification (Removal) Act of 1919 that had opened the door to women becoming magistrates and jurors, Evelyn had reservations about the attention paid to such appointments. Remarking on the sex (invariably female) of the person showed, she argued, just how far women were from achieving real equal opportunities with men. As she put it, 'Woman must, in fact, be thoroughly ignored as a woman before she can be said to be fully recognised as one.'[1]

She was also scornful of the terms of reference for the post. It was to advise on questions affecting the position of women. This could mean everything or nothing in Evelyn's opinion. She disparaged the claim that Mrs Coombe Tennant represented 'the distinctive point of view of the women of Great Britain', arguing that 'a shout of laughter would go up from the civilised world' if a man were given that brief for his sex. Evelyn asked why women should 'be perpetually forced to remain shut up in an intellectual water-tight compartment'. She understood that the insistence on the limitations of women's interests had led to her 'artificial specialisation' in them but saw this as a reactionary rather than progressive development. In her view it would hinder the emancipation of women. Evelyn now argued that problems would be solved only when approached not as women's problems but as human questions.

In her own career Evelyn faced a similar issue about drawing attention to women. In May 1922 the *Manchester Guardian* started a daily Women's Page (though not formally headed as such and initially only covering three columns) 'on subjects which are special to women'. Edited by Madeline Linford, former secretary to the news editor, it was to be aimed at 'the intelligent woman'.[2] It became renowned, provoking debates about the necessity for a space dedicated to women. Evelyn was its first regular columnist. Although there were some other frequent contributors in the 1920s such as Muriel Harris and Catherine Carswell, Evelyn's contributions were unusual in being weekly and signed with her name rather than initials.

The page was a mixture of continuity and change. Women's columns and pages in newspapers were not new. Florence Fenwick Miller had begun her column for the *Illustrated London News* in 1886 and had continued to write it (interspersed with other work such as editing the *Women's Signal* and being on the staff of the *Daily News*) until 1918.[3] In 1895 it had been expanded into a Women's Page. But although Fenwick Miller had progressive views on women's rights, her readership was distinctly conservative and articles had to respect this. In contrast, thanks to early contributors like Evelyn, Winifred Holtby and Vera Brittain, then later spirited feminists such as Mary Stott and Jill Tweedie, the *Guardian* Women's Page, fortified by its ever-vigilant readership, acquired a status of its own.

Evelyn was, however, initially ambivalent about this project. The tone was to be domestic, with articles on subjects such as household economy and the care of children. Evelyn had been writing features on the back page since the Edwardian years. Some had been about fashion with quaint titles such as 'How to Dress in the Water' and 'Harmony in Furs'. She had also written short stories for the paper and weighty pieces of investigative journalism, often without a byline. Her articles commanded respect and occupied at least a full column. She was paid three guineas per article. Now her signed articles were to be for the Women's Page. She protested that 'in nine cases out of ten there is no reason that I can see why they should be on the Woman's [*sic*] Page at all'.[4] The following year she pointed out to C. P. Scott that the fact that her articles were frequently reprinted in the weekly *Guardian* and newspapers all over the world showed that they were not just for women. Moreover, since the format for this page consisted of shorter articles of half a column (payment was three guineas for a column), she was losing out financially.

Anxious not to lose this well-known, experienced contributor, Linford assured Scott that Evelyn's 'very good' articles were usually just under a column in length and worth three guineas each. Scott (whose internal memoranda show that he and Linford needed slightly shorter contributions) assured Evelyn that her articles were 'about the best thing that appear' in the Women's Page. But he then added that if she were happier writing longer pieces, the solution might be to contribute fortnightly rather than weekly. Deeply hurt, Evelyn called this 'a good breakfast before execution'.[5]

She did, nevertheless, continue to write weekly articles for the paper until May 1927 and then fortnightly ones until October 1934.[6] They are a valuable piece of social history, charting shifts in, for example, manners for middle-class women and new labour-saving devices within and beyond the home for the busy professional woman. These included the Bachelors' Mending Service and, especially popular with elementary school teachers, tricycle delivery of what we would call 'fast food' in aluminium containers from a basement kitchen in Bloomsbury.

Some of her Women's Page pieces were on subjects that were probably written to fit in with the spirit of the page rather than because of their own intrinsic interest to Evelyn. She had her share of 'Holiday Frocks for a Little Girl' and tips on how the housewife (or her 'help') might empty refuse without dragging out the pail. Anyone reading such advice could be forgiven for presuming that they were written by a wife and mother living in a family house. But Evelyn was not afraid to be iconoclastic. She poked fun at the clothes displayed in shop windows, seeing them as the fantasies of window dressers and far from the reality of any women she knew.[7] And she could not resist turning even an article on gloves into a political issue. In July 1922 she reported that an all-male committee of MPs had decided that women would have to wear shoddy British gloves since they would not to be able to purchase the superior German fabric gloves. This was called making Germany pay. What an outcry there would be, she wrote, if women declared that men must purchase expensive tobacco from Kent or champagne made in Birmingham.[8]

So, from the start, Evelyn injected the Women's Page with a radical edge. Her article on the 'servant problem' did not solve the problem of how the middle-class housewife of limited means in need of a servant could be reconciled with employees who clearly deserved decent remuneration. But it did suggest that the job should be recognised as a skilled profession and that, instead of trying to turn unwilling typists or factory workers into domestic servants, men should try taking on the job.[9]

Evelyn stressed the importance of striving for the same rights for women and men, arguing, especially after the full enfranchisement of women in 1928, that emphasising women's rights and privileges with reference to their apparently special nature and difference was reactionary. She therefore opposed laws that spared women from, for example, being hanged. Such an approach, she stressed, deflected attention from the basic fact that 'hanging is a relic of barbarism that should not be allowed to exist in a civilised state' (she was active in the National Council for the Abolition of the Death Penalty).[10] She urged co-operation and collaboration between men and women wherever possible. In a talk to the Fabian Society's Women's Group she suggested that greater comradeship between the sexes might prove to be the most important change resulting from women's emancipation.[11]

In the early 1930s Evelyn went so far as to state 'I do not think I should ever have been a Suffragette if I had been a feminist'.[12] She suggested that many who supported the suffragist cause did so from the desire to remove the excuse for separating women's questions from men's. Yet she was, it seems, slightly disingenuously rewriting her own history. She had not supported adult suffrage (with all women and all men having the vote) until the latter part of the war. Rather she had argued for some women to be enfranchised (for women to have the vote on the same terms as men). Indeed, her statements and her practice at the time had shown her to be woman-centred in her approach to politics. Her shift is best understood in the context of interwar debates on feminism and her unease at what she saw as an insistence upon psychological differences between the sexes by those sometimes known as New Feminists. Like the novelist Winifred Holtby, she was more comfortable with an 'Old Feminism' that 'believes in the primary importance of the human being'.[13]

Evelyn was also concerned about the way that women were presumed to be mothers. In a *Daily Herald* story called 'Picnics, Women and War' she questioned assumptions that, for example, women as mothers of the race would naturally oppose war.[14] She stressed that some men displayed a universal respect for life. Evelyn's commitment to international humanitarianism and pacifism was crucial here. This had not been part of her agenda before 1914. Her postwar position as an Old or equalitarian feminist needs to be set against a background of increasing unemployment at home and desperate economic conditions witnessed abroad.

Moreover, much of Evelyn's writing in the interwar years belies her disclaimer. Her newspaper articles show a continued commitment to the interests of women and, even though she was wary of labels, her work was still informed by the experience that she had gained over the years working with and for women. She expressed regret that neither in principle nor practice had it been accepted that a woman had the right to a separate inner life and identity in the same way as a man had.[15] And in the Independent Labour Party's *New Leader* she attacked chivalry as a means of keeping woman in her place.[16] She criticised the assumption that women had no economic identity apart from their husbands and objected to discrimination against married women who, in the current economic climate, were being driven out of employment. As a single woman she objected to the state making marriage synonymous with a woman's occupation.[17] Evelyn was still primarily tuned to women's needs and deplored the fact that the Widows, Orphans and Old Age Contributory Pensions Bill (of 1925) excluded pensions for those whose husbands were incapacitated or had abandoned them. It also, she argued, ignored the children of unmarried mothers.

Evelyn's reservations about certain aspects of interwar feminism become clearer when viewed in the light of a controversial polemical study indicting sex antagonism that was published in 1924. *Ancilla's Share* was written by the woman who had converted Evelyn to suffrage. Elizabeth Robins's bold and angry book was published anonymously but reviewers, Evelyn included, revealed her name. Evelyn agreed that men and women needed to be jolted out of the assumption that, now that women were partially enfranchised, all was right with the world. She recognised that this book supplied that jolt but she maintained that its author underestimated the importance of what had already been achieved. She added 'I furiously disagree with some of the contentions', and she denounced as reactionary the suggestion that all co-operation with men should be suspended until women's position was sufficiently recognised so as to make possible perfect co-operation. Even though Robins rejected the notion of a women's political party, Evelyn saw separatism as the natural and potentially disastrous concomitant of Robins's thesis. Evidence to date did not convince Evelyn that the solidarity of womanhood was a force for effective peace. Nevertheless, she found the book engaging and would always appreciate the way that the actress had brought Ibsen's 'rebel women' to life. So she ended her review admitting that 'You may want to throw *Ancillas's Share* into the fire, but a horribly disconcerting memory of it sticks in your mind'.[18]

Evelyn was not alone in criticising Robins's outspoken words, though she and the founder of *Time and Tide*, the equalitarian feminist Lady Rhondda (who was doubtful whether men's attitudes towards women's work were based on 'sex antagonism'), were nowhere near as dismissive as H. G. Wells, who denounced the book as an artless demonstration of the sex antagonism she indicted.

Nevertheless, Robins chose to answer Evelyn in print, arguing that she had been misunderstood.[19] She distinguished between private and public life, denying that she had suggested the suspension of co-operation with men in private life. She argued that her ultimate aim was for men and women to work together effectually and in harmony but the blunt and provocative statement with which she opened her book ('These pages are not addressed to the masculine mind') did not help her case. Although anxious to correct misinterpretations, Robins was also anxious not to jeopardise her friendship with Evelyn and Henry, so conceded that she was perhaps guilty of some obscurity since Evelyn Sharp was 'so clear-headed and fair' a critic.

In 1926 Evelyn published a memoir of the scientist Hertha Ayrton who had died three years earlier. It too was a weighty tome of three hundred pages that struggled to sell and, as it had been for Elizabeth Robins (also better known for her fiction), this kind of writing was a departure for Evelyn. It was a conventional account of the life of a woman she had greatly admired, the step mother of Edith Zangwill and mother of her close friend Barbara Ayrton Gould. It was written more from a sense of duty than from a genuine desire to write a biography – Barbara had asked her to undertake it – and Evelyn found it hard going, unlike her fictional writing. It took her a year to complete and after the first two chapters Henry wrote in his diary that she 'finds it terrible labour, wishes she had not undertaken it'. She was very 'wretched & querulous'.[20]

The early life of Hertha Marks was synonymous with much of the history of feminism in the late nineteenth century. Her friends had included Barbara Bodichon, Emily Davies and George Eliot (Mirah in *Daniel Deronda* is partly based on her). She became one of Girton's pioneer women students. Louisa Garrett Anderson was one of a number of illustrious women taught mathematics by Ayrton. Evelyn's book is dedicated to another of her friends, Marie Curie. Evelyn had met this renowned scientist in 1912 when on holiday at Highcliffe-on-Sea with Ayrton and her two daughters.

Not surprisingly, it was the scientific research and writing that Evelyn found especially difficult. Chapters with titles such as 'The Hissing of the Electric Arc' would previously have been about magic toys rather than devoted to examining experiments leading to improvements in the illumination in searchlights and cinema projection. Ayrton's work on the properties of the electric arc was recognised when she became the first woman to read her own paper at the Institute of Electrical Engineers. In 1899 she was made their first woman member. This research and her work on the origin of sand ripples (important for understanding coastal erosion) earned her the Royal Society's prestigious Hughes Medal though her gender and marital status prevented her being nominated for membership. Her inventions included a geometric line-divider and, during the war, an anti-gas fan designed to expel poison gas from the trenches, known as the Ayrton Fan.[21]

Evelyn demonstrated how some of Hertha Ayrton's contemporaries gendered her success. She quoted one paper reassuring readers how this physicist was also 'a most charming woman in her home life . . . and in every way a woman' and another remarking on her 'feminine running commentary'. But Evelyn's memoir suffered from being excessively reverential. She also made some sweeping claims.[22] We are told that the scientist was 'born with a passion for justice' and that her whole life had been a preparation for the crisis of Edwardian suffrage. This was the point at which the author's and the subject's lives overlapped. Clearly Evelyn was on more familiar ground here and felt that she owed a lot to Ayrton, to whose home she had gone – as had Mrs Pankhurst – on her release from prison. Yet devoting almost a fifth of this long book to women's suffrage provides a somewhat skewed account. Indeed, in Ayrton's private correspondence with Evelyn, she expressed her wish that the latter could write witty stories rather than 'wasting yourself on Suffrage'.[23]

Evelyn's only other biographical study was of Mary Wollstonecraft. In May 1928 she lectured on her life at London's Essex Hall for the Suffragette Club (known from 1930 as the Suffragette Fellowship) established two years earlier to 'keep alive the suffragette spirit' through several forms of commemoration. This was its inaugural annual lecture. Recognising how the much-applauded notion of service associated with the war was being extended to the prewar suffrage struggle, Laura Mayhall has suggested that this organisation narrowed definitions of militancy by focusing unduly on the importance of imprisonment.[24] Yet although Evelyn's pedigree was impeccable, she chose not to dwell on such activities. Henry's diary described the talk as 'an admirable piece of work', displaying passion and a fine human understanding. He wrote an anonymous and very positive report of it for the *Manchester Guardian*.[25]

Evelyn had been apprehensive but her lecture was well received, the audience being largely composed of elderly people who remembered her suffrage work. She focused on Wollstonecraft as a democrat. The timing was all-important. The Representation of the People (Equal Franchise) bill had been introduced in March and had already passed its second reading in the House of Lords. Here and in the chapter she wrote a few years later for a collection entitled *Great Democrats*, Evelyn was at pains to emphasise the eighteenth-century thinker as a broad-minded idealist. She rejected earlier attacks on Wollstonecraft's morals, not least because she believed that comments on her personal life must necessarily be speculative and therefore problematic. She also chose not to focus on her as a feminist ('which she never was in the narrow sense of the word'). Instead, in line with Evelyn's own beliefs at this stage, she argued that it was only by understanding Wollstonecraft's 'conception of human freedom that one can understand her plea for the freedom of women'.[26]

On 2 July 1928, exactly six weeks after Evelyn's lecture, all women over twenty-one were enfranchised. But on the day of the bill's third reading in the House of Lords, Evelyn had attended Emmeline Pankhurst's funeral. Vast crowds thronged the streets around St. John's in Smith Square. The great, albeit controversial, leader had not witnessed the final triumph but her funeral was in the heart of Westminster, and official mourners as well as spectators would have been well aware of the irony of mounted police making way for the coffin of the woman they had so often confronted.[27]

Two years earlier another suffrage stalwart had died. Gertrude Baillie Weaver had been a friend of Evelyn's.[28] The women had a number of interests in common. A Quaker and pacifist, she was also a novelist who wrote under the name of Gertrude Colmore and she and her husband Harold were founder members of the United Suffragists. They were instrumental in the opening of Britain's first humane abattoir in Letchworth and were the moving spirits behind what became the National Council for Animal Welfare in 1923. Both Evelyn and Henry used the press to promote its annual week designed to draw attention to the plight of animals and birds.[29] Evelyn told a tongue-in-cheek story about the controversial birds' feathers in ladies' hats which the Plumage Bill sought to ban.[30] She advertised 'vegetarian furs' in the *Guardian* and highlighted the need for comprehensive legislation concerning animal slaughter. Indeed, the last article Evelyn contributed to the Women's Page (in October 1934) was called 'Inhuman Custom'. It focused on the need to amend the Slaughter of Animals Act to include the humane killing of sheep and pigs.[31]

Evelyn also asked whether it was still possible to attend the circus and remain a humanitarian. She suggested the difficulty of being 'PC' in the 1920s:

> There is no peace for the tender-hearted in these days of perpetual vigilance. Exhausted with the attempt to eliminate cruelty from what we eat and what we wear, we go to the circus for relaxation, mainly on account of our love of animals, only to be met outside by posters warning us of the horrors involved in performing animal turns and with leaflets containing details so revolting of what is done to the performers in order to make them amuse us that we begin to wonder if the only guarantee of decent treatment for these our fellow-creatures may not lie in the extinction of the whole animal kingdom – or perhaps more justly of the whole race of man.[32]

In the same year, Evelyn published a booklet entitled *Daily Bread* about the co-operative movement. She saw the housewife as 'the pivot upon which it turns'. Evelyn argued that by recognising the woman in the home 'not as a sentimental illusion but as an economic fact', she had been brought out of the home.[33] By 'woman' she meant here the working-class woman, primarily wives and widows, for whom the co-operative store was a real boon. Focusing on London, Evelyn illustrated the welfare, educational and employment opportunities the 'co-op' provided: children's and comrades' circles for the young and the vital work of the Women's Co-operative Guild. To the modern reader, Evelyn's comments on, for example, the 'homely humour' of guild members can seem patronising but the experienced journalist took pains to quote directly from her informants. She also recognised that those employed in the stores would probably sound positive when questioned by visitors who were likely to be co-operators and thus indirectly their employers. Evelyn tried to be unobtrusive and sensitive to members' needs. Virginia Woolf also wrote about the Guild and for four years ran their Richmond branch, but unlike Evelyn, could never quite reconcile herself to the class differences.[34]

Evelyn was asked to write a pamphlet to celebrate the fiftieth anniversary of the Guild. The Guild had started in 1883 with just seven members but now had 72,500 and over 1,500 branches. It fitted well Evelyn's postwar commitment to the Labour movement and her concern for working-class women. In *Buyers & Builders* she admitted that the co-operative organisation still harboured some anti-feminist sentiment (no woman currently sat on the new National Authority of the Co-operative Union). But she meekly accepted that this was to be found whenever men and women were in any kind of political or economic rivalry, suggesting that there was probably less competitiveness in the co-operative movement than elsewhere. Not surprisingly, she was impressed that 'no national or international question, from milk to war, is outside the province of these assembled housewives'.[35] For Evelyn co-operation spelt the negation of war since it involved a commitment to internationalism.

But recent experience of the Labour movement had involved conflict rather than co-operation, most notably in the General Strike of 1926. This strike was the culmination of a crisis that had been gathering pace over the past decade. International competition threatened export markets and the development of alternative sources of power posed challenges. Meanwhile increased worker militancy in a number of key industries was evident from 1915 in areas such as Clydeside and was further fuelled by the Russian Revolution.

Evelyn had already gained a little knowledge of mining communities. She had, as we have seen, visited the Ruhr district in Germany. Ironically, the French invasion that she deplored there had temporarily aided Britain's coal industry. Her first visit to the British coalfields was in late 1919 when the *Daily Herald* sent her as a 'special commissioner' to South Wales and Durham.[36] She compared colliers' houses in the Merthyr area to 'rows of planted cabbages left to run to seed'. Winding gear reminded her of gallows. Like many visitors, she remarked on the 'strange beauty of it all'.

Evelyn's unattributed articles commented on the women's ability to keep homes neat and tidy against the odds. She linked her findings to a plea for state ownership of the mines. This was currently the subject of much debate, having been the majority view of the recent Sankey Commission. The *Herald* was waging a campaign on behalf of nationalisation as demanded by the miners. It printed articles by the six commissioners supporting it. Evelyn's articles on the Durham coalfield reiterated the need for nationalism by looking at pitmen's work and the overcrowding of homes.[37] The Coalition government, however, rejected nationalisation, stoking miners' bitterness. Two and a half years later Evelyn was sent to investigate the financial crisis facing the administrative authorities in the Abertillery district where there was severe unemployment. She tried not to sensationalise, declaring that there had been some exaggerated writing and that people looked 'well and unhappy' rather than starving. [38]

In 1920 trade union membership reached a peak of over eight million (it had more than doubled since 1914).That September Evelyn and Henry undertook a short lecture tour in Cumberland, organised by Catherine Marshall whom they had both known for some years. She had been instrumental in cementing links between suffragists and the main political parties. Having also shifted her allegiance from Liberal to Labour, she had become a leading peace activist. Evelyn and Henry discussed the mining crisis with her, and gave three talks each in villages where their audiences were quarrymen, railway workers and miners. Evelyn spoke twice on 'What the Labour Party Stands For' and once about what she had seen in Germany.[39] They also went to see the Nevinson family's ancestral house at Newby, close to Shap.

In 1921 proposals for wage cuts and the return to independent district wage rates resulted in a three-month national coal strike. Evelyn helped to raise funds for miners' children by, for example, collecting money from people queuing for the theatre in London's West End. The miners were abandoned by railway and transport workers to fight the dispute on their own. Evelyn's fiction reflected the militancy of the times. A May Day story for the *New Leader* has Spring withholding her labour. Summer wants to strike but is badly exploited by Winter who has the shortest hours and lives at the expense of the other seasons.[40]

Evelyn's story 'The Strike-Breaker' told of 'a strike against the community'.[41] Douglas is driving a lorry full of City workers in London. But, instead of expressing admiration, the pretty girl he passes in Holborn calls him a blackleg. Back home, he sips liqueur brandy and hears his family denouncing the ignorant working class and the strike. For the first time he finds their conversation irritating. The next day, his composure restored, he is thanked by a West End Patriots' Emergency Committee and the 'Bolshevik hussy of Holborn' is forgotten. Walking home at midnight he gets talking to a tired old man in the street. Douglas tells him about his day and suggests that he too volunteers. The old man, a road-sweeper, tells his story. His union is bound to come out soon in support of the strike and if they lose he is likely to be unemployed and sacrifice his savings and pension despite having worked hard all his life. Douglas cannot understand why he should strike when it isn't even his battle but, bidding farewell to 'Mr Strike-Breaker' the old man says it's a strike for the future, for his and, perhaps, Douglas's grandchildren and that is why it matters. Douglas is left alone with the stars.

The quiet dignity of somebody used to being overlooked thus disturbs the equanimity of the main, confident character. Such a situation would have been familiar to followers of Evelyn's work. Typically the reader was left to muse on how the latter might reason in the future. This cameo anticipated the atmosphere in 1926. In her memoirs Evelyn recalled how the General Strike revealed how little was known by many people about the lives of those living very close to them.[42]

The return to the prewar Gold standard in April 1925 further exacerbated problems in the mining industry. That summer wage cuts were threatened but temporarily delayed by the extension of a government subsidy and by the establishment of the Samuel Commission to consider the future of the industry. But on 1 May 1926 over a million miners were locked out of their pits pending their agreement to swingeing wage reductions and an extra hour on the working day. A conference of trade union executives approved 'co-ordinated industrial action' in support of the locked-out miners, with the General Council of the Trades Union Congress (TUC) assuming responsibility. A state of emergency had already been declared by Stanley Baldwin's Tory government. After workers at the *Daily Mail* refused to print an anti-strike editorial, at midnight on 3 May, what has become known as the General Strike commenced.

Support for the miners was impressive. Between one and a half and two million workers went on strike. For the first time industrial conflict was co-ordinated by different unions and local organisations such as Trades Councils and Councils of Action.[43] But divisions between the miners, the Labour Party and the TUC surfaced. On the first day of the strike Evelyn and Henry heard the secretary of the Miners' Federation of Great Britain, A. J. Cook, express anger at 'political intrigues' between MacDonald and Baldwin.[44] The moderate TUC leadership represented the situation as an extended industrial dispute, not a political and potentially revolutionary movement, controversially abandoning it after nine days.

Evelyn wrote about those infamous nine days in a personal diary which she called 'The Great Strike. 1926'.[45] Here she recorded what she did and saw and her reactions. Not surprisingly, her sympathies were with the British miners. Although not liking the prevention of freedom of expression, she interpreted the printers' action as 'the most real sign of a possible Revolution that has yet taken place'. It represented 'the helplessness of wealth and material power before the unarmed power of men united in a common purpose'. If, she wrote, workers realise their advantage, 'this will be a real Revolution of the right kind'.

Evelyn also used the diary format to convey to a truncated *New Leader* a sense of what happened on the London streets. It appeared in the paper on 21 May, the weekly paper having suspended two issues out of solidarity with the strikers.[46] Her account for each day covered, at most, several paragraphs. They recorded the writer's visual impressions and feelings. The situation was unique: never before had opponents of striking been effectively organised. The Organisation for the Maintenance of Supplies gave the government the names of about a hundred thousand volunteers on 3 May.[47] Volunteers (blacklegs in Evelyn's terminology) took over transport or enrolled as special constables. She noted that crossing the road had become hazardous, because of the influx of inexperienced drivers of private motors, pirate buses and taxis: 'The first casualties of the great strike have consequently been street accidents.'[48] And she was disparaging about students and 'schoolboys of the middle class, who seem to have invaded London in their best clothes in order to rush round in other people's motor cars'. It was as though the fictional Douglas had, as in Evelyn's fairy stories, sprung to life.

By the third day she was writing in her diary that 'The Revolution is here all right for those that have eyes to see' though these words were omitted in the published version. She described the Council of Action formed by Labour members of Rotherhithe and Bermondsey Council as a Soviet. Much of her information, including some of the material described in the printed version, came not from first-hand evidence but through Evelyn's left-wing postman (postal workers had not been called out on strike by the TUC). He told her that Welsh Guards had been removed to Devonport and confined to barracks as it was feared that they would sympathise with the miners.

Evelyn spent much of her time walking with Henry around the East End: talking to pickets at Wapping and East India Dock, listening to strikers at an open-air meeting and observing lorries crowded with city clerks and young men and women sharing bicycles. She 'wanted badly to bring the scaremongers from Whitehall and Kensington' to the street behind St Katharine Dock where 'lean-faced men in rough working clothes, without collars or spats, stand for weary hours, animated only by their loyalty to their mates and a cause'.[49] The largest concentration of troops was in the docklands. Evelyn was convinced that there had been long-term preparation for such an event.

Many stressed the pacific nature of the strike – not that long ago strikers and volunteers had been facing war together – but Evelyn remarked that the scenes they observed 'would produce revolution and bloodshed nearly everywhere else'. It was ultimately the patience and solidarity of the strikers, 'the spectacle of thousands of workers standing still out of pure comradeship', that impressed both Evelyn and Henry.[50] They attended a church service in St Matthew's Church, City Road, held by a socialist vicar for strikers and their families. It ended with everyone singing 'England Arise'.

To Henry's disappointment, his son Richard was bitterly opposed to the strike. When a Kensington friend told Evelyn that her neighbours were becoming volunteers since they felt the strike attacked the constitution, Evelyn remarked (privately) 'How familiar it all sounds to an old suffragette', adding that women were 'much better at passive resistance than men'.[51] She feared that the men might provoke real force. Hearing that a mediator was needed, she asked (in her personal diary) 'Why don't they choose a woman? They simply don't dream of such a thing!'

On the day the strike had started Evelyn and Henry had spoken to George Lansbury who was with A. J. Cook. Evelyn wrote:

> They fear nothing but the weakening of political Labour in the direction of some formula that would seem to offer a settlement without really doing so; but all agreed that if they yield to this temptation the power of the political over the industrial wing of the movement would be gone for ever & the leaders would have no more power either.[52]

Evelyn was walking to Bethnal Green on 12 May when she saw a sign in a shop window announcing that the strike was over. Confused when a broadcast suggested that the TUC had unconditionally withdrawn, and worried since she believed that the leaders 'had cold feet all through', she was assured at the Parliamentary Labour Club that there was a general agreement. She wrote in her private diary for 12 May: 'A great day'. Her relief was, however, short lived. The next day she heard of the victimisation of strikers, learned that the miners were staying out and how they had been betrayed. She addressed a Friends' meeting, talking about the ethics of passive resistance and breach of contract. She ended her diary for that day by mentioning a terrific thunderstorm after tea. It 'seems to indicate the "Supreme Being" is angry with some one'.[53] The unconditional surrender by the General Council left the miners locked out for a further seven months.

That summer Evelyn and Henry talked to a porter at Victoria Station. He explained that he was in debt for the first time since passengers now tipped him less because he had come out on strike.[54] But it was in the mining areas that Evelyn saw the long-term effects of that 'Angry Summer' of 1926. In 1930 she spent two days in South Wales at the Maes-yr-Haf Educational Settlement established three years earlier at Trealaw in Rhondda Fawr. Initiated by the Swindon Quaker Emma Noble who had visited the area during the summer of 1926, it was the first of a number of voluntary initiatives in the valleys, settlements in which educated outsiders offered schemes providing practical aid and adult education. Between 1921 and 1931 over a third of the population aged 15 to 29 was estimated to have left the district. Now in April 1930, in the aftermath of the Wall Street Crash, with its global consequences and soaring local unemployment, mortality and illnesses, this was one of the most depressed areas of the coalfield. Like Manchester in the 1830s Rhondda had been labelled a problem area. It was subject to considerable press attention and attracted voluntary schemes to alleviate distress.

Evelyn was investigating for the American *Christian Science Monitor*. Her article demonstrates her distance from the Welsh valleys in its lack of appreciation of why the unemployed Welsh miner 'with his passionate attachment to the long narrow valley' was so reluctant to move away if at all possible.[55] She was also characteristically upbeat in her estimation of the achievements of the educational settlement. Emma and William Noble were the wardens and the managing committee was chaired by the philosopher A. D. Lindsay, Master of Balliol.

Philosophy (taught by two Oxford graduates) was one of a number of academic subjects studied there by unemployed colliers. More than fifty clubs had been established locally, providing study for over five thousand people between twenty and sixty, and providing paid jobs one day a week as well as weaving and embroidery classes for women. Yet, although the resources the Friends could supply were appreciated, local people were already politicised and enjoyed a vibrant autodidactic tradition that was not fully in tune with Quaker values.[56] Evelyn was predisposed towards the latter. Briefly assessing the settlement's achievements for a readership thousands of miles away, she focused only on the positive side. Such journalism underplayed indigenous intellectual forces and perspectives.[57]

Evelyn moved on to the Forest of Dean where she spent ten days gathering information about its mines and the Quaker allotment scheme that provided miners with free seeds whilst the council let them have rent-free land for a year. Her article was entitled 'Miners Find New Hope in Tilling Soil'. The Forest of Dean appealed to Evelyn. Indeed, five months later she returned to explore it with Henry and they went down the Lightmore Mine. Whereas 'gray desolation' summed up how Evelyn perceived the Rhondda, this was an area of enchantment for her: 'like a fairy forest'.[58]

But the woman who had gained a reputation for her fairy tales had transformed herself into a serious investigative journalist, examining how voluntarist and state institutions operated in the 1920s and 1930s. She was now read for her sagacious advice on children's futures.

10

The Child Grows Up: configuring childhood in the interwar years

'I wonder when the world will recognise that in every kind of calamity the hardest blows fall first and last and all the time on the babes and children who cannot possibly be blamed for it' wrote Evelyn in her Russian diary.[1] With the experience she had gained of children suffering in Europe and a reputation as a writer of children's fiction, it is not surprising that, with the establishment of the *Manchester Guardian*'s Women's Page in May 1922, Evelyn became known as an expert on childhood. At a time when Freudian theory was being popularised and when there was an outpouring of writings on child-rearing, her weekly articles in the *Guardian* informed readers about voluntary and state educational and welfare provisions from babyhood onwards and resulted in two books, *The London Child* (1927) and *The Child Grows Up* (1929). Evelyn's voice was seen as one of common sense, inflected with an understanding of women's and children's needs that was refreshingly free from jargon. Her interest was genuine but she also knew as an experienced journalist that her openness could encourage others to open up.

After the First World War much energy was expended on studying the psychology of childhood and the role of the mother.[2] Mothercraft had, for some time, been linked to national concerns about improving the health of the nation's young, particularly after the revelations of unfit recruits in the Anglo-Boer War of 1899–1902.[3] Now, presented as a science, it became articulated in national policy. The New Zealand doctor F. Truby King's method for reducing infant mortality was highly influential. The new, regimented method for child-rearing included breast-feeding and strict timetables for training infants designed to change mothers' methods and encourage healthy individuals of sound moral character. Followers of the American behaviourist John B. Watson emphasised obedience and 'habit training' as a means of producing well-behaved, self-reliant individuals. None of this gained Evelyn's support.

In contrast, the child-centred New Psychology was less controlling. It focused on a liberal relationship between parent and child, finding expression in the development of nursery schools, educational psychology, child guidance and psychoanalysis. Clearly there were important differences between middle- and working-class traditions and they, along with geographical discrepancies in the provision of facilities, influenced the popularity of new approaches. Most of Evelyn's investigations involved poor inner-city children. She suggested that the New Psychology reached such children only incidentally, primarily through institutions such as school or the Children's Court.

One of her articles focused on a swimming lesson in Docklands. A child hesitated at the edge of the pool. Suddenly she was thrown in at the deep end by her teacher. 'Every principle of psychoanalysis had been violated', remarked Evelyn, adding that 'if another nail were needed in order to seal Freud and all his disciples in their several coffins' it was apparent when the child swam half a length underwater.[4]

In an article in the *Guardian*'s Women's Page in March 1923 Evelyn made clear her attitude towards advice about childhood:

> If people are really serious in thinking that the limitation of families is a bad thing for the race, they should set about limiting the literature that is poured forth nowadays on the psychology of Childhood. I rarely read a treatise on this absorbing subject without feeling that it would deter any parent from daring to be a parent.[5]

Growing up inevitably involved a degree of suffering, argued Evelyn. She was wary of the over-protective parent and the way that adults patronised children. One of her Christmas stories has exasperated twins declare about relatives: 'What we really want them to do is to behave as if they were grown-ups.'[6] Children, she believed, needed to develop their own natural defences. In her view adults could never really empathise with children. They merely exercised their own, inevitably deficient, memories of childhood. And, she asked, even if child psychologists were on the right track, would children really wish to be understood by their parents? Yet, despite her reservations about the growth in experts and literature on childhood, Evelyn was adding to this by investigating, in a widely read national newspaper, the provision of facilities. In the process she too provided copious advice, contributing to the construction of an image of the deprived London child in the interwar years.

Reporting on a 1923 conference of Labour women discussing the topical issue of the endowment of motherhood (which led to the establishment of family allowances), Evelyn expressed some concern about modern motherhood and the state. The issue had first been raised by Eleanor Rathbone in 1917. She later became well-known for introducing family allowances. Evelyn attended one of her earliest speeches on this subject and recognised the difficulties inherent in helping the children of the underpaid and unemployed whilst maintaining the positive aspects of home life. She asked how this could be done without institutionalising the child or turning the mother into 'an inspected machine for carrying out the regulations of the State'.[7] In her view it was important to stop talking about the mother and child as though they were indivisible. Young children, she reminded her readers, were also the father's concern. She worried that maternity and child welfare were automatically perceived as a woman's question.

So what exactly did Evelyn have to say about children in her weekly Women's Page column?[8] Her focus was primarily on the working-class London child. She travelled round the East End and the poorer parts of Kensington and sometimes went further afield, visiting institutions and societies and providing descriptions of their facilities. Sometimes the column seems like an early version of the Radio 4 Appeal from charities, with Evelyn describing the work of groups such as the National Society of Day Nurseries, the London Children's Gardens and Recreation Fund and the Group Parcels scheme organised by the Quakers for starving German families. These accounts were accompanied by addresses for donations. Many such organisations must have been keen for her to visit them and so help in their fund-raising. Her column also enabled groups such as the State Children's Association to receive free publicity and encourage new members.[9]

Much of Evelyn's writing contained an implicit, if not direct, comparison with her own Victorian upbringing. Although well aware that her very privileged childhood was far removed from the deprived children she was currently investigating, she reworked her experiences to suggest how mores and expectations were being adjusted to the postwar world. She helped to challenge a teleological approach by suggesting that the new was not necessarily better, but more often her concern was not to appear censorious of modernity. She ridiculed, for example, dire forebodings that the younger generation might die of pneumonia from the shorter and fewer clothes they now wore. Rather than criticising the young of the 1920s and wondering what their grandmothers would have said about them, she saw it as more important to consider 'what our grandchildren will say about us when their turn comes to inherit the earth we are now tilling for them'.[10]

Casting herself as a Victorian rebel grown old, she wanted to support modern youth, especially when it was criticised. But she warned against what she called 'Peter Pan' parents who believed that they fully understood their offspring. As early as 1927 she was discussing the problems of parents getting too involved in children's homework. She also made some perspicacious remarks about society's neglect of old age. 'What is wrong with old age?' she asked in 1928.[11] The woman who had treasured her own nurse argued for recognition of the modern nursery-trained children's nurse as a professional worker.[12]

Evelyn lacked credentials in that she was neither a mother nor a professional educationist or psychologist. She sought to validate her position by drawing on memories of her own large family. Since much of her childhood had been spent in Kensington, she qualified as a London child and she contrasted her upbringing – as she chose to recount it – with that of the young people she now observed. She also drew on the past to suggest what all children shared. This invariably involved a somewhat romanticised notion of universal childhood, along with some simplification and generalisation in class terms. As with much journalism, Evelyn's writing focused mainly on the extremes, concentrating on the most needy working-class children and ignoring many of those in families above the breadline, though in the harsh interwar climate economic security was especially fragile. The modern reader of her *Guardian* articles could be forgiven for presuming that postwar society had but two groups: the professionals and the destitute.

A frequent refrain in her articles is that the child takes a cue from a parent and that it is often the parent rather than the child who needs to change and to set a better example. This is reflected in her *Daily Herald* stories.[13] The wisdom of the parents is all-important but children should not be over-burdened with impractical prescriptive literature. Becoming a parent was now a subject for discussion. In an article in the *New Leader*, she declared that 'The outstanding feature of our post-war society is the awakening of parents to the responsibility they take in bringing children into the world'.[14] In this same article, written two years after Marie Stopes had opened Britain's first and much-publicised birth control clinic in London, Evelyn stated that only a nation that made full and decent provision for unlimited families had the right to oppose their limitation.

Evelyn's accounts of the facilities available for London's poorer children lacked a real critical edge. Outlining a scheme organised by the Fellowship of Reconciliation's Hospitality Committee, she appealed for hostesses to take in children from overcrowded homes for a few weeks. She dwelt only on the benefits for the mothers and children, glossing over the potential difficulties of adjustment, the implied critique of working-class mothers and homes and the problems mothers and offspring might face afterwards.[15] Whether advocating Buxted Lodge in Epping Forest where students trained to be nursery nurses by tending the babies of professional parents or the 'jolly spirit' of the Girls' Village Home at Barkingside, Essex, where Evelyn detected real pride in being a Barnardo's girl, she gave the impression that staff and young people were in harmony. The fact that children and staff would have been on their best behaviour on open days and occasions when members of the press visited, and that model pupils might be selected to show her around, does not seem to have had much impact on her assessments. Her comment about the people running Kingsley Hall, the mixed club in Bow founded by the Brethren of the Common Table, says more about her own faith and hopes than about the actuality of charity: 'The community . . . do not talk about abolishing class distinctions, but abolished them long ago.'[16]

Most frequently praised was the Caldecott Community, a boarding school for working-class children in Kent. Run as 'a kind of triple alliance of teachers, parents and children', it had been founded by women graduates. It was an experimental school where children were encouraged to criticise and parents to contribute.[17] This was the closest English approximation Evelyn could find to the Free Schools of Hamburg that so impressed her. Her other benchmark was Russia. She believed that equal educational opportunities were respected there. Interspersed with articles on educational welfare provision in London were accounts of their German and Russian equivalents. She also praised the work of the International Bureau of Education based in Geneva, welcoming initiatives such as its efforts to promote history teaching that was in harmony with modern ideas of justice and international peace.[18]

She sometimes suggested that the institutions she visited lacked equality in terms of gender. A Hamburg home for delinquent boys was criticised because boys were totally segregated from the female sex. In Britain more girls than boys had defective eyesight and Evelyn attributed this to the fact that girls did sewing at school as well as being expected to do so at home. Such duplication she thought inadvisable. Although finding much to praise in London's elementary schools, Evelyn was wary of the emphasis on mothercraft and felt that vocational subjects took up too much time. In *The London Child* she suggested that it seemed 'a curious perversion of educational theory to teach a little girl of the people how to wash and tend a wooden baby', when it was likely that she would be handling the real thing as soon as she returned home. Moreover, 'Little boys, who are not required to learn fathercraft at school, are presumably left to conclude that a man has no more concern with family life than to bring home his wages regularly'.[19]

She was, nevertheless, impressed by the selective central schools of London which concentrated on technical and vocational education. In practice these schools provided secondary education for the most able working-class child and, by the time Evelyn was commentating, they educated almost as many London children as the capital's designated aided and maintained secondary schools.[20] She lavishly praised the girls' central school she saw in Fulham with its emphasis on commercial subjects. Yet she acknowledged without comment the focus on science at Bermondsey's boys' central school (boys in these schools had modern laboratories but girls had no such equipment: cookers were seen as more appropriate for them). Central schools did address the need to train girls but their gendered curricula also helped to replicate gendered job opportunities.

Evelyn's support for these schools was linked to her recognition of the, often unsung, work of teachers more generally, especially in the light of the current 'tendency of Whitehall to spell Economy with a bigger E than Education'.[21] By 1922 'Anti-waste' policies had halved the grant for supplying milk to schoolchildren and over the next two years government expenditure on education fell by just under 10 per cent. Evelyn appreciated how a lack of money affected clothing and, consequently, school attendance. She praised the headmistress of a large elementary school in the East End who sold boots cheap to children, the money going to a hospital. She devoted one week's column to writing about an experienced teacher (originally a pupil teacher aged fourteen) in a boys' school. He inspired his pupils with their nature study lessons on Wimbledon Common.

Evelyn frequently applauded the patience and enthusiasm of London's teachers, calling them heroic men and women who triumphed against the odds (though she was curiously reticent about the Marriage Bar banning married women teachers).[22] Interestingly, despite her own positive experience, she was not in favour of single-sex schools for adolescents not least because her opposition to corporal punishment made her wary of the argument that it enabled male teachers to enforce authority over unruly boys more effectively. And since real life did not segregate the young she felt it pointless to do so in school hours.[23]

She was disparaging about intelligence testing. Cyril Burt, whose part-time appointment to the London County Council in 1913 made him the world's first official psychologist, is the best-known of those who believed that a child's intelligence (seen as 'innate, general, cognitive ability') was the result of hereditary factors.[24] In his view intelligence was a constant and could be measured. It followed from this that mental testing could identify the percentage of pupils most capable of benefiting educationally. Evelyn's criticisms of the National Institute of Industrial Psychology's attempt to discover 'true' vocations included her concern that children were being invited to 'a Barmecide feast of tests for employment that often does not exist'.[25] For Evelyn, the real experts were the teachers and mothers, especially when they worked together.

She recognised that elementary schools were understaffed and overcrowded ('No reasonable person can well expect better results as long as classes hold 40 or more pupils')[26] and that as economic conditions deteriorated so the pressures facing teachers, pupils and parents increased. She also reported on schemes to help the unemployed. In the mid-1920s when there were over one and a quarter million out of work, she praised the Winter Distress League which used its funds to pay unemployed men (at trades union rates) to undertake jobs which did not disturb the labour market further by displacing others. For example, long-overdue redecoration work was carried out in some hospitals. The League also paid for these workers' children to go to the countryside while the work was being carried out.

During the 1920s and early 1930s Evelyn saw inside many places she would otherwise never have visited, from Poplar's municipal wash-house with steam laundry to the Ellen Terry National Home for Defective Blind Children. She was cheered by new approaches such as the Sunlight League's use of sunbathing in orthopaedic work at St

Mary's Carshalton. Any metropolitan facility with a bearing on children's lives might find Evelyn, armed with notebook, on its doorstep, from the pioneering maternity unit opened in 1921 at the Royal Free Hospital, with its integrated approach to a baby's welfare, to the children's library at the Cambridge University Settlement in south-east London.

At a time when many were concerned about the effect of the 'kinema' on young people's morals, Evelyn mocked those who attacked its escapism and sought censorship. In her view, moral dangers could be found anywhere by those determined to find them – even for Jack and Jill going up that hill. However, using an argument that would become familiar in relation to watching television and more recently the use of computer games, she suggested that children's powers of concentration were diminished by the excitement and drama evident in Picture Palaces. She also commented that children were much less likely to read their way through Scott or Defoe than their predecessors were, though she praised the work of children's libraries.

Towards the end of 1922 Evelyn began illustrating her accounts through the device of personalising her subjects. But she retained anonymity by just using a first name. She thereby provided an apparently individual account that aroused sympathy, at the same time suggesting someone who could be seen to be representative of a type, almost a case study. When, for example, she wrote about a day nursery and treatment centre in Wapping, she made her point about the bad housing its children lived in by telling the story of one-year-old Martin. This little boy lived with his parents (an unemployed docker and a rag picker) and two other children in one room by the gas works. He was underweight, had rickets and was almost blind, but within six months of living in the day nursery he had changed into a bonny little lad.

This naming technique, so familiar in psychological studies, had already been used in the *Manchester Guardian*. The paper had serialised a book published in 1910 called 'Young Gaol-Birds'. Its author was Charles E. V. Russell, a former youth worker in Manchester and pioneer of boys' clubs, who became chief inspector of reformatory and industrial schools. His book included case studies of figures such as 'feckless Fred'. Martin's tale and other such stories were used to much greater effect in *The London Child* and its sequel *The Child Grows Up* (one of its early titles had been 'The London Child at the Golden Age'). Here they were extended as the final part of chapters that began with documenting evidence. They enabled Evelyn to draw once more on creative writing. She did, though, find that writing something that was 'neither fiction nor exactly essays' was demanding on top of all the 'roaming about' in tracking down her stories.[27]

Margaret McMillan, a practical reformer who with her sister Rachel opened the country's first school clinic in Bow followed by the Deptford Clinic two years later in 1910, also wrote books on childhood. She was instrumental in shaping Independent Labour Party and Labour Party policy on childhood, family and the State, penning at least a hundred pieces on the treatment of children, many in the *Clarion* between 1905 and 1915. As Carolyn Steedman has argued, McMillan used the allegorical child-figure to exemplify factual articles as part of her campaign to highlight the experience working class childhood in Bradford and Deptford, simultaneously presenting her subjects as invented and real.[28] Indeed, by appearing to give voice to her characters (the child's voice was something that interested Margaret McMillan as an educator), both she and Evelyn moved beyond observation to engage the emotions and support of readers.

Evelyn even used the device, albeit in a more allegorical form, in a *New Leader* story about the Rachel McMillan Nursery School. In 1914 the success of the sisters' Clinic and Night Camps for girls and boys in Deptford resulted in their nearby open-air Nursery School and Training Centre. Evelyn described its garden as a beautiful oasis, and entering the camp like 'going right into the heart of a fairy tale'.[29] After Rachel's death in 1917, Margaret continued their practical experiment, developing a centre for teaching as well as a haven for children and parents in that impoverished part of south-east London.

Evelyn's story was based on first-hand knowledge of the open-air school. A 'rough little urchin' called Angel lives with her grandmother in poverty and poor health. She is unable to see properly, steals and mutters a few lines of the Lord's Prayer after doing something wrong. But her aunt takes her to 'our open-air nursery school'. After four years here Angel is transformed. Her physical development has been nourished and she is so improved that her mother starts being kind to her.

The unorthodox approaches of an educator who believed in little ones sleeping under the stars challenged popular notions about rearing children. But in Evelyn's story the mother has rejected any claim to caring for her child until the change in her daughter makes her recognise a minor miracle. Evelyn's story is invested with biblical significance. Angel's experience is called 'The Coming of the Kingdom'.[30]

In the 1920s Evelyn was keen for some of her fairy stories to be reprinted. She approached the Bodley Head but they suggested instead a book about the London child written for adults. The publication in 1927 of *The London Child* helped to cement Evelyn's reputation as a lay authority on the subject. The *Nation* saw it as 'a delight to anyone who cares about children'.[31] It cost 7s 6d, rather more than Evelyn had hoped, but it included a few colour plates by Eve Garnett – one depicting a summer evening in an impossibly clean London street looking rather like a stage set – and numerous sketches of children. Evelyn called her six chapters 'story-sketches' and explained, rather vaguely, that all the experiences were real and the stories 'nearly all founded on some fact'.[32] She described herself as 'the visitor' but sought to validate her position by stressing familiarity with the vernacular as well as identifying with the locale. When talking about pilfering she explained: '"nicking" we call it in the East End'.[33] She also cited official documents such as Circular 1,371 issued by the Board of Education.

She sought to avoid sentimentality but in the process made some sweeping statements. Telling lies, we are told, was a 'common manifestation of the ironic cockney spirit'.[34] The mix of rewritten press reportage accompanied by stories as exemplars seems especially dated today. She even used the term 'darker London' at one point, a term that suggests the social explorers of the 1880s who discovered, like imperial adventurers, societies so removed from their own experiences. It was difficult to find a tone that seemed appropriate to an adult readership when recounting tales of boys such as the barefooted Dicky who inhabited in his imagination a world far removed from the street on which he scavenged. Evelyn was rather more skilled at writing such tales for children. Much of the material was anyway already familiar to her newspaper readers.

The book was not a commercial success. Nevertheless, press reviews were good. The *Daily News* observed that her sentimentality 'never runs away with her common sense' and the *Bookman* declared that all London ratepayers should have a copy. It would inform them how some of their money was being spent and its understanding tone made it worthy of a place in literature about London.[35]

It was a similar story with *The Child Grows Up* published in 1929. Evelyn described it as good for her reputation but bad for her pocket.[36] In it she remarked that 'a new psychological craze has taken the place of the *fin de siècle* vogue for the Child, and Youth is now the rage'.[37] The expert and the intellectual were her targets once more:

'in continual danger of missing everything except the minutiae and the abnormal'.[38] Carefully presenting herself as 'the unscientific observer' and opening with a reference to her favourite short story, Hans Christian Andersen's 'The Ugly Duckling', she suggested that what was seen as the problem of adolescence was really the product of environment.

A number of Evelyn's articles focused on plans for housing. She was keen for the London County Council to take over more property, reporting on schemes to help poorer ratepayers as well as affordable housing schemes such as Guild housing.[39] She also suggested that many middle-class children would not have succeeded had they faced the obstacles in the way of slum children. Her tone in these years was along the lines of 'There but for the Grace of God Go I'.

Yet this book, especially the early chapters, was more authoritative than *The London Child* since it was based on Evelyn's experience as a member of the Shepherds Bush Advisory Committee on Juvenile Employment. She was by now a close friend of Lillian and Charles Robertson.[40] He had served in the Egyptian Ministry of Education and later sat on the London County Council and chaired its Education Committee. In 1927 he introduced Evelyn to the Advisory Committee, one of twenty-one in London and 162 across England and Wales. Members included teachers, employers, trades unionists, welfare workers and others interested in youth. Their voluntary service was provided at the juvenile branch of the Employment Exchange.

Evelyn's account of the adolescents[41] of London's 'by-streets' examines opportunities for the fourteen-year-old school leaver, outlining the work of the committee in interviewing and placing them in employment and pointing out the importance of day continuation schools. It suggests the difficulties facing the young person aged between fourteen and sixteen, raging against the compulsion that kept them in school until they were fourteen, coupled with a failure to acknowledge those below sixteen as employed persons under the National Insurance Act.[42] They lacked health provision and were treated as cheap labour and were likely to be dismissed once they become more expensive to employ. Evelyn's concern about the fourteen-year-old school leaver had a special meaning for her: this was the age at which she had become a boarder.

Evelyn described with care and humour the committee's attempts to match children to skills, to placate parents and to conduct open evenings. Her sympathies were not with the perfect teenager but with the imaginative one who showed some spirit. Youth for her was a temporary, promising stage that should be respected and not reduced to scientific abstractions and judgements. The surroundings and the provisions needed changing rather than prematurely seeking to turn naturally rebellious young people into adults.

Although published in 1929, Evelyn's book had been written before the Wall Street Crash and its consequences and at a time when unemployment rates in London were well below those in some parts of the country, even though the threat of short-time and unemployment made the years insecure ones for all. It recognised the decline of some of the old trades. One of her 'parables' was about Peter, who had moved with his family to a suburban housing estate after slum clearance. He deliberately 'bunked off' work. Evelyn was also interested in shifts in the treatment of young offenders. In *The London Child* she had praised the work of the practical and capable woman probation officer she visited, and commented that none of the faces of the boys she saw that day suggested delinquency. Yet they all looked ill-nourished, under-sized and poorly fed.[43]

Evelyn had already tackled the subject of class and juvenile crime in a short story.[44] A doctor's son was caught raiding a food store but it was Jane, the leader of the gang, who was headed for prison. The doctor discovered that she was starving and pleaded with the police to let her go home. Otherwise his son would have to stand in the dock of the Children's Court with her. Jane and the doctor's family also featured in a novel Evelyn published in 1925, the same year as Cyril Burt's study *The Young Delinquent* and the establishment of the Departmental Committee on Young Offenders, the precursor to the Children and Young Persons Act of 1933.

This story about a cockney child taken in by the Chalfont family was called *Who Was Jane?* It was a not very convincing account of an unconventional family living in the countryside and committed to children's freedom (the wife was rather less liberated, with no hint of a career, even pre-marriage, and defined by her relationship to other family members, such as the doctor's wife or children's mother). Jane's origins were mysterious and, although it emerged that she had some connection to the local gentry, in a slight twist of the 'True blood will out' tale, she was relieved to find that she was not the young squire's sister but his devoted nanny's grandchild. Described as an urchin and compared to stray animals, Jane was contrasted with the priggish squire's young sister who 'belonged to that class of lady visitor who came interfering' when children stayed away from school.[45]

Jane had led a gang in a raid on a sweet-shop in Hoxton and later, owing to a misunderstanding which had resulted in her returning to London (to Shepherds Bush), came up before the Children's Court. A shocked Dr Chalfont found it 'simply inconceivable' that someone who had lived with his children as a friend should appear before a magistrate and run the risk of going to a reformatory. But the metropolitan magistrate (who admired Dr Chalfont's work with school clinics) placed Jane on probation in the doctor's care and she returned once more to the country.[46]

Evelyn's account of the postwar Children's Court is a sympathetic one. Old Sir William Beryl, the stipendiary magistrate (probably an amalgam of progressive London magistrates Sir John Dickinson, Cecil Chapman, William Clarke Hall and H. L. Cancellor), was portrayed as a kindly and compassionate figure who understood the courage of children, and the place looked more like a schoolroom than a police court.

Evelyn had already visited one of the new-style Children's Courts, held in a mayor's parlour in East London, for her *Guardian* column.[47] She was also favourably impressed by the Boys' Garden Colony at Basingstoke which operated in conjunction with the London Police Court Mission, largely on Cancellor's initiative. In her view it encouraged its residents (employed in a large nursery garden) to be like ordinary members of the community.[48] Her claim, though, that they were never made to feel they were being reformed raises some questions. They had no choice but to fit in with a regime of drill, regular church attendance, lectures and letters home.

She found yet another 'exceptionally well conducted' institution in the Industrial School for Jewish Boys. This article was one of the few to challenge the impression that the London Evelyn scoured was composed of people from the same ethnic and religious background as herself.[49]

Pressure from the Howard League for Penal Reform and the Norris Report resulted in some much-needed improvement in conditions in such institutions in the early 1920s. Evelyn recognised that placing juveniles in institutions curbed their natural spirit but she did not tackle the efficacy of separating parents and children.

Although her writing never suggests it, exposure to the problems facing the young people of the inner city troubled Evelyn. Meeting her at Paddington at the end of 1923 on her way back from 'some model children's reformatory' Henry found her 'distraught' about the situation 'as usual'.[50] Unlike their shared suffrage work or journalism in Europe, parenthood and children were not topics of interest to Henry. Adapting biblical words, he wrote from personal experience that 'Children are a quiverful of arrows that pierce the parents' hearts'.[51]

Evelyn had been returning from a certified home in Cornwall, a 'perfect place for children to learn to be wise'. Young offenders from the Shoreditch Children's Court were sent to this 'Children's Commonwealth', where they lived in cottages and attended village schools. She told readers about Jim whose mother lived in a Salvation Army hostel and wondered, after visiting her son, whether everybody was quite so kind to her Jim when she was not there.[52] Was this Evelyn's gentle way of raising her own doubts?

In 1926 the journal *National Health* emphasised the role now played by women's pages in the daily press.[53] The experience of visits, attendance at conferences, from the Women's International Housing conference to the National Union of Teachers, and familiarity with official reports and professional opinions from both sides of the Atlantic, helped Evelyn to be recognised as a knowledgeable contributor to the understanding of modern childhood and adolescence. She was asked, for example, to open a new shelter at the Children's House in Bow.

In the summer of 1930 Lord Morley responded to Evelyn's article on tinned milk. He had spoken on the subject in the House of Lords and told the *Manchester Guardian* that if, as he hoped, women would soon be made peeresses and Evelyn were selected, there were few people he would rather have beside him on the front bench.[54] Yet he also acknowledged how difficult it was to effect change in this 'utterly unreal assembly'. And despite Lady Rhondda's efforts to take her rightful place in the Lords, not until 1958, after both she and Evelyn had died, did the first peeress take her seat.

Some of Evelyn's leisure interests reflected her investigations into childhood and youth. She and Henry were involved in the early years of the Kindred of the Kibbo Kift (from old English words meaning 'Proof of Great Strength' or 'Be Strong'). Kibbo Kift was founded in 1920 by the Quaker John Hargrave, a former scoutmaster. Fascinated by Saxon myth and the mythology of Ancient Egypt, he was reacting against the militaristic tendencies of the Boy Scouts and pursuing a new model for human society. Kibbo Kift weekend camps advocated woodcraft, seeking to kindle spiritual energies and physical fitness,

LITERARY PROFILES   By JOSS

EVELYN SHARP

Novelist, writer of children's stories. . . . Formerly suffragette, twice imprisoned. . . . Entered literature by way of the "Yellow Book" but denies that the "naughty nineties" were particularly naughty. Recently married, as his second wife, H. W. Nevinson, friend and fellow humanitarian of 30 years' standing.

11. Joss cartoon of Evelyn

and marry symbolism and service. Hargrave was called Head Man. The organisation drew on an amalgam of the ideas on adolescence of the American psychologist Stanley Hall and the utopian notions of H. G. Wells, along with the tribal aspects of scouting, complete with totem poles.[55]

Many years earlier Henry had undertaken his own form of youth work when he trained working-class military cadets in London's East End. He became a founder member of Kibbo Kift, which used (non-military) drill, and briefly sat on its Advisory Council. He enjoyed some of its outdoor activities such as hiking, as did Evelyn, though its elaborate ceremonials, pageants and picturesque costumes are more likely to have appealed to her than Henry. Both approved of its claim to ignore distinctions of age, gender, class and race, and to emphasise world peace and 'brotherhood'. Its flag was a map of the world showing no frontiers.

In May 1923 Evelyn and Henry spent a weekend at the Kibbo Kift's annual 'Al-Thing'. New rules for the order were being discussed. Henry's diary described Evelyn and Emmeline Pethick-Lawrence (a few former suffragettes were members) with a large circle of 'youths and maidens' gathered round a camp fire. He regaled a group with his tales of central Africa.[56] Less than a year later there were splits in the movement. Woolwich co-operative members in particular felt that Hargarve was too dictatorial. Henry was asked to be Head Man. He refused and suggested Evelyn, but she was not interested.[57]

She continued, however, to warn against complacency in the treatment of children. In the 1930s, when the centenary of the abolition of the slave trade was being celebrated, she pointed out that millions of slaves were still being bought and sold. Children were hired for money under the guise of peonage and other forms of child adoption in countries still under British rule.[58] By this time Evelyn's reputation as a writer on childhood had been recognised in several ways.

She was asked to write an accessible account of the June 1931 International Conference on the African Child held in Geneva. Seven years earlier the Declaration of Geneva (Declaration of the Rights of the Child), drawn up by Eglantyne Jebb, had been adopted by the General Assembly of the League of Nations. The latter also created a Child Welfare Committee on which Jebb sat. She was the older sister of Dorothy who had married Charles Roden Buxton. These two sisters had, in the aftermath of world war, started the Fight the Famine Council, the precursor to the Save the Children Fund (SCF). It was followed by the Save the Children International Union (SCIU) in Geneva to rescue starving children living in former war zones.

The large Buxton family, descended from an anti-slavery figure, Thomas Fowell Buxton, were close friends of Evelyn and Henry. Henry had worked for many years on the Balkan Committee with Charles

Buxton's brother, now Lord Noel-Buxton and President of Save the Children Fund. Evelyn and Henry spent many Christmas holidays at the home of another brother, Leland. In the summer of 1926 Evelyn went on holiday with the Robertsons to St Cergues in the Jura. They met Dorothy and Eglantyne Jebb[59] there. In Geneva Evelyn attended the opening of the Seventh Assembly of the League. Watching German and French efforts to make a public reconciliation and hearing Briand give one of the most eloquent speeches she had ever heard, Evelyn wrote in her diary on 10 September: 'One could not help feeling that the League, bad and insufficient and disappointing as it has been, was at last justifying its existence.'[60]

Evelyn had recently given some space in her newspaper column to the SCF's plans in 1926 to create a residential camp school on the Kent coast for poor and sickly London girls. She appealed for funds, warning (in language that does not quite chime with her usual expressions so perhaps she adopted the charity's words rather than her own) that 'ill-conditioned children' in the slums at home constituted 'both a menace for the future & a cause of shame in the present'.[61]

By the late 1920s attention was shifting beyond the European to African children, and the Geneva conference that Evelyn covered represented a milestone in this move. SCIU was keen to 'throw the searchlight upon the problem of the child'[62] and extend the Declaration of Geneva to African children. The 1931 conference sought to pool knowledge and understanding from individuals, groups and governments to realise this. Eglantyne Jebb had died in 1928, but Lord Noel-Buxton was president and his sister Victoria de Bunsen (another friend of Evelyn's) chaired its British Committee. Almost two hundred attended from African and European countries though only seven delegates were black (five of them from Africa). The most positive response to the idea of such a conference came from missionaries advocating an ideology of evangelical philanthropy.

The event was carefully planned and fifteen hundred questionnaires were sent out. They covered stillbirth and infant mortality from pathological as well as social and economic issues, the role of education in preparing children for life, and child labour. Twenty papers were submitted, nineteen of which were discussed. Evelyn's account sought to convey the tone and message of the event in ninety pages. Some of her perspectives are apparent, for example, relief that statistics did not dominate. She also remarked that the introduction of venereal diseases to Africa was 'a terrible indictment of the white

races'. This claim was challenged in the book's introduction by Lord
Lugard, former Governor-General of Nigeria, Member of the Mandates
Commission of the League of Nations (which he attended at the time
of the conference) and of the Committee of experts on Native Labour
of the League of Nations Union.[63] He emphasised instead that slave-
raiding Arabs and bandits were mainly, if not entirely, responsible for
introducing syphilis into the African interior.

In 1929 Evelyn had stressed the importance of what she called
'internationalising the child'.[64] But her task at Geneva was a difficult
one and markedly different from anything she had done before. She
needed to be extremely attentive during the four days of the conference, had to read carefully all the papers and to sum up and put into
readable prose an account of proceedings and viewpoints that did not
necessarily fit her own views but reflected the positions of the participants. Lugard wrote that she 'exactly caught the dominant note of the
Congress'.[65]

Evelyn suggested that children's welfare represented 'probably the
only subject in the world' on which the conference delegates could
conceivably devise a concerted policy.[66] Yet this was complicated by
the tradition of dismissing African adults as childlike. Moreover, Lord
Lugard was associated with the doctrine of trusteeship that essentially
envisioned relations between British and African societies as akin to
those of guardian and ward, even though the doctrine had undergone
various shifts in emphasis, and trust was now essentially conceived as
a duty to ensure the welfare of the imperial ward.

The business of saving the African child was largely approached
through the experience of helping the poor white European child. The
choice of Evelyn as author was significant here. She was already associated with writing about English slum children and the title of her
book *The African Child* echoed her earlier study *The London Child*. And
although Evelyn suggested the difficulties inherent in making deci-
sions about a vast and markedly varied continent, she nevertheless
made the sweeping claim that 'The basic needs of a baby in Kenya and
a baby in Basutoland (or, for that matter, of a baby in a London slum)
are the same'.[67] The emotive picture used on the cover of her book was
an Africanised version of a picture of a white child from England.

Dominique Marshall has pointed out that most participants at
the Conference assumed that natives educated from childhood on
European lines would willingly accept the provision and approaches
of European welfare and education.[68] Evelyn's account includes the

dissenting voice of Mitra G. Sinanan. This London-based Secretary of the League of Coloured Peoples of the British West Indies suggested that focusing on children's rights conveniently avoided addressing political rights. He condemned the British, French and Portuguese 'ruthless and relentless exploitation of Africa' and called for self-determination and self-government for the African people.[69] But Evelyn did not mention the sentiments of James W. Ford, a black American journalist and Communist who denounced all European intervention in Africa as exploitative. However, he had not been officially invited to the event and, as she had been employed to present an official record, for once she had to toe the line.

At the end of the conference it was agreed that the SCIU should form a permanent unofficial centre for documentary research, for exchanging information and experiences and providing links between organisations and institutions as well as stimulating conferences on the protection of African children. The event, as Marshall has suggested, was a valuable snapshot in the history of 'tensions of Empire'.[70] It had exposed some of the problems arising from a predominantly western lens and the tensions inherent in reconciling differing perspectives: those subscribing to an ideology of trusteeship did not see solutions in the same way as either the evangelical philanthropists or the delegates espousing a forward-looking rights-based agenda.

But at the same time, the SCIU's pioneering initiative and focus on children's rights represented an important step forward in the development of human rights. And it is worth noting that in 1970 the Negro University Press reprinted Evelyn's account. She had been part of a seminal and exciting debate. Sadly, though, the rise of European fascism forced attention elsewhere. The energy harnessed in 1931 and the potential for the future that she witnessed and suggested at the end of her book proved to be short-lived.[71]

Another, albeit markedly different, demonstration of Evelyn's expertise as a journalist specialising in children's affairs was her appointment as editor of Japhet's Corner for the *News Chronicle* from 1935. This meant producing a lot of copy over a five-year period: every week she submitted four short informative pieces to appear the following week.[72] They covered topics ranging from old customs to animals and anniversaries of famous events. This section of the paper also ran a children's club. Members of Mr Noah's Ark were known as the Grand United Order of Arkubs (J. F. Horrabin's cartoons depicted the Arkubs). The golden rules were that members should all keep smiling and wear their badges. They were encouraged to take walks, exercise together and find pen friends amongst other members. Weekly competitions were held and members' letters printed. Evelyn found herself writing to many children. But in May 1940 her contributions to the *News Chronicle* ended as wartime newspaper restrictions took effect.

And, as we shall see, war would also force Evelyn and Henry to make dramatic changes in their lifestyles.

11

Defying time and the times

'It was like parting with life, so close are we' wrote Henry in his diary after seeing Evelyn leave for Switzerland in August 1926.[1] He was seventy that year. Evelyn had just celebrated her fifty-seventh birthday. The difficult, long-term relationship had survived and Evelyn and Henry were increasingly dependent on each other. He was about to depart on a fact-finding tour of Palestine. But most of his journeys were now taken with Evelyn as holidays increasingly replaced the assignments both had so enjoyed. Together they challenged the politics and conventions of their age, defying the image of elderly Victorians and writing about older people in a positive light long before the invention of flattering euphemisms for them.

Henry joked that he had founded a League of Age with the motto 'The Older the Bolder'. Evelyn witnessed German youths shift from pacifists to Hitler supporters. In the early 1930s she suggested that fear of future physical incapacity encouraged exaggerated claims for youth. Instead, age with its accompanying spiritual values, should be revered. She advocated an age movement as a counterblast to the current youth movement.[2] If the 1920s represented for her a concern with modern youth, then the 1930s saw her encourage 'senior citizens'.

Evelyn and Henry shared a hobby: folk dancing. It was a fitting one for a couple who had first met skating. He had long commented on how beautifully Evelyn danced (she had first been introduced to folk dancing in Donegal in 1903). She taught the elderly Henry folk dances. Both were determined to keep active. They enjoyed music and came from musical families. Cecil Sharp was renowned for instigating the revival of English folk song and dance. Indeed, it is perhaps surprising that Evelyn was not involved with her brother's work at an earlier date.

But she was a decade younger than Cecil and had not seen much of her eldest brother during her childhood when he was away at school then university. In the 1880s he was assistant to the chief justice of South Australia.[3] He briefly returned to Weston Turville in 1886, recuperating from typhoid, but Evelyn was at boarding school. Cecil then became co-director of the Adelaide College of Music before settling back in England in 1892. In the last two decades of the century he wrote songs and instrumental pieces but it was in 1899 that he first encountered the Morris dancers in Oxfordshire who stimulated his interest in folk music. In 1903 he began collecting traditional songs in Somerset and gave his first lecture on folk song at Hampstead Conservatoire (where he was Principal). During the next four years he collected more than fifteen hundred tunes, seeing them as a means of promoting national identity. He courted controversy over the role of folk music in schools. This was evident in his dealings with the revived Folk-Song Society. Michael Heaney argues that his championing of the use of folk songs in schools was radical but his pedagogical methods reactionary.

Evelyn remained in touch with Cecil, his wife Constance and their four children. But although Cecil spent most of his married life in Hampstead and, like his sister, wrote and taught (for some years he was music master at a boys' preparatory school), they do not seem to have seen much of each other as adults before the 1920s. Cecil had joined the Fabians in 1900 and was interested in Christian Science and spiritualism but he remained more conformist than his sister. When Evelyn was becoming involved in women's suffrage he was music tutor to the Princes Edward and Albert. Cecil did not approve of her activities but after her release from imprisonment in 1913 invited her to join him at the Stratford-upon-Avon dance festival. Evelyn declined, but they agreed that there was no point in quarrelling about suffrage. She told him that she had yet to be convinced that he was a confirmed 'Anti'.[4]

It was Cecil's development of folk dancing that particularly appealed to Evelyn and Henry though they did admire his work in the Appalachians where he and Maud Karpeles collected songs. Morris dancing had become extremely popular in Edwardian England and the Association for the Revival and Practice of Folk Music was started in 1907. A key figure in this and in reviving English folk dance with Cecil was Evelyn's old friend Mary Neal. She had worked at a girls' club with Emmeline Pethick (later Pethick-Lawrence), became a leading suffragette, helped Evelyn with *Votes for Women* and was active in

12. Evelyn's brother Cecil Sharp

the United Suffragists. At first Cecil worked with Mary Neal and her Espérance Girls Club. Before long, however, he was in dispute with her. Their publications reflected their differences over the nature of the Morris dance.

The English Folk Dance Society (EFDS) was founded in 1911 with Cecil Sharp as its director. It expanded rapidly, creating nineteen branches in thirty months. But it was not until after Cecil's return from the United States after the war that Evelyn and Henry became involved.[5] Evelyn's sister Ethel, an accomplished pianist, was already active in the society. Evelyn and Henry attended dance demonstrations, and Evelyn's birthday in 1922 was spent in Cheltenham at the vacation school.[6] They became members of the EFDS executive committee and in the 1930s both sat on the national advisory committee of its successor, the English Folk Dance and Song Society (EFDSS).

Cecil Sharp died on Midsummer Eve 1924. By now both Evelyn and Henry were great admirers of his achievements. In other circumstances they might have been wary of someone who could be accused of eliding socially conservative songs with a national culture. But both Evelyn and Henry displayed a pride in English traditions that was sometimes at variance with their politics. They also recognised what a pioneer Cecil was and how his knowledge and commitment would create a powerful legacy. Cecil had long suffered from ill-health but his untimely death enhanced their praise of his achievements. Evelyn believed in public loyalty to family even though that family might at times be exasperating. Indeed, always modest about herself, she paid lavish tribute to 'the genius of Cecil Sharp' in her articles and memoirs and stressed the inspiration he provided for countless dance students.[7] Evelyn and Henry helped establish a permanent memorial in the form of Cecil Sharp House at Regent's Park, London. Opened in 1930, it remains the headquarters of the EFDSS.

It was during the years immediately after Cecil's death that Evelyn and Henry became most involved in the EFDS. They spent the Easter of 1925 at the Exeter vacation school, attended also by Cecil's daughters Dorothea and Joan Sharp. To Henry's delight, his grand-daughter Margaret took up folk dancing, joining them in Devon the next year. Evelyn helped with the school's organisation as well as dancing, sightseeing and enjoying a display by women sword-dancers. At later schools she dealt with the press as well as dancing in classes with Henry as her partner.

The couple also became regulars at the Christmas school in London, first started in 1920. Here folk songs were sung each morning, followed by classes, lectures and demonstrations, as well as examinations. In 1929 close on a thousand attended. The All-England Festival met at London University. The best dancers were selected to perform at the

13. Evelyn, Henry, Maud Karpeles and Douglas Kennedy folk dancing

Folk Dance Festival which then entertained the public at the Albert Hall. Durham miners, whose average age was said to be seventy, performed sword-dances and there was a team of Danish dancers. It was, Evelyn explained (in a review), the success of Danish folk dancers that had encouraged Cecil to found his society.[8]

In 1927 she was asked to write a book on dancing. *Here We Go Round: The Story of the Dance* for a series on 'The Beginning of Things'. Its yellow jacket was reminiscent of the infamous fin de siècle *Yellow Book* but its content was very different. Evelyn's somewhat antiquarian account told (in 88 pages) how dance had evolved from prehistoric times to the present. Arguing that dance remained the most elemental of all forms of self-expression, she explored a range of types of dancing in different cultures, beginning with the ritual Horn Dancers of Abbot's Bromley in Staffordshire. She included a chapter on 'Dancing for Fun'. This drew on her observations of the dances of the German Wandervögel, of peasants on the frozen Russian steppe and at the Basque Festival where the fandango was danced in brilliant sunshine.

Evelyn went to the festival at Bayonne with the English team and about sixty supporters in April 1927. She wrote about it for the

Manchester Guardian.[9] Her diary shows appreciation of the coast but the hotels and casinos she pronounced 'vile'.[10] The festival began at midnight and the following day dancers snaked their way through the narrow streets before performing in the theatre. Evelyn enjoyed spotting the blue dresses of the EFDS and loved the flounces of the Basque Zamalzain and the very different clownish creations of the West Country Hobby-horse dance. For five days she watched dancers in picturesque settings: in the old square at Bayonne, beneath the walls of a medieval castle and by the harbour at St Jean de Luz. Dance suggested for this international pacifist a positive cultural exchange and expression of natural exuberance: 'It would be difficult to go on hating your enemy if you had to meet him in a dance.'[11]

Peter Ackroyd has called Evelyn's description of inner-city children dancing in the street (in *The London Child*) a symbol of the human imagination triumphing over the city.[12] National dances suggested to Evelyn an international language and understanding, one that politicians at Geneva might usefully heed. At Westminster Cathedral Hall when the EFDSS had its twenty-first anniversary, Evelyn spoke about folk dancing as a bond of peace.[13]

But *Here We Go Round* was criticised in the national press. The *Daily Herald* suggested that it was unlikely to attract the lay reader and took issue with Evelyn's claim that modern ballroom jazz had its roots in the folk dance.[14] This prompted a reader to defend her claim whilst the consensus within the EFDS was one of pleasure at the way in which 'Jazz is nailed to the counter' in what was 'the perfect handbook . . . precisely what every earnest apostle has been awaiting for years'.[15]

Evelyn ran her own country dance class close to home at the St John's Institute and in 1931 did a radio broadcast on folk dancing.[16] She and Henry were still learning new dances at the Malvern vacation school that summer. He declared that 'I have one foot in the grave, but as long as I am alive I shall go on dancing with the other'.[17] He was, however, now seventy-five and before long sciatica dictated that he became an onlooker. His poem 'A Veteran's Song' summed up his regret:

> I've been dancing with the dancers
> All the night till morning grey;
> I have kept the women dancing,
> And they never said me nay;
> But a twilight falls about me,
> They are dancing now without me,
> And I only hear the music as the women dance away.[18]

This poem also suggests something of what Evelyn had to cope with over the years. Henry always had an eye for the beautiful and remained a handsome charmer. He found it difficult to resist flirting with younger dancers such as Dorothy Hall and Edith Humphries despite his awareness of the age gap. Instead of returning home after covering the path-breaking visit of the prime minister, Ramsay MacDonald, to the American president in 1929, Henry went on to Canada with the EFDS. Evelyn wrote dismissively of this 'trailing after the Dancers'.[19] In Toronto he danced at a festival before joining the English folk dancers on their tour across the Rocky Mountains. On his return rumours circulated about him and Maud Karpeles, who had been on the tour.

Maud was twenty years younger than Evelyn. Henry's diary for 1 January 1930 stated that 'ES was evidently hurt & sad at my reputed intimacy with Maud'. A 'terrible letter' from Evelyn on the 10th 'kept me in misery all day'. Henry acknowledged that it was 'All my own fault'. But although he recognised 'the curse that still haunts me in old age, so irresistible' he saw this as part of his nature and so conveniently outside his own control. The folk dancer and poet Ursula Wood (later Vaughan Williams) was part of this circle in the 1930s and has recalled Henry's attraction to and for women and Maud's friendship with him.[20] In May 1931 an anonymous blackmailer left notes at Maud's home and attempted to bribe her housekeeper into revealing details of her employer's personal life.[21] In his diary Henry stressed that no grounds existed for blackmail but Maud was apparently pestered by a private detective for many months.

During this period Evelyn faced further problems within her family. Evelyn may have placed Cecil on a pedestal after his death but her two youngest brothers continued to try her patience. In the early 1920s Algie was out of work and expecting his sister to provide for him. He married again but still periodically turned up at Evelyn's expecting to stay. When Evelyn went to Switzerland with Henry and the Robertsons in 1930, she admitted in her diary that she felt like 'some one freed from an overhanging calamity as Lancelot's affairs are temporarily settled', Ethel was in Rome, Mabel's health seemed better than it had been (though she died two years later) and even Algie was 'quiescent'. Yet just before they returned she wrote 'I wish I did not feel the shades of the prison house already closing round me as Thursday approaches'. And she understood better than most the meaning of such comparisons.[22]

Evelyn rented rooms one summer in a Georgian house in Devon for herself, her sister Ethel and brother Lancelot. He was a diamond jeweller but lost his job in 1930 when his employer took cyanide. This brother had expensive tastes and lived beyond his means. He seemed to expect Evelyn to bail him out but his ever-forgiving sister wrote: 'It is a joy to help Lancelot over his financial crises because he never makes you feel he is under an obligation to you.'[23] She gave him a small weekly subsidy.

Yet in 1932 Evelyn's lawyer informed her that Lancelot intended suing her for mismanagement of the family trust that had caused considerable bitterness over the years. Henry made clear his feelings: 'It is mean & shameful & a terrible & unexpected blow, deadly in thrust.'[24] To make matters worse, Ethel was supporting Lancelot and sending what Henry called 'crazy and abusive' letters to Evelyn. Evelyn decided that the bank should take over the administration of the trust but was deeply hurt by the whole episode which had come just after a specialist warned her of the effect that shock could have on her weak heart.

There were other grave health concerns. In August, Evelyn was admitted to hospital worried that she had cancer of the womb. Her fears were unfounded. She amused herself by jotting down snippets of ward conversation.[25] She initially imagined that the comment 'Mine's fallen five times' came from a mother referring to her child. It was her first time in hospital and it was the poor mothers who concerned her most. She was impressed by the dedication of the nurses and friendliness of patients and noted that medical conditions overrode class in such institutions. She decided that prison was the nearest she had come to such camaraderie. Henry was oblivious to all this and dancing at the summer school. On his return he wrote to Elizabeth Robins:

> And all the time I was enjoying the rush of Malvern my dear ES was in the Royal Free Hospital, suffering as women do for a full week, and saying no word to me about it for fear of spoiling my frivolous pleasure and bringing me back. Now she lies exhausted and powerless.[26]

She was soon home and busy again. Over the years Evelyn helped Henry with obtaining copyright permissions, indexes and the selection of essays for his later books – she and Harold Laski helped to choose extracts for his 1929 anthology *England's Voice of Freedom* – but publishers were now less inclined to revive her fiction. Her papers include fifteen unpublished plays. Evelyn made lists of agents, theatres and actors who rejected *But Why Not?* and *Five Sinners*. This is unusual. The archives of writers and performers tend to include only good reviews and acceptances and this underscores once more Evelyn's lack of self-importance. She noted that Sybil Thorndike, Edith Evans and a host of eminent figures sent enthusiastic letters acclaiming 'Five Sinners' as 'the finest play of the century, but ---'. [27]

Nevertheless, her one-act play entitled *The Loafer and the Loaf* was put on by the Half Circle Players (in the Parliamentary Labour Club) at St George's Hall in 1925 and published the following year. [28] Such fantasies were not to everybody's taste, not least because their mix of humour and politics came close to moralising, albeit through turning conventions on their head. In *The Loafer and the Loaf*, a loaf is taken from a cart, prompting discussion of the right to bread. Love and poverty triumph over respectability. These plays contained too many messages for children to enjoy yet were somewhat fey for adult appreciation.

In 1929 Evelyn decided that she must supplement her diminishing income, not least because of family demands. That summer the publisher Victor Gollancz offered her a post as a reader with a salary of £200 a year. She read numerous manuscripts but the following spring was dismissed (with three months' notice) after rejecting a 'good' book that was snapped up elsewhere. Her work did not really suit modern demands but a disappointed Henry remarked that she seemed more upset at being thought antiquated than at losing the earnings. [29] Early 1932 held out another possibility. The secretary of the Mansion House Armenian Fund offered her the chance of about ten weeks in the summer to visit and write about Armenian settlements. A fee of £100 was offered together with expenses. A very envious Henry encouraged her to ask for more money. She did so, slightly reluctantly. But the plan fell through for want of funds.

It did, however, get Evelyn thinking about writing a book based on her travels. Henry had already published his triple-decker autobiography of more than a thousand pages. Margaret's appeared in 1926. Evelyn's book became a memoir. *Unfinished Adventure* was published in 1933. But, unlike Henry, Evelyn did not really enjoy being in the spotlight. How many other autobiographers apologise for talking about themselves and admit in their introductions that that they are not very courageous? [30]

Evelyn's published story ends (rather than starts) with a significant date: 18 January 1933. As she explains:

> At an age when a woman whose childhood began in the 'seventies should by tradition put on a cap and settle down to enjoy a spinster twilight, I intend to start out on the greatest, because it is the commonest, of all adventures. It is also the most uncertain: that is why it seems unreasonable to leave it, as it is generally left, to the young adventurer. If age and experience have any value at all, they should help and not hinder the explorer who sets out to sail the uncharted seas of married life.[31]

Evelyn had always enjoyed seeing herself as a rebel. A few years earlier she had posed a question with a somewhat modern ring in the *Manchester Guardian*: 'What is wrong with old age?' Aged sixty-three, she once more challenged convention though, ironically, in the most conventional of contexts. She and Henry became engaged in December 1932.

Margaret had died six months earlier. She had been ill for some time. In 1929 Henry had returned from the United States to find her in a nursing home. A non-malignant growth on her colon was removed. The following two years were punctuated with physical and mental illness. She even tried to drown herself in the bath. Suffering from delusions, she believed there was a plot to assassinate her and her beloved son Richard. Richard wanted her put into an asylum but Henry thought this cruel and was also aware that there were periods of lucidity so preferred to pay for care at home. Henry cut down on engagements but still got out and about. On 4 June 1932 he stayed in Cambridge as Sir Arthur Quiller-Couch's guest. Returning the next day he found Margaret unconscious. She died from kidney failure at home on 8 June.

Just hours after Margaret's death Henry wrote in his diary about her in a tone that seems callous but reflects just how tragically ill-matched this couple had been. He recalled her energy and humour but dwelt more on their differences. It had been a 'mistaken engagement' and 'dismal marriage'.[32] Less than a fortnight later he was discussing the future with Evelyn. In December Frederick Pethick-Lawrence noticed that Evelyn was 'specially brilliant & lovely' at the Folk Dance and Song Festival. His wife Emmeline wrote to congratulate them on their engagement, saying that it was 'the perfectly right & natural & happy thing' that two such wonderful comrades 'should no longer be separated at all but that your lives should be made one'.[33]

The national and provincial press made the most of this unusual engagement. 'It created the liveliest interest in literary circles' declared the *Western Mail*.[34] Pictures of the two mature, eminent journalists appeared with captions such as 'Literary Romance'. Most concentrated on Henry's fearless exploits. The *Daily Despatch* declared that Evelyn was as notable as Henry: 'As a mere girl she was a light in modern literature.'[35] Henry explained that they had been 'comrades and colleagues in a great many causes'. When interviewed they both emphasised their radical credentials and shared beliefs. Evelyn mentioned that Mr Nevinson was always on the side of militant women and had smuggled a letter to her in Holloway sewn inside the hem of a dressing gown.[36]

Evelyn's summary of the last chapter of her autobiography declares somewhat disingenuously, 'I find a fellow-traveller'.[37] She had, of course, decades earlier found the man answering that description. Friends had long been aware of their closeness. At the beginning of 1931 Laurence Housman had referred in a letter to 'your dear man' and sent 'love to you both'.[38] One cherished friend who had long welcomed Evelyn and Henry as a couple was Edward Carpenter. Henry wrote from Cologne in 1923 to tell Carpenter that when they were home again 'be sure we will come to see you as one of our greatest joys'.[39] Evelyn and Henry used to visit him at Millthorpe near Sheffield and then at Guildford. Both addressed the vast gathering – estimated to be fifteen hundred strong – at Millthorpe in 1930 to mark the first anniversary of his death. Evelyn, whom Carpenter had called 'a noble creature', spoke about his youth and his belief in women's equality. Henry noted in his diary that her words moved people to tears.[40]

Evelyn had become Henry's constant companion, whether on dancing holidays or at events such as the Oxford Recitations established by his old friend John Masefield to discover talented verse speakers (Henry was one of the judges). They also still enjoyed country walking. In the autumn of 1925 she stayed in the York youth hostel with her old suffrage friend Mary Postlethwaite. Henry joined them a few days later and, armed with rucksacks, they all set off to walk along Hadrian's Wall before moving on to the Lake District, For Evelyn this 'walking tour' was 'one of the most delightful holidays I have ever taken'.[41]

Evelyn tended to work on holiday, not least because there were press deadlines. Staying on the Sussex coast with Mary Neal in 1924 to recuperate from 'slight strain from overwork', she wrote a *Guardian* article on Poplar municipal wash-houses and a message for Eva Gore-Booth to read out at a Deputation to the Home Office supporting the abolition of capital punishment. Nevertheless, she found it easier to relax than did Henry. On the eve of their 1929 holiday in northern France with Victoria de Bunsen (one of the Buxtons) and her two sons and two teenage girls, the veteran correspondent confided in his diary that he 'felt sad & unwilling about this tour without definite object: for "rest" and "pleasure" are no object for me'.[42] It was the first time he had been a tourist abroad since he had accompanied the Toynbee Travellers on an educational tour to Greece in 1894. Whereas Evelyn's holiday diary expresses her great joy in being on holiday, Henry's mentions 'silly rhyming games' in the evening. But for Evelyn their sightseeing reawakened happy memories of the *Yellow Book* days, especially when they visited Dieppe.

Both were, however, enchanted by an excursion to Chartres. Evelyn called the cathedral 'one of the great moments of my life':

> The miracle of Chartres has stirred me as I have been stirred only by the 5th & the 7th Symphonies [Beethoven's], & the Agamemnon & HWN's description of the Suvla landing, and parts of David Copperfield & parts of the Gold Rush where Charlie Chaplin touched depths for the fraction of a minute, & a Greek winged statue of a woman without a head whose name I don't know. You can't talk about Chartres, you can only wonder how it was that you were just saved from dying without seeing it – as you might so easily have done.[43]

For Henry too, glimpsing the cathedral at the end of a narrow street was 'overwhelming' and 'one of the supreme sights of my life, on the level with the acropolis, or the 7th symphony, or the Agamemnon'. He had to admit that it was 'One of the great days of life'.[44]

Yet these remarkably similar sentiments expressed on the same day in their respective diaries represent are not simple, impromptu examples of the congruence of Evelyn and Henry's interests. That evening at dinner they had discussed with Victoria and young Bernard de Bunsen what had most impressed them in life and ranked these experiences. Their diary entries reflected this particular conversation.

Nevertheless, they had a lot in common and when Henry was asked to address a big meeting to celebrate the release from prison of

JOURNALISTS MARRY.—Mr. Henry W. Nevinson, the veteran war correspondent, and Miss Evelyn Sharp, author of a number of children's books, after their wedding at Hampstead yesterday. On the right is Mr. C. R. W. Nevinson, the bridegroom's artist son.

14. Evelyn and Henry's wedding on 1 January 1933. Henry's daughter Philippa stands behind him with her daughter Margaret to her left. Henry's son, the artist C. R. W. Nevinson, is on the right of the picture, poised to make a quick exit

the Labour leader Tom Mann on the day originally selected for their wedding, they both felt that they should postpone it. So Henry gave his speech on 17 January 1933 and he and Evelyn were married the next day at Hampstead Town Hall.

The previous Christmas Day Ramsay MacDonald had written to Henry:

> The best of all my Christmas news has been a letter saying that Evelyn and you are going to marry each other. My regard for both of you is such that I am almost bold enough to exercise a hitherto unused prerogative of the PM and insist upon being your best man . . . It is perfect.[45]

But such a suggestion was not quite so perfect for Evelyn and Henry. The prime minister's presence[46] would have transformed the occasion into a public event and anyway, though fond of him as an individual, Evelyn had serious reservations about MacDonald's position as leader of a National Government. So they held a private, family ceremony. Evelyn's friend Charles Robertson and the international journalist

S. K. Ratcliffe, whom Henry had known since the start of the century, were witnesses.

Several weeks later the Nevinsons held a reception for 150 guests at Sidney and Gertrude Parry's London home (Gertrude was Roger Casement's cousin and an old friend of Henry's). During the first few weeks of their marriage they were as busy as ever though Evelyn took a brief break from writing her *Guardian* column. They socialised with friends, enjoyed a cocktail party held by Henry's artist son, did some writing, went to Cecil Sharp House and saw several films. Going to the cinema was now one of their favourite pastimes along with listening to wireless concerts and gramophone records. Evelyn spoke in Bolton at a women's luncheon club, Henry lectured to a hundred schoolboys and both were present at a large Caxton Hall meeting against capital punishment. They attended Galsworthy's memorial service at Westminster Abbey and were driven home afterwards by Sylvia, daughter of Henry's old lover Nannie Dryhurst (who had died in 1930).

In June 1933 they were lent a house on Lake Windermere by an old school friend of Evelyn's. They stayed there with the Robertsons. The Lake District had long been one of Henry's favourite places. Another visit was made to the old Nevinson home at Newby. They met Arthur Ransome, who 'talked admiringly' of Evelyn's novel *The Youngest Girl in the School*.[47] In the autumn they visited the Parrys in Cushenden, Northern Ireland. Evelyn wrote simply: 'Both these holidays belong to those rare interludes in life when one is too happy to have anything to write about.'[48] The next year, despite bad weather and the realisation that they could not walk as they used to, they visited the Hebrides with the Robertsons. Evelyn called it 'the finest holiday we have yet taken together'.[49] On marrying she had moved into 4 Downside Crescent. On returning, the sight of a new blue and white bathroom and a Hampstead home full of flowers was a welcome contrast to an empty attic flat.

But married life in Henry's home also required tolerance. Henry's frequently fractious offspring had to be placated. The volatile and self-absorbed Richard was in ill health. Henry sadly commented that the 'sunshine' had been taken out of him.[50] When he told his children about his impending marriage, Philippa wrote 'a nice letter' (though Henry's nephew John L. Nevinson, always keen for gossip, believed that Philippa's daughter Margaret felt displaced). Son Richard responded by telephoning to say 'Oh, I suppose that's all right'. But his wife Kathleen told Henry: 'You must not expect us to be intimate with you & her. An occasional lunch perhaps?'[51] When Evelyn came to take measurements for her furniture, Henry noted how she valiantly 'tried to make friends'.

Evelyn was a sociable person. Each year she held either a Christmas tea party at her rooms or a dance (for at least seventy) at St John's Institute. Downside Crescent, described by Henry's nephew, John L. Nevinson, as a 'cheerless, uninhabited house'[52] remarkable only for its paintings by Richard, now became more like a home. Evelyn and Henry began a tradition that Christmas of hosting an annual sherry party. Guests included friends such as Vera Brittain, Winifred Holtby and Sir William Rothenstein (who did a drawing of Evelyn in 1933).

Just a couple of months after their wedding, a sapphire that Lancelot was having set split. Henry advanced him £30 towards repaying the costs. It was money that the Nevinsons could now ill afford. In the disastrous international economic climate Henry lost £1,000 from an investment. Evelyn had moved from John Street to nearby 104 Guildford Street at the start of 1932 and on leaving had to pay £100 to clear her new lease. Meanwhile the end of Henry's *Baltimore Sun* work in 1933 was closely followed by the end of Evelyn's fortnightly *Manchester Guardian* articles (though she still did some reviewing). Henry started selling books and pictures. A gift of £360 from admirers (largely eminent themselves) gathered to honour his achievements at the Criterion in the summer of 1933 was therefore especially welcome, not least because health problems now added to the Nevinsons' costs.

Henry had become diabetic and spent their first wedding anniversary in hospital. He remained there for a fortnight, receiving twice daily visits from Evelyn. He needed regular insulin injections and a special diet. The following month he was ill with a hernia. In the spring, to help revive his flagging spirits, they went on a three-week Gallipoli cruise organised by the Royal Naval Division (8th Corps). Henry had free passage (Evelyn travelled half-price) in return for his two lectures with lantern slides on the Gallipoli Campaign and one on Athens. There were seven hundred passengers aboard the *Duchess of Richmond*. It was not Evelyn's idea of fun. Cruises, she felt, were better suited to the young and sporty. Always a hopeless sailor, she was seasick on the way out and back as they crossed the Bay of Biscay. She admitted in her diary that Henry had little patience with shopping or 'mooching round'.[53] And she felt somewhat hypocritical travelling with so many professional soldiers. If they criticised the Gallipoli Campaign it

15. William Rothenstein's pencil drawing of Evelyn in 1933

tended to be in terms of the mistakes of the High Command rather than questioning the politics that made such conflict possible.

Gallipoli revealed to Evelyn 'the whole wickedness as well as the stupidity of war'. She was deeply moved by the sight of Anzac Cove and Chocolate Hill where Henry had been wounded in 1915, but the 'brooding melancholy & the sense of waste & futility & tragic heroism associated with the Expedition was almost unbearable'. She wondered how the kind people sharing their table would react if they knew what she really thought about it all.

But when the ship moored opposite the entrance to the Golden Horn and Evelyn caught her first sight of Istanbul, she was enchanted by the mosques, the Byzantine mosaics being uncovered in the cisterns and the treasures of the Seraglio. She enjoyed seeing the Grand Bazaar despite being pestered to make purchases. It was a fascinating time to be in the former Constantinople. Atatürk's reforms, creating a westernised, secular society, were affecting everyday life. Evelyn knew Halidé Edib Adivar, politician, writer and pioneer of Turkish women's emancipation and was interested in the views of the young male guide who declared that women were now 'free & equal with us'[54] but admitted that the older generation preferred the banned veil and fez.

On the way home the ship anchored off Piraeus and Evelyn at last visited Henry's beloved Athens. 'Of course I can't describe it', she wrote in her diary about the Acropolis, well aware that any praise would be hackneyed and banal. But it was, she wrote, the 'final touch of perfection' to be there with the 'Grand Duke'.

Despite her reservations about cruises, three years later Evelyn and Henry boarded the *Cairo City* at Marseilles for a Greek island cruise. This Anglo-Hellenic tour was to be Henry's farewell to Greece. Many of these cruisers were well versed in the subjects (such as ancient Greek sculpture and temple architecture) of the accompanying lectures. But whereas Henry was in his element discussing classical topics with academics such as the Cambridge literary scholar F. L. Lucas, Evelyn admitted in her diary that she felt 'quite an untravelled ignoramus' because she could not provide a discourse on Apollo or Hera.[55] She enjoyed Naomi Mitchison's moving and well-delivered lecture on Socrates. Henry wrote in the *Spectator* that Mitchison retold 'beautifully' the 'irresistible story of Socrates'. But his diary was less charitable, noting that she tried to lecture on slaves and women in ancient Athens.[56]

Evelyn was deeply impressed by the ancient sites, particularly Delphi:

> Even 200 cruisers and various clumps of information dealt out by excellent Professors could not take away the feeling of standing where the Delphic Oracle once drew all Greece to consult here.

But the tour was a strain. Henry was now in his eighties. He caught a chill and fever after visiting Crete, so they had to forgo seeing Cyprus, the next port of call. Much of the terrain on land was rough and steep. At Delos, where Lucas recited passages from Homer, Henry fell down the steep side of the amphitheatre – he had, of course, resisted taking the safe path – but escaped with a bruised forehead and shin. This we know from Evelyn's diary. Henry did not mention it in his account. He did, however, refer to ES (as he still called her) being seasick. He recovered quickly and they enjoyed a day visiting his old friend William Miller in Athens. Like Evelyn, he treasured the 'amazing spiritual life & beauty' of Delphi. But they found the cruise costly and tiring. Henry had to acknowledge that he was far from agile and Evelyn needed to be constantly alert in case he stumbled. On their way home they were jerked back into a harsh present: in Salerno they saw walls plastered with 'Il Duce' posters.

As they sailed to Italy Evelyn noted in her diary that *The Poisoned Kiss* was being performed at the Juilliard School of Music in New York. This was the comic opera with music by Ralph Vaughan Williams and libretto by Evelyn. She had become acquainted with the eminent British composer in 1924 through the EFDS. The following year Vaughan Williams conducted the folk song class and addressed the Easter school in Devon. He was a song collector and, from 1932 until his death in 1958, the society's president. He composed a handful of operas, starting with the romantic ballad opera *Hugh the Drover* in 1910. It is not known exactly when he approached Evelyn to collaborate with him but she was already writing lyrics for him in June 1927. The following month she was corresponding with John Lane about performing rights and publication as some of the characters and incidents were based on Richard Garnett's story *The Poison Maid*.[57]

Nathaniel Hawthorne's 'Rapaccini's Daughter' provided the other main source for the story. Published in 1936, *The Poisoned Kiss* was described as 'A Romantic Extravaganza'.[58] The main character Tormentilla is a magician's daughter who has been trained to poison the first man she kisses. Henry declared the first act 'excellent' and was astonished at the ease of Evelyn's comic verse. The libretto's contemporary references and witticisms, however, soon made it seem dated.[59] There are comments on a car in its garage and shingled tresses and 'perms'. Evelyn was fascinated by the fashions of the postwar modern woman. Tormentilla's maid Angelica gives her a cocktail of 'arsenic, vitriol with a dash of cocaine and a bryony berry to give it pep'. Modern devices such as central heating are mentioned.

Yet there is also a beautiful duet with Tormentilla and Prince Amaryllus. Continuing the botanical theme, this is called 'Blue Larkspur in a Garden'. Evelyn had loved the larkspur in the garden at her old home at Weston Turville. But her diary shows that she wrote the words in a Guernsey garden overlooking the sea in the summer of 1927 on one of her working holidays. She stayed in digs outside St Peter Port and went out daily, composing songs on rocks and beaches. She spent a few nights on the tiny island of Sark 'at once so welcoming and so aloof, that the traveller who lands there is instantly caught by the magic of it'. She was fascinated by local superstitions. In an article in the *Contemporary Review* she described small stone ledges jutting out on the chimney side of old cottages. They were reputed to be seats for witches who, according to local legend, were the offspring of fairies.[60] She also tried less fanciful Jersey but in late June it was full of tourists and not conducive to work. Every few days she would send material to Vaughan Williams. After three weeks Evelyn sailed home, writing two songs en route.

Whilst working on their venture, Vaughan Williams told Evelyn: 'We've really got to make up our minds whether this is to be a musical comedy or real comic opera.'[61] They were conscious of the need to work out the balance between drama and music, yet the end product still seems to be a hybrid. With her reputation for witty fairy stories, it had made sense for Evelyn to undertake the libretto. But although she had written the words for a light-hearted song called 'The Cherub',[62] collaborating with Dr Vaughan Williams (which is how Evelyn's letters addressed him) was unlike anything she had done before. Moreover, she was used to writing books and articles which, once printed, were completed. Here was a piece of work that continued to be developed as performances prompted further revisions.

Vaughan Williams made detailed suggestions from the outset. Evelyn was undaunted and both correspondents remained good-natured with each other (he was also very fair in terms of shared royalties). She was prepared to disagree about the plot, arguing for example, against his suggestions for Act II as they meant that little action would be left for the final act. She did, however concede (despite some limited experience of having plays performed) that she did not know what might be most effective on stage: 'You have written operas and I haven't.' Moreover, she believed that 'the music must decide finally' because it was the more important of the two.[63]

Vaughan Williams sent Evelyn detailed letters with specific suggestions for improvements. He was keen not to sound too prescriptive, so tempered his comments with remarks such as: ' I hope you will pay *no* attention to any of my suggestions – every one works better with a *free* hand – & as you have already discovered I find you are right & I am wrong usually.'[64] But they would be immediately followed by another example of what might be changed. After sending what he called 'an awful rehash of your text' and suggestions for Act III, along with requests for new songs, he added 'I expect on receipt of this you will chuck the whole thing – & I shd not be surprised – but I hope not as I've managed to nab one or two rather nice tunes'. Some years later, in an unsigned newspaper article, Evelyn admitted that as a librettist she had found Vaughan Williams full of surprises: 'So exasperating at one moment in unexpected demands, and then overwhelmingly disarming in his words of generous praise.' 'Furious spurts of enthusiasm' would be followed by complete silence.[65]

By early January 1930 the opera was ready for sending out though Vaughan Williams professed to have no idea of where to place it and asked Evelyn if she would try 'hawking it round'.[66] There were concert versions performed in London and Gloucester but it was six years before it was fully staged. Further revisions were made before it opened at the new Arts Theatre in Cambridge. They were told that the evening's entertainment must not start before 8.30pm 'so Dons may digest their dinner' and it had to end by 11pm in order for undergraduates to get back into their colleges. This meant 'cutting to the bone' so Vaughan Williams suggested that he cut twenty minutes of music and Evelyn twenty minutes of dialogue.[67]

On May Day 1936 Evelyn and Henry attended rehearsals in Cambridge. Vaughan Williams's second cousin, Gwen Raverat, designed the set with Elisabeth Vellacott. The first performance took place on the 12th. Henry called it 'a real triumph at last' for Evelyn.[68] Vaughan Williams and Evelyn were called on to the stage at the end by an enthusiastic audience. Six days later it transferred to Sadlers Wells, London, where it was again well received by its audience though press reviews tended not to be so positive.[69] Vaughan Williams suggested that they should not worry about the press since those who saw the opera clearly enjoyed 'our joint effort' and some had come came three times. He had, however, more suggestions for improvement. Amateur performances in Liverpool, Bristol and Bridport seem to have gone down well. Yet although one of the most revered of British composers, Vaughan Williams is not best remembered for operas. Not until 2003 was a recording made of *The Poisoned Kiss*.[70]

But dance, marriage and music tell only part of the story of Evelyn and Henry in these years. They were also increasingly concerned about the effects of economic depression and the rise of fascism in Europe. The postwar boom had been short-lived. More than two million were without jobs in the United Kingdom by the winter of 1921–22. Although the late 1920s saw some relative improvement, the Wall Street Crash of 1929 had worldwide effects. The years between 1931 and 1935 witnessed Britain's worst unemployment figures. Once again over two million were officially classified as unemployed (actual numbers were rather higher) throughout this period. The winter of 1932–23 saw one quarter of the insured working population out of work.[71]

Evelyn and Henry still cared about social issues and wanted to make their voices heard. Evelyn was well aware of how employment prospects were deteriorating for the young. By the early 1930s the majority of her *Guardian* articles contained some, if not detailed, reference to the plight of the unemployed. In 1932 she wrote a piece about a promising lad of seventeen whose good job was already in the past. Beaten by circumstances with parents who were also victims of the Depression, he had collapsed from starvation. The Juvenile Advisory Committee found him another job, but it was one he loathed, requiring less skill and paying lower wages. He was one of the 'good children of the State' with crushed ambitions.[72]

Had Evelyn's books about London childhood and youth been written a few years later their tone would have been grimmer. She was furious that an attempt in 1930 to raise the school leaving age was unsuccessful – not until 1944 would children have to stay in school until they were fifteen – and she advocated as an emergency measure a decree to keep all children in education until they were eighteen. Cinemas and theatres could be used in the mornings, with films used for teaching. Idle factories could be turned into classes. In her scheme of things, unemployed mechanics, artists, actors and intellectuals would become teachers whilst disarmament would serve the useful function of enabling soldiers and sailors to help build rather than destroy the future. She saw education as the vital way forward.

Her fear was that if 'hungry idleness and boredom and disillusion-ment' were the only offerings, people were unlikely to resist war fever when it broke out again.[73] As she put it in November 1932:

> I sometimes wonder whether it is realised how strong a factor in future war is this profound dissatisfaction of the soul, now throbbing from end to end of the civilised world; for if the arts of peace are to be thus with-held from millions, can we expect them to resist the adventure of war when it is once more dangled before their eyes?[74]

Evelyn disparaged those who suggested that the unemployed pre-ferred to be idle. The scenes she had witnessed in Germany in 1931 made her nervous about heroic youth in search of a crusade, whether in Italy or closer to home: unemployed youth would become 'the prey of Hitler types' who had learned the 'trick of firing souls in the wrong direction' unless powerful voices were found to counteract this.[75] 'The Dictator's great ally' was 'the starvation of spirit and body'.

Evelyn promoted positive examples of international harmony such as the message broadcast annually from 1922 by the children of Wales 'to the boys and girls of every country under the sun'. In 1933, at the same time as schoolchildren from seventy countries were replying to the Welsh children, sixty-five members of the League of Nations were being told that it was impracticable to continue even discuss-ing disarmament. Such juxtapositions were a frequent feature of her columns.[76] Although she viewed the League's achievements as disappointing, she applauded the way it had made peace propaganda respectable. She stressed in June 1934 that it remained the one body that 'stands between us and a relapse into the old Europe of intrigue and tyranny'.[77] What it needed to focus on was 'the building up of a habit of peace among the ordinary people of the world where there is now a habit of war'.

She also advocated the work of the Friends International Service Council and praised small multi-national ventures such as the Quaker-run hostel in Geneva and the Youth House in London's Camden Town, along with experiments to promote self-help amongst the unemployed and a hostel in London for working lads from the Welsh valleys. She visited the Grith Fyrd (peace and army) Camp in the New Forest, the first of a number of practical, non-militaristic cultural experiments for unemployed young men run by the Woodcraft Order of Chivalry.[78]

Evelyn had some harsh words to say about the image of pacifism. Pacifists needed to make peace seem more appealing. She had been part of the spectacle and theatre of suffrage and felt that pacifists could learn from the suffragettes' acute awareness of marketing style, novelty and visual impact. Yet time was not on the pacifists' side. Warmongers had grasped how to attract youth. It was therefore vital, she argued, to reclaim the young from the militarists and fascists, to use bands, flags (she ridiculed the pacifist use of white – the colour of the shroud), ceremony and stirring propaganda 'for the glory of pacifism'.[79]

Evelyn declared that pacifism was on trial everywhere. It was, she wrote, easy to be a pacifist immediately after a war but in 1933 it required courage. 'The fight to make a country worth fighting for', demanded, in her view, 'more courage, heroism and loyalty to a high ideal of patriotism than any war'.[80]

But Evelyn and Henry were not merely armchair activists. In February 1934 Robert Kidd formed (and became secretary of) the National Council for Civil Liberties (NCCL) to challenge the encroachment on the liberty of the individual. Evelyn attended its inaugural meeting and was one of eighteen elected to its first executive committee.[81] There was concern about the *agents provocateurs* and police baton charges that had greeted the 1932 Hunger Marchers on their arrival in London. On the eve of the 1934 Hunger Marchers' arrival in London, fifteen members of the new NCCL, including their founder and secretary, Ronald Kidd, Evelyn and Henry, Laski, Wells and Dr Edith Summerskill, signed a letter to the press. It complained that the police demand that shopkeepers should barricade their windows had unnecessarily fomented a sense of impending danger, as had the Attorney General's hint of the possibility of bloodshed. Yet, the letter stressed, the discipline of the marchers was said to be excellent. Concerned about this encroachment on the liberty of the citizen, the NCCL members explained that their new council would uphold and promote civil liberties by monitoring proceedings over the next few days and investigating reports.[82] Evelyn and Henry both attended Hyde Park on 25 February and were relieved to find 'all very quiet but determined'.[83]

In 1936 Henry became the NCCL's second president, replacing E. M. Forster. Freedom of speech and association were increasingly under threat and the NCCL was especially concerned about the rise of British fascism. Evelyn and Henry were also active in English PEN (Poets, Essayists and Novelists) and keen to uphold freedom of expression internationally. In June 1938 when Henry was its president they travelled to Prague for a PEN congress. The prime minister welcomed them. There were five days of talks, debates, dinners and sight-seeing in Prague, including a performance of *Romeo and Juliet* in Wallenstein's old palace. They particularly enjoyed the company of the writer Karel Čapek. The delegates took a motor-coach to Bratislava then travelled into the mountains, entertained by local PEN members. Henry had to make several speeches. His voice no longer had much strength and he was concerned that the microphone was not functioning well. But the writer Margaret Storm Jameson, who was present (and succeeded Henry as president), later told Evelyn that:

> I used to watch Henry looking at you when he began to make a speech & I don't think it is fancy that he drew strength from you as he spoke, until his voice rang out like the trumpet it had always been.[84]

Two months later the Munich Agreement was signed and Sudetenland, the German-speaking mountainous area of north Czechoslovakia, was peremptorily handed to Germany. Henry denounced Neville Chamberlain's 'Peace for our time' as 'Peace with Dishonour' and, after being accused of being political at a PEN dinner, resigned his presidency. The day after his resignation, Hitler crossed into Sudetenland. In mid-March 1939 German troops occupied the rest of the country and 'our beloved Czechoslovakia ceased to exist'.[85]

In the years leading up to the war Evelyn and Henry also attended anti-fascist demonstrations and through the NCCL helped to monitor the interpretation of legislation such as the Official Secrets Act. When Lord Runciman was announced as the guest of honour at a Society of Authors dinner to be held in November 1938, Evelyn wrote to protest. In August the Runciman Mission had been sent to Czechoslovakia by Chamberlain to report on the Czech–German question. Evelyn (who sat on the society's pension fund committee) argued that it was not the time 'to go out of one's way to honour somebody who was associated with the calamitous series of events' and returned her ticket for the event. In her view, writers 'of all people' should avoid any semblance of support for those who 'willingly or unwillingly were parties to a betrayal which has opened the way to further suppression of thought & persecution of opinion in Europe'.[86] The secretary then informed Evelyn that Lord Runciman would not, after all, be attending the dinner.

When Evelyn saw the opening of the seventh assembly of the League of Nations in 1926, Briand and Stresemann's speeches and shaking of hands had given her hope.[87] Briand's dramatic statement that 'La Guerre est finie entre nous' would, she wrote in her diary, make it much more difficult than ever before for a new war to develop. Yet, reproducing these words in 1933, Evelyn added a note of caution, suggesting that her words had struck 'a more hopeful note than subsequent events have perhaps warranted'.[88] Seven years later, on 13 October 1940, and two days after Henry's eighty-fourth birthday, the veteran reporter of war and the denouncer of war were bombed out of their Hampstead house.

12

War and widowhood: Chipping Campden and Kensington

For a long time Evelyn and Henry resisted leaving Hampstead despite pleas from friends for them to escape the Blitz. Evelyn had rented small flats all her adult life until moving to Henry's spacious home at 4 Downside Crescent. The house had been new when Henry and his family had moved there almost forty years earlier. Evelyn and Henry were both deeply attached to London. Even when forced to leave, they felt, as Evelyn put it, 'horribly like deserters'.[1]

At the outbreak of war they had blacked out their windows and taken other precautions. Two German refugees came to lunch weekly. Gradually Evelyn and Henry's finances became more precarious. Evelyn's *News Chronicle* work ended, reducing their income by a third. The diminishing demand for their journalism (exacerbated by space needed for war news and the shortage of paper) led Evelyn's solicitor to suggest they move to a flat in the suburbs. This they sturdily resisted. They briefly considered giving up their maid Marguerite Scott, but Evelyn was now seventy and their house was large, so she stayed on. During the first year of the war Evelyn and Henry carried on much as before, still going to NCCL meetings (arguing against the internment of friendly aliens) and to other groups such as the Anti-Slavery Society. They attended more and more funerals, for old friends such as J. A. Hobson and George Lansbury.

By the summer of 1940 Henry was noting that more frequent air raid warnings were taking their toll on Evelyn's nerves. They made a little sheltered room on the ground floor of their house. Nearby there were crowds sheltering at Belsize Park Tube. Days and nights became punctuated by wailing sirens. On 1 September Henry wrote noted that there had been 'only' three air warnings, but on 7 September the Blitz began.

The first local fatality came two nights later when two houses in

Upper Park Road were struck. In a twenty-four-hour period three large bombs fell very near the Nevinson home, damaging some of their windows and ceilings.[2] Night after night that autumn London was bombarded. On average 160 bombers were attacking nightly. There were air raids for seventy-six consecutive nights (excepting 2 November when the weather was too bad to attack) with particularly devastating effects on east London. As Mollie Panter-Downes, London correspondent for the *New Yorker*, put it, 'For Londoners, there are no longer such things as good nights; there are only bad nights, worse nights and better nights.'[3] In one September week Henry recorded thirty air raid warnings. Between 8.30pm and 5am heavy bombing was frequent and sometimes their house shook and swayed. 'We miss the sunshine', he lamented, 'for many windows are boarded up and we live like things forbid'. They packed suitcases, ready to flee should the house collapse. Richard's studio was struck by an oil bomb. His two latest paintings were in the bath so survived intact and, remarkably, only one picture was seriously damaged though Evelyn found the place in chaos. A bomb wrecked Cecil Sharp House.

On 1 October water supplies were cut and nine days later a bomb exploded on the road about twenty yards away from Evelyn and Henry's home. 'We came very near to death & ruin', he wrote, adding that Evelyn and Marguerite were 'chilled with shock'. He did not admit his own fears. Henry's birthday began with a hissing bomb. It prompted him to write a short review of his life in the precious diary that he still kept. Two days later even the veteran war correspondent had to confess to experiencing a 'Day of terror'. There had been some short raids in the morning on 13 October but at 7.30 that evening they heard a rushing, hissing sound followed by a huge explosion in the garden just beyond them. Nearly all the windows at the back of the house were blown out and the base of a 250-pound bomb struck their roof. Evelyn had just left the front room. Ten minutes later another bomb whined past and burst a few streets away bringing down three houses. Evelyn, Henry and Marguerite cowered in the kitchen but were unhurt. The house was covered in thick dust, splintered wood from the windows and acrid smoke. They made up beds in the shelter.

There were neither gas nor water supplies and many holes in the roof. They were vulnerable to further attack so Evelyn and Henry had no choice but to move out. There had already been fatalities in the next road. On 19 October the Nevinsons left their home. They travelled to

High Ridge, Kingsbourne Green near Harpenden to share a rented house with Helen and Douglas Kennedy of the EFDSS. Henry was distraught at leaving his home: 'I have seldom touched such depths of misery', he wrote, 'and age quenches hope'. Military service and evacuation were depleting the population of Hampstead. Just before the war the borough had ninety thousand residents. By 1941 their number had been reduced by more than a third.

A few days later they took a Green Line bus 'home' to survey the damage and collect possessions from a darkened house. Books and furniture had to be left behind. Evelyn was in better spirits in Hertfordshire but Henry was inconsolable. He was, though, at least aware of his sentiments: 'All cheerful except my self-centred self.' At the beginning of November a hired car took them and their meagre possessions to the Cotswolds. Evelyn and Henry had decided to move to Chipping Campden.

Visiting in March 1934, Evelyn had written in her diary, 'scarcely a motor passes our window though we are right on the main street'.[4] Campden had been at the height of its prosperity in the early fifteenth century as a centre for the collection and exporting of wool. It then became a quiet market town with its Cotswold stone, thatched roofs, cherry orchards and houses that all boasted a name rather than number. Evelyn described it as a fine place, 'passed over by tourists who rush along the main road to Broadway'. This would change, stimulated by G. M. Trevelyan's description in 1942 of its High Street as 'The most beautiful street now left in the island'.[5] But in 1940 it was unspoilt and Campden, with its monthly cattle mart in the centre of town, seemed a world away from London and the Blitz.

There was another reason for choosing Campden. It had become the home of close friends. Evelyn had known the Oxford-educated socialist writer Joseph Clayton since the 1890s. He had long been a friend of Henry's (the Claytons had lived in Hampstead) and both Jo and Margaret had been active supporters of women's suffrage. Jo recalled how much he had enjoyed the excuse for 'elevenses' of damson wine and the 'light & warmth & amusement' Evelyn and Henry had provided on their visit to the town in 1937.[6] Evelyn loved reading detective stories and enjoyed discussing them with Jo, who, unlike Henry, also devoured them.

The Nevinsons moved into rooms in Stamford House, Campden, paying £6 weekly for board and lodging. The house was owned by Miss Sunderland-Taylor, a former headmistress, and was within walking distance of the Claytons' cottage. 'Sunny' had an excellent library that helped Henry complete the volume on Thomas Hardy that he had been writing under increasingly difficult conditions in London, whilst Evelyn enjoyed reading authors such as P. G. Wodehouse. They supplemented their reading with books lent by friends and by using the county library that was open for one hour a week. But they missed their own collection of books, found the old stone house cold and dark, and had only one private room. Their landlady could not cope easily with the catering. Rationing and Henry's need for a special diet for his diabetes made daily life more difficult. Evelyn travelled to Evesham in search of his food.

They stayed less than two months at Stamford House. Their next temporary home was in the centre of town at the sixteenth-century Kings Arms. Evelyn and Henry had stayed at this hotel in the High Street before the war. They now had a bedroom and their own sitting room and the hotel provided meals. The Gordon Highlanders drilled beneath their window. Evelyn was ever alert to witty comments and heard one say 'Well, this place might suit Shakespeare all right, but give me Aberdeen'.[7]

The Nevinsons were not short of friends. Campden attracted the artistic. C. R. Ashbee had moved his Guild of Handicraft there at the start of the century. One new friend was Nina Griggs, widow of the visionary pastoralist Frederick Griggs who had designed their arts and crafts home. The Nevinsons became friendly with the Mackails at Cotswold House. Henry had first met J. W. Mackail (former Professor of Poetry at Oxford, Greek scholar and civil servant) in 1905. His wife Margaret was Edward Burne-Jones's daughter. The Nevinsons attended 'Cotswold Winter Evenings' and the debating society at the Town Hall. In one debate on the motion that the modern want of reticence was bad for morality and literature, Evelyn spoke against reticence. Henry defended it.

Campden now had many evacuees. An east London school had moved there and Evelyn spent one morning a week peeling potatoes and carrots for the midday threepenny school dinners. Yet, although she wrote that she and Henry were warmly welcomed and that people 'fell for' him immediately, neither of them felt at home.[8] A couple of visits to London to see their old house and attend PEN lunches, visit Algie and admire Richard's pictures at the Royal Academy only made them more homesick and underlined Henry's increasing frailty. The man of action hated not being in the thick of things. He attached the words

'In Exile' to his letters and the theme of exile dominated his verses. 'A Village Exile' refers to the 'terrifying silence' of his present location whereas 'London, my home' is 'the centre of the living earth'.[9]

Evelyn had other losses: both her sister Ethel and Cecil's daughter Dorothea died. Richard and Philippa rarely visited, and, when Henry's daughter did come, she upset him and annoyed them both by eating their meagre rations. There were, though, welcome food parcels from the United States and Canada, and a couple of wealthy Americans even sent cheques. Thomas Jones wrote on behalf of the Pilgrim Trust with a surprise offer to Henry of £100 annually for life for 'national service' unrecognised. But that life was drawing to a close.

Henry's diabetes was taking its toll on his mobility. He had become very thin and was frequently in pain. He and Evelyn were also depressed at the war news which now took precedence in his diary. In June 1941 they made their final move together, taking unfurnished rooms in the Victorian wing of the vicarage attached to St James, the splendid early perpendicular wool church known as the cathedral of the Cotswolds. People offered furniture. Henry had his own study and Evelyn a writing-table in the dining-cum-sitting room. Even though putting pen to paper was increasingly hard for Henry, it was integral to his very being. Evelyn was more and more preoccupied with looking after him though she too was determined to keep writing. She reviewed Marie Belloc-Lowndes's biographical study of her family, *I Too Have Lived in Arcadia*, for the *Manchester Guardian*.[10]

The Nevinsons now had their own kitchen and independence but this put pressure on Evelyn who had to organise meals once more. Rent, though, was less than they had been paying, there were magnificent views and, Henry wryly noted, it was convenient for the churchyard. But they were on the edge of town and not in sympathy with the views of their landlord, O'Loughlin, a strict Irish Protestant minister. It was a wet, windy summer. They felt dislocated but well aware that it was not an appropriate time to voice complaints.

Evelyn adapted to Campden's social life better than Henry. But his misery affected her. As she told one friend just after moving into the vicarage: 'He has at times been so profoundly homesick and miserable that I have been in despair.'[11] She had to deal with his considerable correspondence as well as her own.

By September Henry was using a bath chair and Evelyn pushing him round town. On his eighty-fifth birthday he was delighted to receive a copy of his PEN publication on Thomas Hardy. Henry's letters to friends now bade them farewell, and, although he composed some verses, he dozed a lot. Their London home had been made more or less habitable and, a year after leaving it, they were still dreaming of returning and hoped to have a trial few weeks there. Looking after an invalid was, however, taking its toll on Evelyn and on 19 October she had a nasty fall as she carried the supper tray down the stairs. She landed on her back, bruised, shaken and in pain.

Then Henry fell, cutting his legs badly and forcing an end to the diary that he had maintained for almost half a century. Evelyn, at his request, wrote the last few entries from 21 October. Refusing to stay in bed, he fell again several times that day and cut his eye. He almost died the next day then rallied a little. This was the pattern for the next fortnight. A nurse took up residence. Richard and Kathleen came one day and grand-daughter Margaret visited. Evelyn's loyal friends Lil and Barbara arrived. By 8 November Henry was only semi-conscious, Evelyn constantly by his side.

The next afternoon parishioners walked beneath his window to the Armistice Sunday service. Evelyn wrote in his diary that 'There was a flaming red sunset right across the sky and the reflection of it was across the room'.[12] Henry stopped breathing – he just 'slept away' – not long after six o'clock but 'his face did not change, or become less beautiful'. Evelyn held his hand until Lil and Nina Griggs took her away.

Henry was cremated at Golders Green on 13 November 1941. Among those attending were friends – many very elderly – family, Members of Parliament and representatives of societies such as the Balkan Committee. Henry's bearers were from Campden. On the coffin was Evelyn's laurel wreath. The crematorium was crowded. Respecting Henry's wishes, no words were spoken. Henry's old friend the composer Martin Shaw played folk songs and dances on the organ. The committal was accompanied by the slow movement from Beethoven's Seventh Symphony.

Henry had wanted his ashes scattered on 'any field or mountain or river of the England I loved so well'. On 23 November Evelyn went to Tewkesbury, throwing them at the confluence of the Rivers Avon and Severn 'as the current set towards his beloved Shrewsbury'. It was mild, sunny weather, quite unlike the storm that had followed his death. So, Evelyn wrote, 'I felt his turbulent spirit was perhaps at last at peace'.

There were many obituaries. Henry's papers include almost fifty of them. But, as a number of Evelyn's friends noted bitterly, *The Times* used an obituary that had been written some years earlier.

It mentioned Margaret but not Evelyn. Two days later Janet Leeper added an Appreciation in the paper which pointedly referred to 'his beloved wife Evelyn'.[13] Richard featured in the majority of other obituaries though a number alluded to Evelyn's devotion and her own achievements. Like the famous Webbs, Evelyn and Henry had enjoyed a distinguished partnership and had been, as Beatrice Webb once wrote of herself and Sidney, 'curiously well combined'.[14]

On 11 December PEN and the NCCL held a memorial meeting for Henry Nevinson at Caxton Hall. Vera Brittain, E. M. Forster, Noel Brailsford, General Sir Ian Hamilton, Emmeline Pethick-Lawrence and others paid tribute to the war correspondent, writer and champion of liberty in many campaigns and countries.[15] Richard and Philippa attended. Evelyn was profoundly glad to have been there but relieved when it was over.

Personal tributes kept her busy. She wrote letters to accompany Henry's gifts of books (such as Gibbon for the historian J. L. Hammond). Writing on Boxing Day to J. H. Whitehouse about his appropriate bequest of Ruskin's works, Evelyn mentioned that she had already received 340 letters.[16] They brought some comfort. Maude Royden wrote how Evelyn and Henry's happiness had lit up a room like a lamp. The scholar and editor G. P. Gooch stressed that 'The greatest thing in his life' was their love for each other and Katie Ratcliffe echoed the sentiments of many by saying how they enhanced each other.[17] Margaret Storm Jameson told Evelyn how 'casual little things' Henry had said showed how 'you were woven into his life by memories, going back years and years' and how clearly he depended on her 'as an anchor and centre'.[18]

There seemed little point remaining in Chipping Campden. By mid-December Evelyn was staying with neighbours at 12 Downside Crescent, undergoing the unpleasant task of clearing up and emptying her former home so that it could be put on the market. In a letter to the Society of Authors she remarked 'When the world is behaving so horribly what does it matter if one person has stopped being happy?'[19] After Christmas she returned to Kensington where she had lived as a child and young woman. Evelyn's solicitor owned 23 Young Street. His office was on the ground floor. Evelyn moved into a vacant flat on the floor above, paying a 'wartime rent'. Once nicknamed 'Becky' Sharp, she now lived opposite Thackeray's old home. Although her first winter back in Kensington was bitterly cold winter, it was mercifully free of air raids.

Evelyn was Henry's Literary Executor, and she occupied herself during the first half of 1942 by sorting out his affairs and seeing through the publication of his Pelican anthology *Words & Deeds*. At times, though, she was so overwhelmed with loneliness that she confessed to being 'nearly beaten'.[20] The book should have appeared during Henry's lifetime.[21] It had been the idea of George Ridley MP, and Henry and Ridley had worked on it from early in 1941. Ridley, who later chaired the Labour Party's National Executive, was a former railway worker and lifelong admirer of Henry's work. He had started work aged fourteen and spent his first earnings on Henry's *Essays in Freedom*.

The publication of what Henry called his 'Sixpenny Immortality' was, however, delayed owing to the war. The printing trade was de-reserved so suffered from a lack of staff and the paper quota was reduced. Aware that time was running out, in July 1941 Ridley had told Penguin that Nevinson did not have long to live and that it was 'the hope of his life that he may see his book in print'. It was not to be. Although Evelyn had finished the proofs by September 1941, it was not published until the following July when she helped to publicise it. At the same time the lack of new publications in juvenile literature unexpectedly led to the sale of about two thousand of the remaining stock of her old Macmillan children's books.

In February 1942 a radio tribute to Henry as the 'foremost of war correspondents, champion of freedom' was introduced by Richard.[22] Evelyn also did a radio programme that year, a six-minute script on Ibsen for a Home Service series on books that made history. It was broadcast on 26 June and she was one of three speakers. Sir George Arthur 'who had witnessed it all', spoke about the sensation Ibsen's plays had caused when first produced in London. The modern critic Alan Dent commented on the playwright's dramatic mastery. Then Evelyn recalled the social consequences of his work on England, revealing 'with moving sincerity' the meaning of the plays for women's emancipation. She explained how the journalist and novelist Richard Whiteing had taken her in April 1891 to see Elizabeth Robins as London's first Hedda Gabler and the impact the play and actress made on her. The reviewer for the *Listener* was struck by the 'sheer broadcasting ability' of the two veterans. It was remarkable that 'two survivors of the hansom-cab epoch should take to wireless as a duck to water'.[23] Evelyn enjoyed herself. The BBC noted that the material was 'very good' and that she had a 'pleasant voice' (an attribute that others also commented upon).

A former teacher called Vere Hodgson, now in her early forties, saw a new stage production of *Hedda Gabler* in October 1942. She found it gripping yet puzzling and noted in her diary that 'I was rather at a loss to know what all the emotion meant. Have a vague idea that Ibsen showed the New Woman, and that his plays were considered very advanced.'[24] Evelyn, who understood only too well the play's significance for late Victorians, also saw it that month. She commented how, in the early 1890s:

> Hedda stood for the rebel woman, a type of all the women then struggling for freedom of one kind or another, and she played it full of the spirit of revolt and with bitterness. There was no humorous side of it for her or for most of the women who saw her performance and read into it their own indignation with the lot of the average woman who could call neither her property nor her soul her own in those days.[25]

Now, she noted, it was partly played for laughs, impossible when first performed since 'It was no laughing matter in the 80s and 90s to make a mistaken marriage'.

Evelyn's words were written in her new diary. After taking up Henry's long-standing diary when he was forced to leave off, she began her own daily recording nine months after his death. It was a bid to get back into the habit of writing. The diaries show Evelyn determined to get out and about. She travelled by Tube and went to the hairdresser's as well as facing bomb alerts, war-induced illness and the horror at 'the immensity of the crime of war'. Unlike her earlier holiday diaries which had been full of humour and joy, these daily recordings resonate with loneliness. Evelyn began writing at 10am on Sunday 2 August 1942. After a relationship spanning forty years, Henry had spoken his last words to her at that precise time on Sunday 11 November 1941. Henry had been ill during the summer, the war news had been grim and 'there was nothing, one felt, to look forward to'. But, 'compared with my unhappiness now, that was very heaven. I had my beloved.'[26]

Evelyn had her seventy-third birthday two days after starting her diary. She took her brother Algie and his wife Helen out to lunch (they too lived in Kensington) and Gertrude Parry came to tea. Evelyn suspected that she shocked her sister-in-law with 'my tolerance towards the modern standards of sex relationship among the young'.[27] She was supportive when the various romantic entanglements of Margaret Caulfield (Henry's grand-daughter) did not work out.

Friends still rallied. The wealthy Florence Lamont sent parcels from New York of marmalade, orange juice, magazines, soap, hairpins and clothes, all of which were eagerly welcomed in the face of shortages, expense and rationing. But many friends were no longer alive and, as Evelyn put it, Henry had 'made my life a glory and it is desolate without him'.[28] Blackouts made days short and evenings long.

Evelyn gradually began to be busy again. She wrote that she was never happy 'unless using myself to the last ounce of my strength'. At the end of August she started voluntary work for the Friends Service Council at Friends House which was developing a postwar educational scheme. She helped most weeks with filing, folding circulars and transferring money from British-based refugees to France. At the Famine Relief Council in Brook Street she sorted press cuttings for the Greeks. She still saw old friends such as the Robertsons. Cecil's daughter Joan (who worked for the fire service) came when she had time. There were PEN lunches, Evelyn joined the University Women's Club and proofread Frederick Pethick-Lawrence's autobiography.

But it was writing that really mattered: 'there was no happiness like the glorious feeling of having written something that was worth writing' she had observed in her first diary entry and she later admitted that 'Nothing will dispel my melancholy until I do some real work'. It was difficult, however, in the midst of the uncertainty and disasters of war, quite apart from personal grief, to concentrate on any sustained writing. 'I think', she wrote on 29 October, 'one of the worst effects of Nazism has been to rob us – at least those of us who are past middle age life – of the future and to turn the present into a turmoil about which one cannot think at all'. And whereas the diary of Kensington-based Vere Hodgson evinced an unflinching belief in Churchill as the greatest leader Britain had ever produced, Evelyn demonstrated no such faith.

But news of an air raid in the Dieppe area got Evelyn thinking about her holidays there in the 1890s and this led to an article about her memories. To her delight the *Manchester Guardian* published it on their leader page in August. It was just the boost she needed and the words she wrote when it was printed suggest how central her writing was to her sense of self. She commented that she was cheered considerably 'for I was beginning to feel I should never be a person again'.[29]

There followed reviews, obituaries, short features in the miscellany column and some longer articles. She wrote several tales about 'Aunt Jane', such characters enabling generational comparisons.[30] In one non-fictional piece she made a plea for supplies to help Greek children, ending with a genuflection to Henry's hero: 'We cannot afford to be without these young champions of the creed of Pericles.'[31] Evelyn was asked to write an article marking the twenty-fifth anniversary of women first winning the vote in Britain. Here she applauded women's suffrage as part of 'those rebel movements which down the ages have helped to build up the ideal of human liberty for which the war is being fought to-day'.[32] She did express regret at the indifference of so many young women to the political power they possessed but was pleased that social reforms, once branded 'women's matters' and dismissed, were now embraced by government. Men and women stood side by side in war and peace in a way that would have caused scandal when she was young. This assured Evelyn that real progress in human relationships had been made as well as vital legislative change.

Writing was not helped by problems with eyesight and high blood pressure. And to add to her problems, Evelyn lost Everard, her much-loved eldest nephew (Lewin's son). He had not really recovered from the death of his own son, an airman killed in action. Evelyn remained a Christian but her belief had been shaken. On the anniversary of Henry's death she met a recently widowed friend and commented 'I have not her unbounding faith, but enough of it to be able to discuss the after-death question with an open mind'. In August 1942 her stepson Richard had a stroke, caused by sunstroke and overwork from stretcher-bearing in the Blitz (against medical advice). His eyesight and speech were affected and his right hand paralysed.

The Downside Crescent house had been left to Evelyn, Philippa and Richard. It was in a very dilapidated state but when a purchase offer of £650 was made (it had cost £1,225 when Henry and Margaret bought it in 1901) Philippa initially rejected it. Evelyn, usually scornful of amateur psychology, wrote that it was part of her 'horrible desire to hurt Richard whenever she can'. She believed that this was 'buried in childhood' and at the root of all her 'difficult behaviour'.[33] The house was sold cheaply in October.[34] Evelyn was not struggling financially and was helped by a small windfall from Henry's American investments. Yet, as she wryly put it, 'I have dreaded being a widow who is left comfortably off'.[35]

At the end of 1942 she began compiling a selection of Henry's work that had either not appeared in book form or was unpublished. This included three essays he had named 'Visions' (originally intended for a volume he had never had the chance to produce) and his final, incomplete verse, 'Peace'. It gave Evelyn some purpose over the following months though she found its preparation demanding. It reminded her how she and Henry had worked together on their manuscripts, and she was anxious to do justice to him. She obtained a little secretarial help from the *Guardian*, and neighbours and friends such as Lady (Helen) Young helped with the index. Evelyn arranged the material according to subject, and included a couple of pictures of Henry, one an informal snapshot taken on their holiday on Skye. She was delighted when Gilbert Murray agreed to write a short introduction and arranged for Oxford University Press to publish it. Murray made it clear that these were not Henry's finest offerings – those were already in print – but this writing was informed by a compelling combination of sensitivity and reflection allied to passionate indignation.

Visions and Memories finally appeared in December 1944. It sold out immediately[36] and was reprinted the following year. Henry's papers include forty reviews, many of them written by eminent poets and writers, including John Betjeman, Leonard Woolf and George Orwell.[37] Fascinated by the contradictions between the man of letters and man of action, many reviewers dwelt more on Henry's life than on the specific works featured in the collection. Some, like Compton Mackenzie, used the space to recall personal memories. But others commented on Evelyn's judicious selection and moving words. The *World Review* thanked her for a 'wise, refreshing and wholly delightful book'. Stephen Gwynn's review drew attention to Evelyn's arrangement of the book. He praised both 'ES', author of children's books, and Nevinson the famous journalist, stressing that throughout the period between the two wars he had 'as good a comrade as ever came to any man of letters'. Henry Harben thought it 'a masterpiece of editing' to place the essay on the futurist Marinetti between pieces on Roman literature and on miracles prompted by a reading of the medieval 'Aurea Legenda'.[38]

But Evelyn was not well when she made this compilation. Influenza in the spring of 1943 was followed in the summer by 'a sort of breakdown as a climax to the events of the past two years'.[39] Armed with thrillers, Henry's poems and Plato's *Republic*, she spent a week in a nursing home.

Upheavals in Evelyn's personal life were accompanied by the horrors and uncertainties of war for someone who called herself 'one of the world's few remaining Die-hard Pacifists'.[40] After the previous war Evelyn had toured the Netherlands lecturing in order to raise funds to help care for underfed German children. These children, guests in Dutch homes, had been seen as a hopeful sign for future international understanding. Evelyn asked 'Where are these German children now?' and answered 'In the S.S. waiting to destroy the land of their former playmates and hosts'.[41] She had opened the second volume of her diary on 11 February 1943 with her concern about 'the immensity of the crime of war'.[42]

Her brand of patriotism was not common. In October she wrote: 'I cannot bear to think of what we have done to Berlin, not because I love Berlin but because I love England more.'[43] She declared that German atrocities could not be criticised considering what the Allies were doing.[44] The longest piece selected for *Visions and Memories* is an essay about another of the figures Henry admired, the renowned German poet and writer Goethe. Evelyn was, however, sensitive to how this might be received and had taken advice as she had not wished to affect adversely the reception of her late husband's work.[45] 'Whatever happens to Nazi Germany', she wrote, 'the immortal soul of the nation that bred Beethoven and Goethe cannot be stamped out'.[46]

Evelyn was fascinated to see how Russia, previously so derided, was now heaped with praise. Vere Hodgson wrote how she was 'Terribly sorry for those dear people in Leningrad', adding that 'The Russians are doing marvels and have the Germans on the run in the snow'.[47] Hodgson was living and working (for a Christian charity) not far from Evelyn. She had holidays in Chipping Campden in 1943 and 1944 and even met there some of Evelyn and Henry's old friends such as Mrs Heaton (who visited Evelyn in Young Street in 1943). Evelyn and Vere Hodgson may have both been Kensington war diarists but they expressed diametrically opposed views. Describing an acquaintance as 'an unrepentant Pacifist', Hodgson added 'even now [1942] she will not admit that their Propaganda has largely led us into this mess'.[48]

Evelyn was increasingly pessimistic about the future: 'I do not suppose that in my lifetime there will ever be a world in which friends will be able to travel and to meet and to talk with sanity and ordinary human feeling'.[49] In March 1942 her correspondence included the words '*when* [my emphasis] the invasion comes'.[50]

Although Kensington had been free from attacks when Evelyn first returned there, in the spring of 1943 night alerts began. There were three warnings before 4am on 17 May, two more the following day and a further two the day after that.[51] By early June Londoners faced once again air raid warnings more or less nightly. The wailing sirens, the sound of guns and the hiss of the new explosive incendiary bombs introduced the previous summer, seemed a world away from quiet Chipping Campden. Evelyn noted, though, how people appeared to be resigned to the situation.

Early 1944 saw the 'Little Blitz', implying comparison with 1940–41, though it was small too when the raids on Germany were considered. Kensington had its share of raids. In February the Carmelite Church was burnt out, the Albert Hall damaged and Evelyn and fellow tenants spent long periods sheltering in the darkness downstairs in the lawyers' offices. By March, when the trees in Kensington Gardens were laden with almond blossom, several of Evelyn's friends were lucky to escape with their lives as their homes and furniture were destroyed. Barbara was now living nearby in a bomb-damaged flat where the whistling wind made her feel as though she were living on a yacht. Defence had its price too: many were casualties of anti-aircraft guns and rockets.

The worst night was 14 March when a hundred bombers flew over London. When Evelyn emerged after the All Clear, she saw that Kensington Church was ablaze. Seeing it the next day Vere Hodgson neatly described it as looking 'nearly too tired to stand upright'.[52] But the block of flats in Kensington Church Street where Algie and Helen lived had also been hit. Evelyn went out late in search of them. Their flat had been spared but seventy-year-old Algie had carried heavy pails of water to extinguish the flames on the stairs and suffered a heart attack. In early May he died. Evelyn was deeply upset. He was her little brother, the one she had always sought to protect. Evelyn had a sweet tooth and he used to give her his sweet rations. She had shared her American food parcels with him. With Henry no longer there to disapprove of Algie, Evelyn had grown closer to him again and since returning to London had seen him most days. Only Evelyn and Ronald were left from that large Sharp family, and Ronald lived in Canada. Joan, Evelyn's niece, offered to live with her but she would not hear of it.

Evelyn was delighted at news of the fall of Rome then the successful D-Day landings in early June. Then a period followed that was guaranteed to keep Londoners' nerves on edge. Retaliation had arrived in the form of the V-1, flying bombs nicknamed doodlebugs or buzz bombs because of their noise. These pilotless planes were packed with high explosives and often struck by day. There was a direct hit on St Mary Abbot's Hospital. On 19 June as Evelyn was going out to lunch and the streets were crowded, a flying bomb could be heard approaching 'like a gigantic bumble bee'. It came down in Kensington Church Street. Alerts did not help much since she found there was little she could do to protect herself. She now slept behind a screen in her living room and covered her head with an eiderdown and pillow.

Between 25 June and 28 July the doodlebug stopped Evelyn from writing her diary. A lunchtime overhead bomb came down on a block of flats in Fulham. Evelyn lived very close to Barkers department store. The store's windows were broken time and again. A spotter on the roof of the bakery gave special warnings but there was little time to take much action. Evelyn recalled 2 July as 'one long succession of alerts and crashes'. Vere Hodgson too wrote that 'life is one long air-raid Alert, and things that go bump in the night'. All her household was living on the ground floor. She remarked that the atmosphere of the Big Blitz had returned and that there was 'Apprehension in the air': 'To walk from Kensington to Chelsea one has to think deeply in case one is killed en route.'[53] Buses were empty in the evenings, people went down into the shelters early and there was an absence of people on the streets.

Railway stations were crowded as many thousands fled London. Friends tried to persuade Evelyn to leave. To appease them she stayed a few nights with the Robertsons in Golders Green, sleeping in their reinforced kitchen behind a steel shutter and at least got some rest and a little company. She was anxious not to be running away or leaving others to face the problems. But, somewhat reluctantly, on 11 July she went to Devon to stay with her nephew Christopher (Lewin's son) and his wife Kathleen. After standing with several hundred people for two and a half hours at the station, she finally secured part of a seat for the six-hour journey.

For the next few weeks 'the little aunt', as they called her, had a complete change. Christopher was a local doctor and they lived on a smallholding close to Dartmoor. A Canadian airforce man on leave and a woman bombed out of her Kensington (Harrington Gardens) flat were also seeking refuge there. Evelyn stayed in bed until midday and everybody helped with the animals and fruit picking. Her eyes had been troubling her and in many ways it was a tonic but this household's outlook was markedly different from Evelyn's: 'No one feels about the world and the future as Henry and I do.'[54] This was evident from their reactions to her account of the General Strike. Evelyn mentioned attending a meeting in May 1926 and they asked on whose behalf she was speaking. When she replied that it was the strikers, 'There was a sudden dead silence then Kathleen exclaimed "Good Lord!"'.

Aware that she did not fit in, despite her relatives' kindness, as soon there was a momentary lull in the doodlebugs in mid-August, Evelyn returned to London. In her absence a bomb had dropped on nearby De Vere Gardens and the Lyons Restaurant on the corner of Earls Court Road had been destroyed when full of people eating lunch. Vere Hodgson had heard four doodlebugs pass her roof in as many minutes. On 2 August ninety-seven flying bombs had exploded in the London area. As soon as Evelyn reached London there was an alert and one of the worst weeks for bombs followed.

A brief visit to the Pethick-Lawrences in Surrey to celebrate the centenary of Edward Carpenter's birth saw Evelyn back with friends of like mind, including E. M. Forster. She then returned to Chipping Campden for three weeks. She had spent a week there the previous December, staying with old friends Felix and Tatiana Crosse, and even participated in a public debate. But this second visit was marred by illness: jaundice and high blood pressure.

Grief, the noise and strain of war all contributed to Evelyn's poor health. She was seventy-five in 1944, and in addition to heart problems she now suffered from boils, ear ache, a bad back and, increasingly, difficulties with her sight, exacerbated by the dust in the air after bombings. She braved courses of manganese injections. She hated it when prevented from working but knew that resting her eyes helped. And the disruption from bombing made it even more difficult. Her doctor told her that she had been overworking for years but writing was what made her feel alive.

She was pleased when the *Manchester Guardian* asked her to send a short piece about a folk song lecture she had attended, since this was 'the one thing I can do – *write*'. Although she could not convince others, she was adamant that her illnesses occurred because she had been prevented from writing.[55] At the beginning of the year she had been forced to explain to the newspaper that, as a result of a very bad report from the occulist, she was temporarily obliged to turn down an article.[56]

In November, with V-2 rockets loudly proclaiming their presence, she felt too ill to do anything for a month. Between 8 September 1944 and late March 1945 over a thousand rockets fell on Britain, about half of them hitting London. It was an extremely cold winter. Yet Evelyn retained her humour, writing in her diary that her swollen face looked like the west side of a Gothic porch. She wished she were not 'such a crock' since she wanted to work for prisoners of war and trace missing persons.

It was not just her personal health causing concern. Evelyn also worried about Richard. She visited him frequently after his stroke and was anxious about the impact of the strain on his wife. She was touched when, in March 1945, the usually undemonstrative Kathleen told her how fond they had both become of her. Richard was now confined to a wheelchair and by the autumn of 1945 his speech was incomprehensible. Yet three landscapes completed with his left hand were exhibited at the Royal Academy in 1946. Despite having been warned more than two years earlier that he had, at most, six months to live, with Kathleen's help he survived until 7 October 1946. Richard was in his mid-fifties and died just five years after his father.

The pressure of living in west London in 1944 saw Evelyn and Vere Hodgson reflecting on the future. During the worst of the bombing in July the latter was despondent: 'I have not much further real hope for our poor old civilisation. The brain of man has gone so far beyond his morals that the only thing to do is to scrap him and start again.'[57] But, reflecting on the year, Evelyn thought that mankind's apparent lapse into barbarism might be a temporary aberration and that at least it forced people to think. Clinging to her faith, she refused to believe, even at the worst moments, that 'man's creation is a failure'.[58]

Just after the American assault on Iwojima and their retaking of Manila in February 1945 Evelyn expressed her distress at the way war news was broadcast. She believed that 'we and our supposedly Christian Allies are deteriorating in our conduct of the war'. Not one to believe in retribution, she admitted that 'our attitude towards the enemy we are successfully destroying, is playing havoc with my sense of restraint'.[59] Evelyn recorded the last flying bomb on 24 March (in Bayswater) and what proved to be the final rocket attack three days later. On 30 March she wrote that for the first time she thought it might be 'the beginning of the end'. That was the day when Hitler committed suicide. But Evelyn was tired of being told that the war news was generally splendid. She was relieved that Henry was spared the sight of destruction and agony as the allied armies advanced into Germany. At the same time she was shocked by the revelations of the 'hideous atrocities' in German prison camps and 'it is dreadful to be no longer able to make any effective protest myself'.

On 5 May, the day that German forces in the West surrendered, Evelyn noted the lack of 'any extravagant transports of joy or triumph here in London'. Relief combined with the details of German atrocities, seemed to have numbed people. She quoted an elderly man she met who had lost three sons and fifteen nephews. 'What have I to wave a flag about?' he asked. The end of war in Europe was celebrated on 8 May. Evelyn stayed at home on VE (Victory in Europe) Day, listening to Parliament on the radio and taking coffee with her neighbour. On the second day of celebrations there were crowds and flags everywhere though exhaustion was evident. Naomi Mitchison echoed this in her Mass-Observation diary, writing of celebrations in the West End: 'Most women had lipstick and a kind of put on smile but all but the very young looked very tired when they stopped actually smiling.'[60] Evelyn felt her age and found it difficult to realise that the nightmare was really over for Londoners. The day ended well with a PEN meeting where she met members from Paris including the French author Vercors.

Although in her mid-seventies Evelyn still attended a number of literary events. She was now a Fellow of the Royal Society of Literature and in June chaired a memorial lecture given by Desmond Macarthy in honour of Sir Frederick Wedmore. Evelyn had known the elegant art critic Wedmore as 'a man about literary London' in those halcyon days of the 1890s. He had been very kind to the young writer. She dreaded giving a short speech at the memorial meeting but admitted that it went down well.[61]

At the beginning of July the doctor told Evelyn that she was suffering from malnutrition. She also had shingles in both eyes and it later spread to her ears. But her indomitable spirit is well demonstrated by the way she kept going despite the pain this caused over the next two months. After the initial diagnosis, she wrote 'No wonder I feel down and out' but the next day she had her hair waved. And on 5 July in the first general election in Britain for ten years Evelyn helped out at the local polling station at Kensington Square. When the clerk explained what to do, she could not resist telling him 'You see, I helped to win the thing'.[62] This was followed by her attendance at the AGM of the Professional Classes Aid Council (where she represented the Society of Authors from 1943 to 1948). It helped to relieve professional men and women's financial distress.[63] The day was completed by a visit to her friend Helen Young.

News of the Labour Party's sweeping victory on 25 July surprised and delighted Evelyn. She wrote in her diary that the size of the majority had 'left everyone gasping'. Attlee now led the first Labour government to have its own parliamentary majority. Evelyn expected speedy reforms everywhere. Back in 1942 she had been 'much roused' by the Beveridge Report, describing it as 'one of the best efforts in social improvement that we have ever seen in this country, I think, since it makes as little class distinction as can be made without a Revolution in an old country like ours'.[64] But less than two weeks after the 1945 election, came news of the worst kind. Evelyn was horrified to hear of the secret development of the atomic bomb and its devastating effect at Hiroshima. The way that Churchill announced it made her feel 'physically sick and shocked beyond any experience I yet had of being shocked'. [65]

During these summer months of grappling with shingles and the events leading to the final Japanese surrender at the beginning of September, Evelyn, like her contemporaries, attempted to resume everyday life in a society that was undergoing profound changes. Her diary records the mundane as well as the momentous events. On 1 August she tried to make plum jam but it boiled over and covered her kitchen. 'Why do I try to be domestic?' she asked. The answer was that she did not need to try since her good friends the Crosses had suggested that she live with them. They were moving from Chipping Campden to a house just ten minutes away at 9 Eldon Road.

Evelyn was torn. The arrangement had a lot of advantages. Although undergoing necessary repairs, it was an attractive four-storey house. For a very fair rent that included heating and meals (which she would take with her friends) she was being offered two 'delightful' rooms for herself and her books on the first floor. She even protested, to no avail, that she should not have the best rooms in the house. The Crosses would look after her if she were ill. It was an elegant building in a quiet street and it was handy for the Kensington shops.

Henry was fond of Felix and Tatiana and Evelyn appreciated their stimulating conversation. She saw this as the greatest delight of old age, especially appealing because it was not dependent on physical gifts or charms. They were an interesting couple. Tatiana was born in Georgia but brought up in Moscow and was Tchaikovsky's niece. Evelyn enjoyed her astute observations. Felix was her third husband, part of the family that owned Crosse & Blackwell. A Balliol graduate, he had lived abroad and worked in the Foreign Office in the First

World War. He had translated a book on Bismarck from German into English. Evelyn did not always agree with the Crosses' political views but during her Campden visit in 1943 made the somewhat belated discovery that 'real differences of opinion and outlook in some directions need not stand in the way of real understanding and even affection in personal relations'.[66] Felix reminded her a little of Henry. He was interested in helping her collect together some of her stories and essays. Evelyn was flattered: 'the idea thrills me' she wrote, 'I bask in his admiration of my work'.[67] All three enjoyed 'fairy tales and animals and laughter and fun'.[68] Tatiana called Evelyn a Bolshevik and she retaliated, declaring her friend a bloated aristocrat.

Evelyn was concerned about the potential loss of her independence. She had spent the majority of her adult life living on her own and in March 1942 had told S. K. Ratcliffe that 'I would always rather live alone than with the wrong person, and choosing the right person is a risky business to which I don't feel equal'[69] She wrote in her diary that if she could have someone to live with without compromising her freedom she would not suffer from fits of depression. But she suspected that only during her brief married life had that been possible.[70] She was well aware that, whilst her heart approved the move, her reason hesitated. But all her friends seemed to think it a good idea, so she moved into Eldon Road at the end of October 1945.

It was not a success. At first she luxuriated in the company and care. She remained there for a year but moved in November 1946, not least because she did not wish to spoil a precious friendship. The Crosses had wanted her to stay but the experiment had confirmed what Evelyn had earlier suspected. She now, understandably, romanticised her marriage with Henry and believed that 'I am not the right person to live with anyone after the perfect companionship of my Henry'.[71] Another bitterly cold winter with gastric chills had not helped. But the real problem was that 'I simply could not write at 9 Eldon Road, and I am only half alive when I cannot write'.[72] Evelyn felt that Henry would have understood this, defined as he too was by writing.

So, for the fifteenth time in her adult life, Evelyn moved to a house opposite Olympia at 13 Russell Road. Most probably it was W. L. Clark who secured the large room for her. Clark had been Evelyn's electrician in Young Street. He had endeared himself to Evelyn by admitting that he been an avid reader of Henry's books and her *Daily Herald* stories. He and his wife lived in the ground floor flat at 13 Russell Road. The house was very close to the noisy railway but Evelyn focused on its advantages. Her room looked on to the backs and gardens of the Kensington High Street end of Holland Road and accommodated her books and some of her most valued pictures and furniture. She had the use of a small kitchen and domestic help several days a week. The main occupants and owners were three 'delightfully kind & tactful ladies', a professor's widow, daughter and stepdaughter, who made the house feel like a home without encroaching on her independence.

Despite more problems with her eyes – Evelyn now had cataracts – she was determined to keep busy. She helped Noel Brailsford edit some of Henry's best published work in verse and prose for a third posthumous collection. It appeared in November 1948 as *Essays, Poems and Tales* and contained extracts from ten of Henry's books. But it had been a long time in the making. Early in 1945 Evelyn had visited Brailsford to discuss a collection, concerned that if she undertook yet another editing job it would mean that 'I shall not be able to touch my own work again'.[73] And 'Writing my own book would make me happier than anything else cld now'.[74] Yet she was anxious to secure Henry's posthumous fame. To her relief it was agreed that Brailsford would find a publisher (he got a contract with Victor Gollancz), make selections and edit the book. In January 1946 Evelyn told Florence Lamont that she was helping Brailsford with editing but that he had gone to India for some months (for the *New Statesman*).[75] They were still discussing the final selection over a year later.[76] They agreed to divide the advance but that Evelyn should have any further royalties.[77]

In his Introduction Brailsford ranked Henry among the masters of the essay form, claiming that his essays deserved 'a lasting place, with the journalistic work of Hazlitt and Lamb, in the treasury of English literature'.[78] Reviewers were reverential but saw the essays as part of the past rather than the postwar present. Anticipating more recent critiques of the 'sound-bite' society, one suggested that current readers were restive and concerned with the immediate.[79]

Evelyn was also associated with an earlier era. J. G. Wilson, managing director of the prestigious London bookshop Bumpus (where Evelyn bought all her books) was keen for her to publish more fairy tales. She believed that her fairy stories represented the best of her writing. In 1932 one of her fairy tales had been displayed as a nineteenth-century classic in an exhibition on the history of illustrated books for children at the Victoria and Albert Museum. Now she collected together more than a dozen of the stories she had published between 1897 and 1928. Wilson was very enthusiastic and in June

1948 told Evelyn he would try to find a publisher.[80] But illness seems to have prevented Evelyn taking this further.

After she left Young Street, diary entries became sporadic. Significantly, there were none for the year she spent at Eldon Road and only in March 1947 did she recommence her diary. She then wrote daily for the best part of three months. When possible she went out to lunch though for six or seven weeks that spring she was confined to her room through illness. She made a new will in April then decided she 'must be frivolous or die at once' so made a hair appointment, renovated her hats and bought a chic French silk frock. It made a change from 'the homespun of my recent life which was beginning to cloud my whole outlook'.[81]

The daily diary ends on 30 April with Evelyn attending an 'excellent' PEN dinner with her friend the mountaineer Geoffrey Young as her guest. She met there old friends such as Eleanor Farjeon. Only two more entries survive: for 1 and 2 May 1947. Evelyn now dictated her letters to a typist and spent much of her time listening to classical gramophone records and reading. In the last available entry she recorded only three hours' sleep but this was because she had been engrossed in a thriller by Ngaio Marsh.

Although she noted that her diary was continued in a fifth volume, tantalisingly there is no trace of this amongst her papers. We know from her correspondence that she visited Emmeline and Frederick Pethick-Lawrence in the summer of 1947 but was not well enough to attend Emmeline's eightieth birthday party in October (complete with birthday cake in suffrage colours). By late January 1948 she was in a nursing home and apparently 'fine', her mail being answered by a Miss G. C. Brown. In May her address was the nursing home at 32, Woodville Gardens, Ealing. By April 1949 she was nearby at the Methuen House Nursing Home at 13–15 Gunnersbury Avenue. And there she stayed for more than six years.

Evelyn died at this nursing home on 17 June 1955.[82] She was aged eighty-five, the same age as Henry had been when he died. Her obituary in the *Manchester Guardian* noted that her death 'breaks one of the few remaining links between those who fought for women's emancipation and those who now possess it'.[83] It added that her recent life had been 'clouded and circumscribed by the failure of her sight'. That was a cruel fate for someone whose passion was writing.

It seems as though her last years were especially lonely. There remained a few loyal friends and her niece Joan Sharp. Little can be gleaned about these last years though Frederick Pethick-Lawrence, now Lord Pethick-Lawrence, provides a clue. He visited Evelyn frequently in the late 1940s and early 1950s. In an affectionate tribute published the month after she died, he explained that in her eighties she needed the care and attention of a nursing home. 'Up till a little while before she died', he wrote, her face would 'light up with interest as we shared some reminiscence of the suffrage days'.[84] Elizabeth Robins also visited but she was very old and frail and died in her ninetieth year in 1952. The loss of many of those Evelyn cared for – Barbara Ayrton Gould died in 1950 – in addition to the death of Henry, her greatest friend, must have added to the despondency. Her death certificate for June 1955 shows that at some stage she became senile as well as suffering from hardening of the arteries.

But it would hardly be appropriate to end the story of Evelyn's life on such a note. Here was a resilient, creative woman who never wallowed in self-pity and retained her sense of humour. 'Miss Sharp seems to have enjoyed every minute of her life' declared the reviewer of her autobiography for the *Times Literary Supplement*.[85]

An incident that the elderly Evelyn recounted in a letter dating from October 1945 demonstrates that persistent humour. She had boarded an omnibus (this public space had been the setting for a number of her stories) and was promptly told by the conductress to move quickly.[86] Evelyn replied: 'Give me a chance, I am seventy-six'. A girl sitting near whispered to her friend 'Well, that's a whopper, anyway'. Evelyn Sharp smiled.

Appendix 1: Evelyn Sharp's major publications

Novels

Adult fiction

At the Relton Arms: A Novel, John Lane, The Bodley Head, 1895
The Making of a Prig, John Lane, The Bodley Head, 1897
Children's fiction
The Making of a School Girl, John Lane, The Bodley Head, 1897, Oxford
    University Press, 1989
The Youngest Girl in the School, Macmillan, 1901, The Cottage Library, 1936
The Other Boy, Macmillan, 1902
The Children who Ran Away, Macmillan, 1903
The Child's Christmas, Blackie & Son, 1906, New Jersey: Avenel Press, 1991,
    1999
Nicolete: A Novel, Constable, 1907
The Story of the Weathercock, Blackie & Son, 1907
The Hill that Fell Down, Blackie & Son, 1909
What Happened at Christmas to Nancy, Pat, Elfie and Baby, Blackie & Son, 1915
John's Visit to the Farm, T. Nelson & Sons, 1920
Who Was Jane? A Story for Young People of All Ages, Macmillan, 1922
Young James, Macmillan, 1925

Books of short stories

Stories for adults

Rebel Women, A. C. Fifield, 1910, New York: John Lane, 1910, United Suffragists
    1915, reprinted 1975, Portrayer Publishers, 2003
The War of All the Ages, Sidgwick & Jackson, 1915
A Communion of Sinners and Other Short Stories, George Allen & Unwin, 1917
Somewhere in Christendom: A Fantasy, George Allen & Unwin, 1919
Stories for children
Wymps and Other Fairy Tales, John Lane, Bodley Head, 1896, 1897
All the Way to Fairyland, John Lane, Bodley Head, 1898

The Other Side of the Sun, John Lane, Bodley Head, 1900
Round the World to Wympland, John Lane, Bodley Head, 1902
Macmillan's Story Readers (3 vols.), Macmillan, 1903
Lessons, R. Brimley Johnson, 1904
Micky, Macmillan, 1905
The Victories of Olivia and other stories, Macmillan, 1912

Published plays

The Loafer and the Loaf: An Incredible Episode in One Act, Labour Publishing Co,
    1926

Non-fiction works

The London Child, Bodley Head, 1927
Here We Go Round: The Story of the Dance, Gerald Howe, 1928
The Child Grows Up, Bodley Head, 1929
The African Child: An Account of the International Conference on African Children,
    Longmans, Green & Co, 1931, Westport, Conn.: Negro University Press,
    1970

Biography

Hertha Ayrton 1854–1923: A Memoir, Edward Arnold, 1926

Autobiography

Unfinished Adventure: Selected Reminiscences from an Englishwoman's Life, The
    Bodley Head, 1933, Faber and Faber, 2008

Pamphlets and booklets

Fairy Tales As They Are, As They Were and As They Should Be, Brighton: D. B.
    Friend, 1889
The Little Enemy Friends Relief Committee, 1920
Brothers, Friends Relief Committee, 1922
In The Volga Valley, Friends Relief Committee, 1922
Daily Bread, Ernest Benn, 1928
The Problem That is Germany, Friends Service Council, 1931
Buyers & Builders. The Jubilee Sketch of the Women's Co-operative Guild 1883–
    1933, Women's Co-operative Guild, 1933

Libretto/verse for music

The Poisoned Kiss, or, The Empress and the Necromancer: A Romantic Extravaganza, Oxford, Oxford University Press, 1936 (music by Ralph Vaughan Williams)

The Cherub, Reynolds, 1922 (original verse by Evelyn Sharp, music by M. E. Marshall)

Contributions to books

'Lost Fairy Tales' in Mrs Aria (ed.) *The May Book*, Macmillan, 1901

'The Castle with the High Bell' in Netta Syrett (ed.) *The Dream-Garden. A Children's Annual*, John Baillie, 1905.

'Mary Wollstonecraft 1759–1797' in A. Barratt Brown, *Great Democrats*, Ivor Nicholson & Watson, 1934

Introduction to Winifred Wilkinson, *Students Make Their Lives*, Allen & Unwin, 1935.

Edited collections

H. W. Nevinson, *Visions and Memories*, Oxford, Oxford University Press: 1944 (collected and arranged by Evelyn Sharp).

In addition to writing regular stories, features and reports for the *Manchester Guardian* (from 1904), *Daily Herald*, *Votes for Women* (which she edited for six years) and the *New Leader*, Evelyn Sharp's numerous articles and short stories in annuals, magazines and newspapers included six stories for adults in *The Yellow Book* and stories for children in *Girls' Realm* and the *New Chronicle of Christian Education*. She had a regular slot in the *News Chronicle* between 1935 and 1940. Her first stories for children were 'My Favourite Brother', *Atalanta*, September 1894, '"The Eldest Sister" As She Really Is', *The Idler*, October 1895. She published a number of stories in *Atalanta* in the 1890s. Other significant articles or stories for adults appeared in the *Nation* and the *Listener* 9 July 1942 (based on her broadcast on the Home Service), *Contemporary Review* and the American *Christian Science Monitor* and *New York World*. She also published short poems in, for example, the *Westminster Gazette*.

Appendix 2: 'The Cheap Holiday and What Aunt Joanna Thought About It'

By Evelyn Sharp. From the *Daily Herald* 6 August 1923

The little aunt sat and dreamed, while Cousin Paul and his wife gave the family a picturesque account of the wonderful holiday they had spent in Germany. 'Most enjoyable time I ever had', boomed Cousin Paul. 'Hotels excellent, if you know your way about; cooking perfect –'.

'And all dirt cheap!' supplemented Cousin Mary, who regarded herself as existing primarily for the purpose of supplementing Cousin Paul. 'A five-course dinner, wine, coffee and liqueurs – for 4½d.! Just fancy!'

The family, in unison, fancied. Gratified at the effect already made, Cousin Paul proceeded to embroider. 'For about a halfpenny you could travel to all the places worth visiting in the Umgebung – I should say, the neighbourhood,' he explained; and the family, applauding, noted with clannish pride that cousin Paul had returned home a linguist.

'Yes,' chimed in Cousin Mary, 'and we travelled right from the South of Germany to Hamburg – or was it Dresden, Paul? – for *eight-pence*. Only think!'

The family only thought. Cousin Paul appeared to be making calculations. 'No, my dear', he corrected; 'that was on the way out. Coming back, the mark had slumped again, and owing to my fore-thought in not taking return tickets it cost us only five-point-three pence.' He turned to the silent aunt, anxious that no one should be excluded from the approving chorus. 'How's that for a holiday, Aunt Joanna?' He roared at her jovially.

The little aunt jumped. She had been in the family – though not of it – for upwards of 60 years, but she had never quite got used to being roared at. 'It sounds to me very mathematical, dear,' she said, with her conciliatory smile. 'I never could do sums, so perhaps it is a good thing my travelling days are over.'

But Cousin Paul, who never asked questions for the dull purpose of getting them answered, had already forgotten her, and was embarking on a florid description of the purchases he had made.

'*I* didn't want the things; but your Cousin Mary – well you know what women are!' said Cousin Paul, though, whatever might be said of those to whom this remark was addressed, this was certainly not one of the things that Paul knew.

'Well, dear, everything was so *cheap*,' simpered Cousin Mary, who had listened so long to Paul's definition of women that it had now begun to fit her nicely. 'You couldn't expect any true woman to resist a fur coat – oh, but a *ravishing* fur coat, girls! – that was going for a few shillings. It would have been simply *wicked*, wouldn't it, Aunt Joanna?' Fortunately Aunt Joanna was not really expected to unravel this ethical problem.

The little old aunt never knitted; and it is possible that Satan, in his search for idle hands, saw Aunt Joanna's folded in her lap, and was, consequently, responsible for the excursion her spirit took in the next few minutes. But it may have been equally ascribable to a passage in the letter that lay in the under-pocket of her grey alpaca gown.

'We have had nothing but a little weak cabbage soup for days,' wrote Freda, the Professor's wife, 'Everything is now sold except poor Mamachen's fur coat, which we were trying to keep because of her rheumatism; for alas! We can no more buy fuel or warm underclothing . . .'

Suddenly Aunt Joanna was looking in at the neat Berlin apartment where she had spent such happy holidays in the past. But the great carved sideboard was gone; so was the stuffed sofa on which the favoured visitor was invited to sit. The round polished table and solid oak chairs were no longer to be seen, nor the big clock, nor the handsome crimson carpet. A gaunt old lady sat on a stool in the corner of the room, and moaned as if in great pain. At the window, a man with despair in his eyes, his frame bent and shrunken, stood looking hopelessly out. As Freda stole from the room with the fur coat over her arm, Aunt Joanna saw that even the wedding ring was gone from her thin finger.

Up from the street below, in a voice strangely like cousin Mary's, floated the gay remark of the passing tourist: – 'after that enormous lunch I simply can't *face* tea yet awhile. Let's go and buy that diamond ring instead!'

'Don't you believe it,' Cousin Paul was saying, as Aunt Joanna's spirit wandered back again into the family circle. 'There's plenty of everything in Germany. Haven't I seen it with my own eyes?'

'Shops filled with luxuries' chorused his wife. 'Furniture, clothes, jewels – well, they must come from *somewhere*, mustn't they?'

'I am an observant man,' resumed Cousin Paul, whose knowledge of women was only equalled by his knowledge of himself; 'and you may take my word for it, there's no more distress in Germany – than there is in this country!'

'God help the poor souls!' was the quite amazing remark that came from the spot in the family circle where Aunt Joanna appeared to be sitting. It was, however, so incredible a remark that those who heard it at once attributed it to their excited imagination.

'And to think,' was Cousin Mary's parting observation when the visitors took leave, 'that we very nearly went to Belgium, where the mark, or whatever it is, hasn't slumped at all! Wouldn't it have been *tragic?*'

No doubt, it was a sense of awful tragedy happily averted that made the little old Aunt relapse suddenly into hysterical laughter. The family charitably attributed it to her customary eccentricity.

Notes

Place of publication throughout is London unless otherwise stated. For the full titles of Evelyn's books see Appendix 1. Abbreviations are as follows: BLPES (British Library of Political and Economic Science Archives Division); DH (*Daily Herald*); ES (Evelyn Sharp); ESNP (Evelyn Sharp Nevinson Papers, The Bodleian Library, University of Oxford); HWN (Henry Woodd Nevinson); HWNP (Henry Woodd Nevinson Papers, The Bodleian Library, University of Oxford); MG (*Manchester Guardian*); MGA (Manchester Guardian Archives, The John Rylands University Library, The University of Manchester); NL (*New Leader*); UA (*Unfinished Adventure*).

Introducing the Rebel Woman

1 *MG* 16 November 1932.
2 The subject of this biography is *not* Evelyn Adelaide Sharp, Baroness Sharp (1903–85). Daughter of a radical Liberal vicar, and born in Ealing (where the writer Evelyn Sharp died), Baroness Sharp was an eminent civil servant who, in October 1955, became Britain's first female permanent secretary. The two Evelyn Sharps sometimes received each other's mail in the 1940s.
3 ES, *UA*, p. 57.
4 Jill Liddington, *Rebel Girls: Their Fight for the Vote*, Virago Press, 2006, p. xii.
5 Blurb for the American edition of ES, *Who Was Jane?*, Macmillan, 1922.
6 ESNP, MSS. Eng. Lett. d278, 16 June 1933, d279, nd.
7 *Women's Bulletin* 16 July 1955.
8 *Guardian* 3 May 2008. *UA* is now back in print in the Faber Finds series.
9 See Hilda Kean, 'Searching for the Past in Present Defeat: the Construction of Historical and Political Identity in British Feminism in the 1920s and 1930s', *Women's History Review* 3/1, 1994, p. 72.
10 Two hundred or so individuals kept war diaries for the social research organisation Mass-Observation.

11 *Christian Science Monitor* 30 June 1920.
12 See Chapter 2 and Appendix 1 for references to these.
13 Letter to Francis Sheehy Skeffington, 15 August 1912, MS 21,623 (1), Sheehy Skeffington Papers, National Library of Ireland, Dublin.
14 Elizabeth Robins, *Way Stations*, Hodder & Stoughton, 1913, p. 226.
15 See Chapter 4 and Appendix 1. Carolyn Christensen Nelson, *Literature of the Women's Suffrage Campaign*, Toronto: Broadview Press, 2004, p. 293.
16 *MG* 10 August 1928. Eleanor Mills with Kira Cochrane, *Journalistas: 100 Years of the Best Writing and Reporting by Women Journalists*, Constable, 2005, pp. 55–6, includes her *MG* article 'The Rebel on the Hearth'.
17 Wendell Harris, 'H. W. Nevinson, Margaret Nevinson, Evelyn Sharp: Little-known Writers and Crusaders', *English Literature in Transition 1880–1920* 45/3, 2002, p. 299.
18 Angela V. John, *War, Journalism and the Shaping of the Twentieth Century: The Life and Times of Henry W. Nevinson*, I. B. Tauris, 2006.
19 Labour politician and supporter of women's suffrage.
20 31 March 1918, 6/257, Lansbury Collection, BLPES.

1 From Evie to Becky Sharp

1 *Who Was Jane?* and *The Young James* were two of her titles. See Appendix 1 for a complete list.
2 ESNP, MSS. Eng. Misc. c499b/2. In '"The Eldest Sister as She Really Is"' in *The Idler*, October 1895, pp. 245–7, she explored the 'tyranny' of the eldest sister and how well youngest sisters understood them and their ways.
3 ES, *UA*, p. 73.
4 ESNP, MSS. Eng. Lett. d277, Jane Sharp to ES, 30 June 1909.
5 Evelyn stated that her mother was in her ninetieth year when she died in February 1915. Census records show her to have been eighty-five. Her mother's marriage certificate reveals that she was twenty-six when she married, not twenty-seven as Evelyn claimed. The family order was: Mabel (b. 1857), Ethelreda known as Ethel (b. 1858), Cecil (b. 1859), Bertha (b. 1860), Llewelyn known as Lewin (b. 1862), Neville (b. 1864, d. 1865), Oswald (b. 1865, d. 1870), Ronald (b. 1867), Evelyn (b. 1869), Lancelot (b. 1871) and Algernon, known as both Algie and Ben (b. 1875).
6 ES, *UA*, p. 19.
7 *Ibid.*, p. 18. No further mention of this tragedy has been found in Evelyn's writings.
8 One story called 'Nurse' tells how the adult narrator and brother Lionel reverted to childhood submissiveness when taking their old and eminently capable Nurse out for the day. ES, *Lessons*, p. 169.
9 *MG* 3 April 1929.

10 ES, *The London Child*, p. 1.

11 ESNP, MSS. Eng. Misc. e635, 3–8 December 1943.

12 *MG* 12 August 1925.

13 For childhood in other large families see Barbara Caine, *Bombay to Bloomsbury: A biography of the Strachey Family*, Oxford: Oxford University Press: 2005 (ten children), and Revel Guest and Angela V. John, *Lady Charlotte and An Extraordinary Life*, Stroud: Tempus, 2007 (ten children). See too Leonore Davidoff, 'Kinship as a Categorical Concept: A Case Study of Nineteenth Century English Siblings', *Journal of Social History* 39/2, 2005, pp. 411–28.

14 *MG* 21 October 1925.

15 *Ibid.*, 26 May 1908.

16 ES, *The Other Boy*, p. 19.

17 *MG* 26 May 1908.

18 *UA*, p. 40. Her account of the life of Beatrice Webb (née Potter) stressed her large family (she was one of nine girls) and that her family did not value her intellectual ability. *MG* 1 May 1943.

19 Cecil's correspondence suggests his fondness for his father but belief that his mother had no affection for him. Cecil Sharp MS. Collection, Box 7, CJS/7/6. 1893 Letters, EFDS, Cecil Sharp House, London.

20 *UA*, p. 43.

21 Its popularity was not confined to middle-class girls since it was taken by public libraries. Sally Mitchell, *The New Girl: Girls' Culture in England, 1880–1915*, New York: Columbia University Press, 1995, p. 11.

22 *Atalanta*, July, September 1890.

23 *Ibid.*, July 1889.

24 Evelyn encountered the artist Walter Sickert on a family holiday in Southwold so he may have been the basis for this story.

25 ES, 'Village Hampdens in the 'Eighties: A Reminiscence', *Contemporary Review* 932, August 1943, p. 110.

26 See Wendell V. Harris, 'John Lane's Keynote Series and the Fiction of the 1890s', *PMLA* 83, October 1986, pp. 1407–13.

27 ESNP, MSS. Eng. Lett. d276 added in 1935 to the envelope of Lane's acceptance letter of 10 November 1894.

28 Stephen Gwynn, *Experiences of a Literary Man*, Thornton Butterworth, 1926, p.142, Margaret D. Stetz and Mark Samuels Lesner, *England in the 1890s: Literary Publishing at the Bodley Head*, Washington DC: Georgetown University Press, 1990, p. 43.

29 For debates about the naming and shaming of the New Woman in the mid-1890s see Sally Ledger, *The New Woman: Fiction and Feminism at the Fin de Siècle*, Manchester: Manchester University Press, 1997.

30 See too ES, 'The Wrong Sort of People' in *The War of All the Ages*, pp. 219–24.

31 ES, *At the Relton Arms*, p. 124.

32 Quoted in Katherine Lyon Mix, *A Study in Yellow: The Yellow Book and Its Contributors*, Lawrence, Kansas: University of Kansas Press, p. 238.

33 More than half a century later Evelyn referred to her desire to 'write uninterrupted, for which I have sacrificed so much ordinary happiness since I first ran away from home and upset my darling Mother'. ESNP, MSS. Eng. Misc, e636, 22 April 1946.

34 ES, *The Victories of Olivia*, p. 250.

35 See too ES, 'Something about the Children I have Taught', *Atalanta*, December 1897, March, July 1898.

36 ESNP, MSS. Eng. Misc. e639. See too her lectures on London, e637.

37 She was still a member in the 1930s when it was known as the New Victorian Club.

38 Netta Syrett, *The Sheltering Tree*, Geoffrey Bles, 1939, p. 89.

39 This critique was much more clearly articulated by Evelyn during the next decade (see Chapter 4). See too Carolyn Christensen Nelson, *British Women Writers of the 1890s*, New York: Twayne, 1996, p. 94, which compares women contributors to the *Yellow Book* with New Women Writers and their more explicit challenges to gender relations. In some instances women writers belonged to both categories.

40 Joan Smith, *Femmes de Siècle: Stories from the 90s: Women Writing at the End of Two Centuries*, Chatto & Windus, 1992.

41 She remained wary of schemes to help distressed gentlewomen. In a later, unpublished, novel, an impoverished singer who had left home to earn an independent living comments 'As long as you offer charity to women in reduced circumstances, you are asking society to manufacture women in reduced circumstances'. ESNP, MSS. Eng. Misc. d671.

42 Probably the Church of England's Maurice Hostel Women's Settlement (which her friend Rev. Percy Dearmer was involved with) or the Girls' Guild of Good Hope.

43 *MG* 23 Aug. 1933.

44 ES, *UA*, chapter IV.

45 Penelope Fitzgerald, *Charlotte Mew and her Friends*, Harvill Press ed., 1992, p. 61, notes the gender division between the *Yellow Book* contributors. Whereas its male writers seemed to encapsulate fin de siècle decadence, its female writers were strong and lively.

46 *MG* 15 April 1943.

47 Sally Ledger, 'Wilde Women and *The Yellow Book*: The Sexual Politics of Aestheticism and Decadence', *English Literature in Transition* 50/1, 2007, pp. 9–10.

48 Gwynn, *Experiences of a Literary Man*, p. 137.

49 F. R. Rolfe (Baron Corvo), *Nicholas Crabbe or The One and The Many: A Romance*, Chatto & Windus, 1958, p. 42.

50 ESNP, MSS. Eng. Lett. d278, ES to Elspeth Graham, 16 April 1933.
51 HWNP, e625/4, 14 May, 7 July 1932.
52 See too *ibid.*, 13 August 1935, e626/2.
53 ESNP, MSS. Eng. Misc. d668, 19 August 1942.
54 ES, 'Dieppe!' *MG* 24 August 1942.
55 ES, *UA*, p. 78. Donald Gray, *Percy Dearmer: A Parson's Pilgrimage*, Norwich, The Canterbury Press, pp. 100–8.
56 See ESNP, MSS. Eng. Misc. c499b, d671.
57 Arnold Bennett, *The Journals*, Harmondsworth, Penguin, 1971 ed., p. 45.
58 HWNP, e615/1, 27 September 1908.
59 For women's journalism see Anna Sebba, *Battling for News: The Rise of the Woman Reporter*, Sceptre, 1994, Fred Hunter, 'Girl Reporters: Entry, Training, Career and Networking in Late Victorian England', paper given to the Research Society for Victorian Periodicals Conference, 1992, Hunter, 'In Pursuit of a Profession: Teenage Girls Learning Journalism 1890–1940', paper given to the Social History Conference, 1998, Barbara Onslow, *Women of the Press in Ninteenth Century Britain*, Macmillan Press, 2000.
60 William Hepworth Dixon edited the *Athenaeum*. See Valerie Fehlbaum, *Ella Hepworth Dixon: The Story of a Modern Woman*, Aldershot, Ashgate, 2005.
61 *MG* 23 August 1933.
62 Owen Ashton, 'Henrietta Stannard and the Social Emancipation of Women, 1890–1910' in Ashton, Robert Fyson and Stephen Roberts (eds) *The Duty of Discontent: Essays for Dorothy Thompson*, Mansell, 1995.
63 Hunter, 'Girl Reporters', p. 12.

2 Writing for the young

1 Published by D. B. Friend in Brighton.
2 A chapter on the school play was added. The heroine, her brother and his friend are the same as in her 1894 *Atalanta* story 'My Favourite Brother'.
3 Margaret D. Stetz and Mark Samuels Lasner, *England in the 1890s: Literary Publishing at the Bodley Head*, Washington DC: Georgetown University Press, 1990, p. 61.
4 For Evelyn's books for children see Appendix 1. ES, *The Making of a Schoolgirl*, 1989 edition, p. 6.
5 Sheila Ray, 'School Stories' in Peter Hunt (ed.), *International Encyclopaedia of Children's Literature* 1, 2nd edition, Routledge, 2004, p. 469. See too Deborah Gorham, 'The Ideology of Femininity and Reading for Girls, 1850–1914' in Felicity Hunt (ed.), *Lessons for Life: The Schooling of Girls and Women 1850–1950*, Oxford: Basil Blackwell, 1987, pp. 53–8.
6 See Beverley Lyon Clark, *Regendering the School Story*, New York: Garland Publishing, 1996, p. 7.

7 ES, *Lessons*, pp. 100, 103.

8 ES, 'My Favourite Brother', *Atalanta*, September 1894.

9 This was Britain's first women's physical education college. It later moved to Dartford, Kent.

10 *Christian Science Monitor* 30 June 1920.

11 HWNP, e626/1, 29 May 1933, Obituary in *MG* 20 June 1955.

12 Elizabeth Robins, Introduction to ES, *Rebel Women*, 1915 edition.

13 In with ES, *The Other Boy*, p. 9.

14 Sue Simms and Hilary Clare (eds), *The Encyclopaedia of Girls' School Stories* 1, Aldershot: Ashgate, 2000, p. 294.

15 In a story called 'Pamela, the Infant and the Right Man' in ES, *The Victories of Olivia*, p. 273, she captures nicely the position of the Head Girl held in awe by four hundred girls 'in a kingdom that she had conquered for herself'. Yet she is dethroned as soon as she returns home and has to resume her customary role as the youngest sister in the family.

16 Microfilm of Reader's Reports, 1st series, vol. mclxxvii, Macmillan Archives. MS. 13151, 5 December 1900, Cambridge: Chadwyck Healey, 1982.

17 Miss Sparks becomes Miss Parks in her 1922 story recalling end of term performances of Molière's plays, *MG* 2 January 1922.

18 ES, *The Youngest Girl*, p. 54.

19 See Valerie Sanders, *The Brother-Sister Culture in Nineteenth-Century Literature from Austen to Woolf*, Palgrave, 2000.

20 See Gillian Avery, 'The Family Story' in Hunt, *International Companion Encyclopaedia*, p. 454.

21 Microfilm of Reader's Reports, vol. mclxxix, MS. 13985, 19 December 1901.

22 ES to Maurice Macmillan 26/33, 21 December 1901, 26/33, 26 December 1901, Macmillan Archives, University of Reading.

23 *Ibid.*, Maurice Macmillan to George P. Brett, 28 October 1903.

24 ES, *Lessons*, pp. 85–116.

25 See Sheila Rowbotham, *Edward Carpenter 1844–1929: A Life of Liberty and Love*, Verso, 2008.

26 ES, *The Child's Christmas*, 1991 edition, p. xiii. This Annual is shorter than the original 1906 publication and similar to the abbreviated 1915 version (see Appendix 1).

27 *Atalanta* October 1895 to September 1896.

28 Kathryn Hughes, *The Short Life and Long Times of Mrs Beeton*, Fourth Estate, 2005, p. 390.

29 ES, *Macmillan's Story Readers. Book 11*, p. 33, first published as 'The Other Point of View' in the *Westminster Gazette* 13 June 1902.

30 ESNP, MSS. Eng. Misc. d672/7. See too ES, *Nicolete*.

31 For suffrage see Chapter 4.

32 ES, *The Victories of Olivia*, p. 13.

33 *Ibid.*, p. 284.

34 ESNP, MSS. Eng. Misc. d672/6.

35 Grimms' tales were available in English from 1823 and Andersen's from the mid-1840s. See Ruth B. Bottingheimer, 'Fairy Tales and Folk Tales' in Hunt, *International Companion Encyclopaedia*.

36 Advertisement in ES, *The Other Side of the Sun*.

37 Margaret Drabble (ed.), *The Oxford Companion to English Literature*, new edition, Oxford, Oxford University Press, 1985, pp. 548–9.

38 The similarity between 'The Palace on the Floor' in this collection and Edith Nesbit's 'The Town in the Library' (1901) is discussed in Julia Briggs, *A Woman of Passion: The Life of E. Nesbit 1858–1924*, Penguin ed. 1989.

39 *All the Way to Fairyland* is dedicated to Geoffrey and Christopher Dearmer, along with Evelyn's nephew Everard and Margaret Hannay and her son (taught by Evelyn). *Micky* is dedicated to Christopher Dearmer, Evelyn's godson.

40 Quoted at the back of ES, *All the Way to Fairyland*. Lewis Carroll/Charles Dodgson published his own fairy tale in two volumes in 1889 and 1893. *Sylvie and Bruno* was expanded from a short story of 1867.

41 ESNP, MSS. Eng. Lett. d277, 26 December 1907. The artist for this book, for *The Child's Christmas* and for *What Happened at Christmas* was Charles Robinson.

42 *Yellow Book* XII, January 1897. See the similarities with the *Yellow Book* story by Vernon Lee (Violet Page), 'Prince Alberic and the Snake Lady', discussed in Carolyn Christensen Nelson, *British Women Fiction Writers of the 1890s*, New York: Twayne, 1996, pp. 90–1.

43 See Lisa Chaney, *Hide-and-Seek with Angels: A Life of J. M. Barrie*, Arrow Books, 2006.

44 *The Academy* 18 December 1897.

45 In 'The Weird Witch of the Hollow Herb' in ES, *The Other Side of the Sun*.

46 'The Girl with Rough Hands', *DH* 1 May 1921.

47 For other examples of reversed plot lines see Jack Zipes (ed.), *The Oxford Companion to Fairy Tales*, Oxford: Oxford University Press, 2000, pp. 157–8.

48 In Zipes (ed.), *Victorian Fairy Tales: The Revolt of the Fairies and Elves*, Methuen, 1987, pp. 361–72, originally published in *Girls' Realm* January 1900.

49 ESNP, MSS. Eng. Misc. c499b/8.

50 *Ibid.*, d672/2. The short story version of this entitled 'The Hundredth Princess' appeared in ES, *The Other Side of the Sun*. Here it ends with the king vowing never to kill anything again, to the great delight of the little rabbits. For an attack on the sport of shooting see ES,'Lost Fairy Tales' in Mrs Aria (ed.), *The May Book*, Macmillan, 1901.

51 *Ibid.*, d672/4. Compare this with her story 'The Prince's Umbrella' in *Atalanta*, January 1898.
52 John Masefield to Evelyn Sharp, MS. Eng. Lett. c269, The Bodleian Library, University of Oxford.
53 In 'The Tears of Princess Prunella' in ES, *The Other Side of the Sun*, the princess speaks so kindly to a deaf child that he hears again. He had been given the gift of being deaf to every sound that was not beautiful. In 'The Wymp Magician', Juniper Jerry, who has the gift of communication with animals, but cannot walk, is disenchanted and gains mobility, *Little Folks* December 2003.
54 ESNP, MSS. Eng. Misc. d672/5. The short story was first published in *Atalanta*, December 1896, then appeared in ES, *All the Way to Fairyland*.
55 See Chapter 12.
56 In an advertisement in ES, *Micky*.
57 *The Library Journal* 1 October 1922.

3 Fellow traveller: meeting Henry Nevinson

1 This chapter should be read alongside Angela V. John, *War, Journalism and the Shaping of the Twentieth Century: The Life and Times of Henry W. Nevinson*, I. B. Tauris, 2006, chapter 5.
2 ESNP, MSS. Eng. Misc. e634, 7 August 1943.
3 HWNP, e611/3, 30 December 1901.
4 *Ibid.*, 3 February 1902.
5 *Ibid.*, 15 February 1902.
6 *Ibid.*, e612/1, 19 September 1902.
7 ESNP, MSS. Eng. Lett. 21 December 1903.
8 HWNP, e612/3, 6 January 1904.
9 *Ibid.*, 28 January 1904.
10 See Chapter 2.
11 HWNP, e612/3, 26 February 1904.
12 Angela V. John, 'A Family at War: The Nevinson Family' in Michael J. K. Walsh (ed.), *A Dilemma of English Modernism: Verbal and Visual Politics in the Life and Work of C. R. W. Nevinson*, Newark, DE: University of Delaware Press, 2006, pp. 23–35, Angela V. John, 'Margaret Wynne Nevinson: Gender and National Identity in the Early Twentieth Century' in R. R. Davies and Geraint H. Jenkins (eds), *From Medieval to Modern Wales: Historical Essays in Honour of Kenneth O. Morgan and Ralph A. Griffiths*, Cardiff: University of Wales Press, 2004, pp. 230–45.
13 HWNP, e617/3, 11 January 1913.
14 See Chapter 11.
15 15 June 1942 in manuscript papers compiled by Mrs Dryhurst's daughter Mrs Maire Gaster held by the family. Henry's diaries were kept in a strong

room in Evelyn's solicitor's office after his death. Her own diary gives no indication that she read them (except for a diary about Toynbee Hall). She may have recognised that it was wiser not to do so.

16 *DH* 24 October 1919.

17 *MG* 20 June 1955.

18 See John, *War, Journalism*, p. 99. It may have stood for Diana. Henry had recently read George Meredith's *Diana of the Crossways* whose eponymous heroine is a writer. The story is based on an incident in the life of Caroline Norton, who became a champion of women's legal rights.

19 HWNP, e612/3, 30 November 1904.

20 *Ibid.*, e613/2, 8 January 1906.

21 ES, *UA*, pp. 111–19.

22 HWNP, e613/3, 13 May 1906.

23 *Ibid.*, 19 May 1906.

24 *Ibid.*, 5 June 1906.

25 *Ibid.*, e614/2, 15 October 1907.

26 *Ibid.*, 11 December 1906.

27 *Ibid.*

28 *Ibid.*, e614/1, 8 March 1907.

29 *Ibid.*, 19 February 1906.

30 *MG*, 8 January 1908.

31 *Ibid.*, 30 March 1906.

32 *Ibid.*, 28 March, 10 May 1906.

33 *Ibid.*, 6 June 1906.

34 See John, *War, Journalism*, chapter 5.

35 HWNP, e614/2, 11 October 1907.

36 *Ibid.*, e615/3, 7 August 1906.

37 ES, *The War of All the Ages*, p. 224.

38 HWNP, e625/4, 6 May 1910.

39 *Ibid.*, e617/2, 6, 7, 13 May, 4 June 1912.

40 *Ibid.*, e616/4, 20 September 1911, e617/3, 19 January 1913. Brother Ronald had emigrated to Canada.

41 *Ibid.*, e617/4, 24 April 1913. Henry later admired Cecil Sharp. See Chapter 11.

42 See Chapter 4.

43 HWNP, e617/4, 3 June 1913.

44 P. M. Young, 'Friends Pictured Within' in R. Monk (ed.), *Elgar Studies*, Aldershot: Scolar Press, 1990, pp. 89–91.

45 For an exploration of how Henry handled this see John, 'A Family at War'.

46 HWNP, e617/1, 1 December 1911.

47 ESNP, MSS.Eng.Lett. d277, 7 August 1907.

48 HWNP, e614/1, 27 February 1907.

49 *Ibid.*, 10 June 1910.
50 ESNP, MSS. Eng. Misc. d668, 23 November 1942.
51 Evelyn was invited by Hardy to a party at Max Gate a couple of years later when spending a holiday at Lulworth Cove with her sister. Clodd denounced Evelyn's suffrage 'methods of agitation' as 'unwise and also mischievous'. ESNP, MSS. Eng. Lett. d277, 23 February 1908.
52 ES, *UA*, p. 96.
53 HWNP, e613/1, 18 September 1905.
54 See Peter Searby, *A History of the University of Cambridge. Volume III 1750–1870*, Cambridge: Cambridge University Press, 1997, p. 644.
55 See Rachel Rich, 'Ordering Dinner on Display: Bourgeois Manners and the Emergence of a Restaurant Culture in Paris and London, 1850–1914', History Seminar, Aberystwyth University, 2006.
56 HWNP, e613/4, 27 April 1907.
57 ES, *Macmillan's Story Readers*, p. 96.
58 *Nation* 6 January 1912, 17 March 1923.
59 Most notably in his 1901 collection *The Plea of Pan*.
60 See Chapter 6.
61 ESNP, MSS. Eng. Lett. c278, 16 January 1913.
62 HWN, *More Changes: More Chances*, Nisbet, 1925, p. 333. *MG* 12 July 1910.
63 ES, *UA*, p. 76.

4 Words in Deed: women's suffrage

1 ES, 'The Babe', *Votes for Women* 3 January 1913, p. 207.
2 Angela V. John, *Elizabeth Robins: Staging a Life 1862–1952*, Stroud: Tempus, 2007, pp. 203–4.
3 ES, *UA*, pp. 129–30.
4 *Ibid.*, p. 128.
5 *Daily Chronicle* 13 October 1900, ESNP, MSS. Eng. Misc. d669.
6 *Ibid.*
7 ES, *UA*, p. 131. Since the Representation of the People Act of 1884, two-thirds of adult males could vote in national elections. Yet all women, along with children, lunatics and criminals, were denied this right.
8 *Ibid.*
9 ESNP, MSS. Eng. Lett. d277, 2 April 1909.
10 1 August 1909. Harry Ransom Humanities Research Center, University of Texas at Austin.
11 *MG* 14 March 1928.
12 Museum of London, Book of Suffragette Prisoners, 58.87/65.
13 *Votes for Women* 3 September 1908. See too 14 May 1908.
14 HWNP, e614/4, 26 March 1908.

15 *Ibid.*, e616/3, 1 February 1911. A slightly different version of this is reproduced in HWN, *More Changes*, p. 332. Henry added that 'Iron tears rolled down Ellis Griffith's cheeks'. He was Under Secretary of State at the Home Office.

16 She could not recall which organisation invited her. But since the request came via the WSPU and was for a lecturer on the militant movement, it was unlikely to have come from their moderate Danish Women's Associations' Suffrage Federation (Danske Kvindeforeningers Valgrets Forbund) and probably emanated from the National League for Women's Suffrage (Landsforbundet for Kvinders Valgret).

17 See ES, *UA*, pp. 102–110, for her Danish tour.

18 According to a letter she sent Henry. HWNP, e615/2, 21 January 1909.

19 Richard J. Evans, *The Feminists*, Croom Helm, 1977, p. 80.

20 For the stories discussed below see ES, *Rebel Women*, Warrington, Portrayer Publications, 2003 edition, and Katharine Cockin, Glenda Norquay and Sowon S. Park, *Women's Suffrage Literature* 4, Routledge, 2007, for reprints of 'Shaking Hands with the Middle Ages', ' "Votes For Woman – Forward!"' and 'The Person Who Cannot Escape'. 'Patrolling the Gutter' and 'The Women at the Gate' are reprinted in Glenda Norquay (ed.), *Voices & Votes: A Literary Anthology of the Women's Suffrage Campaign*, Manchester: Manchester University Press, 1995. The latter, along with 'Shaking Hands with the Middle Ages', is reprinted in Carolyn Christensen Nelson (ed.), *Literature of the Women's Suffrage Campaign in England*, Toronto: Broadview Press, 2004.

21 Jane Eldridge Miller, *Rebel Women: Feminism, Modernism and the Edwardian Novel*, Virago Press, 1994, p. 143.

22 See Laura E. Nym Mayhall, *The Militant Suffrage Movement: Citizenship and Resistance in Britain, 1860–1930*, Oxford: Oxford University Press, 2003, chapter 3, for how suffragettes staged exclusion, most notably the WSPU 'Rush' of the House of Commons, 1908, and the Women's Freedom League's 'Siege of Westminster', 1909.

23 HWNP, e615/1, 14 October 1908.

24 Liddington, *Rebel Girls*, Krista Cowman, *Women of the Right Spirit: Paid Organisers of the WSPU 1904–18*, Manchester: Manchester University Press, 2007. See too Maroula Joannou's recognition of how *Rebel Women* challenged popular misconceptions of suffragettes, 'Suffragette Fiction and the Fictions of Suffrage' in Maroula Joannou and June Purvis (eds), *The Women's Suffrage Movement: New Feminist Perspectives*, Manchester, Manchester University Press, 1998, p. 105.

25 *MG* 27 February 1908. See too Maria DiCenzo, 'Gutter Politics: Women Newsies and the Suffrage Press', *Women's History Review* 12/1, 2003, pp. 15–33.

26 *MG* 12 July 1910.

27 For photographs of this shop see Diane Atkinson, *The Suffragettes in Pictures*, Museum of London, Stroud: Sutton Press, 1996.

28 ES, *UA*, p. 139.

29 Antonia Raeburn, *The Militant Suffragettes*, Michael Joseph, 1973, p. 79.

30 *Nation* 22 February 1908.

31 *MG* 25 November 1910.

32 *Ibid.*, 8, 12–22 August 1912.

33 *Ibid.*, 8 March 1912.

34 ESNP, MSS. Eng. Misc. c499a.

35 However, the first imprisoned suffragettes had been placed in the First Division.

36 ESNP, MSS. Eng. Misc. d277, December 1911.

37 HWNP, e617/1, 2 December 1911.

38 *Nation* 6 January 1912. See too Angela V. John, '"Behind the locked Door": Evelyn Sharp, Suffragette and Rebel Journalist', *Women's History Review* 12/1, 2003, pp. 5–13.

39 ES, *Rebel Women*, p. 25.

40 *Nation* 6 January 1912.

41 In ES, *The War of All the Ages*, p. 64. See too Louisa Garrett Anderson's letter to her mother, Elizabeth Garrett Anderson, telling how the rows of faces in the prison chapel made her want to cry. Louisa Garrett Anderson Papers, 7LGA/12/6, 26 March 1912, The Women's Library, London.

42 *Votes for Women* 1 November 1912.

43 ESNP, MSS. Eng. Misc. d277, 30 June [1909].

44 *Ibid.*, 25 March [1911].

45 HWNP, e617/1, 22 November 1911.

46 ES, *UA*, p. 139.

47 ES, *The War of All the Ages*, pp. 136–7. See too her stories in this book about siblings. A brother who enjoys the good life and incurs debts is alienated from his suffragette sister whom he sees as irresponsible. But when she has to recuperate in a nursing home he is shocked at the hypocrisy of their aunt and uncle who are more concerned about disclosure of this shameful secret than about the damage to their niece's health. He begins to understand why she is a suffragette. *Ibid.*, 'Three Boys', pp. 201–11.

48 Elizabeth Crawford, *The Women's Suffrage Movement: A Reference Guide 1866–1928*, Routledge edition, 2001, pp. 671–3.

49 ESNP, MSS. Eng. Misc., 2 January 1908.

50 HWNP, e617/1, 9 December 1911.

51 *Ibid.*, 11 November 1911.

52 *Ibid.*, 22 November 1911.

53 Lord Pethick-Lawrence, *Fate Has Been Kind*, Hutchinson, 1942, pp. 88–9.

54 Dramatised in the television series *Shoulder to Shoulder.*
55 *Women's Bulletin* 16 July 1955. See John Mercer, 'Making the News: Votes for Women and the Mainstream Press', *Media History* 10/3, 2004, pp. 187–199, for the paper's history.
56 Elizabeth Robins, *Way Stations*, Hodder & Stoughton, 1913, p. 276.
57 MS21, 623(1), 15 August 1912, Sheehy Skeffington Papers, National Library of Ireland, Dublin. See too ES to P. Willcocks, 21 June 1912, Willcocks Papers, Devon Record Office.
58 *Votes for Women* 8 March 1912.
59 An all-party Conciliation Committee drafted a Conciliation Bill in 1910 proposing limited women's suffrage. A modified bill was on the verge of being passed in 1911 but the government announced an impending Manhood Suffrage Bill that could be amended to include women's suffrage, effectively ruining the Conciliation Bill. Militancy was resumed. The 1912 Conciliation Bill was defeated by Irish Nationalists withdrawing support and erstwhile Liberal and Conservative supporters or abstainers voting against it.
60 Louisa Garrett Anderson Papers, 7LGA/1/3/6, 26 March 1912.
61 See Chapter 2.
62 She did other organisational work too, for example helping to disseminate information when suffragette prisoners were on hunger strike in April 1912.
63 HWNP, e617/2, 1 April 1912.
64 *Ibid.*, 8 December 1912. In a letter to Evelyn, probably written soon after she had gone into exile, Christabel compared receiving the paper to 'rain on parched earth' and added 'I thought it just right in every way'. She stated what might go in the news columns. ESNP, MSS. Eng. Misc. March 1912 [?]. However, Frederick Pethick-Lawrence also sometimes told Evelyn what to cover in the paper. Pethick-Lawrence Papers, 9/30, Letter to Christabel Pankhurst, 4 August 1912, Wren Library, Trinity College, Cambridge.
65 See Chapter 3.
66 HWNP, e617/2, 4 September 1912.
67 *Ibid.*, 27 August 1912.
68 *Ibid.*, e617/2, 28 November 1912.
69 ES to Elizabeth Robins, 14 October 1912, Harry Ransom Humanities Research Center.
70 See note 59 above for the Manhood Suffrage Bill. June Purvis, *Emmeline Pankhurst: A Biography*, Routledge, 2002, p. 208.
71 *Ibid.*, 3 May 1913.
72 HWNP, e618/1, 24 July 1913.
73 ES,*UA*, p. 146.
74 HWNP, e618/1, 25 July 1913.
75 ESNP, MSS. Eng. Misc. d277, 27 July [1913].

76 Evelyn wrote to the Home Secretary to complain about this alteration of her sentence.
77 HWNP, e618/1, 28 July 1913.
78 ESNP, MSS. Eng. Misc. d277, nd [1913] and 29 July 1013.
79 HWNP, e618/1, 30 July 1913.
80 ES, *UA*, p. 205.
81 HWNP, e618/1, 11, 16 October 1913.
82 ESNP, MSS. Eng. Misc. d277, March 1912 [?]
83 *Ibid.*, 14 June 1912.
84 *Ibid.*, 12 October 1913. In her reflections on the first twenty-five years of women's enfranchisement for the *MG* (6 Feb. 1943), Evelyn remarked that the militant movement was associated with Mrs Pethick-Lawrence, Elizabeth Robins, Mrs Pankhurst and Lady Constance Lytton (in that order) making no reference to Christabel.
85 See Chapter 5 and Angela V. John, 'The Privilege of Power: Suffrage Women and the issue of Men's Support' in Amanda Vickery (ed.), *Women, Privilege, and Power: British Politics 1750 to the Present*, Stanford, CA: Stanford University Press, pp. 243–52.
86 ESNP, MSS. Eng. Misc. d277, nd [1912?].
87 *MG* 17 November 1943.
88 HWNP, e618/2, 21 January 1914.
89 Evelyn refers to Murray coming 'between us all those years ago, just before the last war, and our friendship seemed broken'. She adds 'I have always felt a great love for her', ESNP, MSS. Eng. Misc. e635, 1 November 1943. On the 3rd she refers to a letter from Louisa that 'seems to suggest that she never faltered in her love for me'. See too Johanna Alberti, *Beyond Suffrage: Feminists in War and Peace 1914–28*, Macmillan, 1989, pp. 115–16. Evelyn wrote her Obituary for the *MG*. Between 1915–19 she was Chief Surgeon at the Endell Street Military Hospital, the only official army hospital staffed entirely by women.
90 HWNP, e618/2, 18 March 1914.
91 *Ibid.*, e618/3, 8 July 1914.

5 Working with war

1 Sylvia Pankhurst suggested to Henry that her mother's attitude to war was attributable to two factors: going to school in France soon after the Franco-Prussian War and the influence of Christabel. Sylvia believed that her sister was demoralised by comfort and that she (Christabel) had always opposed their father for being generally progressive rather than wholeheartedly pursuing one advanced cause.
2 *Votes for Women* 6 February 1914.
3 Laurence Housman, *The Unexpected Years*, Methuen, 1937, p. 298.

4 Evelyn objected to proposals for protective legislation that targeted women. See her letter 'The Case for Restricting Drinking Hours', *MG* 19 November 1915.

5 Deirdre Beddoe, *Out of the Shadows: A History of Women in Twentieth-Century Wales*, Cardiff: University of Wales Press, 2000, p. 71.

6 ESNP, MSS. Eng. Misc. d672/13.

7 ES, *A Communion of Sinners*, 1917.

8 *Ibid.*

9 'A Civilian Looks Back', *MG* 8 November 1933.

10 ES, *The War of All the Ages*, p. 66. The following accounts are based on stories from this and the 1917 collection of short stories.

11 *Ibid.*, p. 98.

12 *Ibid.*, p. 73.

13 *Ibid.*, pp. 59–65.

14 *Ibid.*, p. 53.

15 ES, *A Communion of Sinners*, p. 61.

16 ES, *Rebel Women*, p. 12. See Chapter 4. Angela Smith, *Suffrage Discourse in Britain during the First World War*, Aldershot: Ashgate, 2005, p. 16.

17 ES, *UA*, p. 157.

18 ESNP, MSS. Eng. Lett. d276, 7 November 1914.

19 HWNP, e618/4, 22 November 1916.

20 See June Hannam and Karen Hunt, *Socialist Women: Britain 1880s to 1920s*, Routledge, 2002, p. 181.

21 HWNP, e620/4, 12 July 1918.

22 See 'The Wounded Tommy' in ES, *The War of All the Ages*, pp. 47–52.

23 She had established the Hull House Settlement in Chicago and was well known in feminist and pacifist circles.

24 WIL, 1st yearly report, BLPES.

25 HWNP, e618/4, 17 April 1915.

26 *Ibid.*, 22 April 1915.

27 Johanna Alberti, *Beyond Suffrage: Feminists in War and Peace, 1914–28*, Basingstoke: Macmillan, 1989, p. 54. Jill Liddington, *The Long Road to Greenham: Feminism and Anti-militarism in Britain since 1820*, Virago Press, 1989, p. 105.

28 ILP pamphlets, 16/1915, BLPES.

29 Notably the *DH*, *MG* and *Bristol Times and Mirror*.

30 The words 'For Peace and Freedom' were added to Women's International League at the Zurich congress of 1919 where it was also decided to site the international headquarters of WIL at Geneva. Sybil Oldfield, 'England's Cassandras in World War One' in Oldfield, '*This Working-Day World': Women's Lives and Culture in Britain, 1914–45*, Taylor & Francis, 1994, pp. 89–100.

31 WIL yearly reports 2/1, 2/2, BLPES.

32 See Chapters 6 and 8.

33 Karen Hunt, 'Journeying Through Suffrage: The Politics of Dora Montefiore' in Claire Eustance, Joan Ryan and Laura Ugolini (eds), *A Suffrage Reader: Charting Directions in British Suffrage History*, Leicester: Leicester University Press, 200, p. 168, Elizabeth Crawford, *The Women's Suffrage Movement: A Reference Guide 1866–1928*, Routledge edition, 2001, pp. 671–3.

34 HWNP, e620/2, 3 July 1917.

35 *Votes for Women* February 1918. It first appeared in the *Herald* the previous summer.

36 *Christian Commonwealth* 1 August 1917.

37 7/354, 21 June 1917, Lansbury Collection 6/257, BLPES.

38 She received £75 a year from the Trust Fund set up by her father in 1891.

39 HWNP, e602/2, 7 August 1917.

40 HWNP, e620/3, 18 May 1918.

41 Their Southwark club carried on as the Women Citizens' Club.

42 HWNP, e620/3, 28 January 1918.

43 ES, *UA*, p. 169.

44 ESNP, MSS. Eng. Lett. d277, 25 November 1916.

45 HWN, *More Changes*, p. 331.

46 ESNP, MSS. Eng. Lett. c277, 11 January 1918.

47 *Ibid.*, c277, 19 March 1918. See too similar letters from Dorothy Pethick (15 November 1917) and Harriet Newcomb (11 January 1918).

48 HWNP, e620/3 16 March 1918.

49 *Ibid.*

50 ESNP, MSS. Eng. Misc. b102/c and c/2.

6 The relief of peace: in Weimar Germany

1 WILPF 2/2, BLPES.

2 *MG* 7 April 1919.

3 HWNP, e621/2, 25 January 1920.

4 *Nation* 17 April 1920.

5 Some of her stories also appeared in the *New York World*.

6 This was a precursor to the Universities Committee of the Imperial War Fund.

7 See Chapter 5. Evelyn's *Guardian* column advertised their international work in, for example, France and China. *MG* 20, 27 April, 26 October 1927.

8 HWNP, e620/4, 12 July 1918.

9 Barbara first stood for Parliament in 1922. She became an MP (for North Hendon) in 1945. She sat on the executive committee of the Labour Party for nearly twenty years, chairing it in 1939–40.

10 See Sybil Oldfield, 'Mary Sheepshanks Edits an Internationalist Suffrage Monthly in Wartime: *Jus Suffragii* 1914–19', *Women's History Review* 12/1, 2003, pp. 119–31.

11 ES, *UA*, pp. 173–4.

12 *Nation* 12 April 1919.

13 *Ibid.*, p. 174.

14 See Angela V. John, *War, Journalism and the Shaping of the Twentieth Century: The Life and Times of Henry W. Nevinson*, I. B. Tauris, 2006, Chapter 1.

15 ES, *Somewhere in Christendom*, p. 20. See Chapter 8 below for discussion of this.

16 ES, *A Communion of Sinners*, p. 11.

17 *NL* 26 December 1924. See too *DH* 23 December 1920, 19 April 1922. For Bolshevik labels see Chapter 8.

18 David F. Crew, *Germans on Welfare: From Weimar to Hitler*, Oxford: Oxford University Press, 1998.

19 Ruth Fry, *A Quaker Adventure*, Nisbet, 1926, pp. 305–6.

20 WILPF, 2/2, BLPES.

21 HWN, *Last Changes: Last Chances*, Nisbet, 1928, p. 158.

22 John, *War, Journalism*, pp. 180–1.

23 ES, UA, p. 172. See his similar claim in the *Freeman* 7 July 1920.

24 See his powerful article in the *Nation* 15 February 1919.

25 Elizabeth F. Howard, *Across Barriers*, Friends Service Council, 1941, p. 12, Introduction by HWN.

26 See Joseph Roth, *What I Saw: Reports from Berlin 1920–33*, Granta 2004 ed.

27 ESNP, MSS. Eng. Misc. e630.

28 FEWVRC, General Committee Report 4 May 1920, Friends House Library, London.

29 ES, *UA*, p. 182. See too *DH* 14 July 1920.

30 ES, *UA*, p. 180.

31 Fry, *A Quaker Adventure*, p. 333.

32 ES, *The Little Enemy*, 1920, leaflet no. 26, FEWVRC/10/1/9. The Save the Children Fund and Salvation Army also contributed funds towards feeding these children.

33 ES, *UA*, p. 188.

34 Mark Pottle (ed.), *Champion Redoubtable: The Diaries and Letters of Violet Bonham Carter 1914–1945*, Phoenix ed. 1999, p. 148.

35 ESNP, MSS. Eng. Misc. e630.

36 *Ibid.*

37 *DH* 7 October 1920.

38 FEWVRC, Germany sub-Committee, 25 August 1920.

39 For example, in 'One of the Family', Jo's prejudiced family learns that the

girl he met when stationed on the Rhine was the daughter of an impover-ished railway official. *DH* 1 April 1921.

40 See Chapter 8.

41 *MG* 8 October 1920.

42 ES, *UA*, p. 197.

43 *DH* 6 December 1920.

44 FEWVRC, General Committee, 30 November 1920.

45 It is interesting to compare Evelyn and Henry's journalistic assign-ments with the work of Martha Gellhorn and Ernest Hemingway. For the latter see Kate McLoughlin, *Martha Gellhorn: The War Writer in the Field and in the Text*, Manchester, Manchester University Press, 2007, pp. 117–26.

46 By the mid-1920s Dorothy Thompson (daughter of an English Methodist minister though she grew up in New York) and Sigrid Schultz were based in Berlin for American newspapers. See Nancy Caldwell Sorel, *The Women Who Wrote the War*, New York: Perennial edition, 2000, chapter 2. Charlotte Haldane is recognised as the first British woman war correspondent for her 1941 journalism from the Soviet Union (Judith Adamson, *Charlotte Haldane: Woman Writer in a Man's World*, Macmillan, 1998). But Evelyn and other women in these years were operating in far from pacific arenas.

47 Translated and quoted by Marion Löffler, 'Kate Bosse-Griffiths (1910–1998)' in Bernhard Maier, Stefan Zimmer and Christiane Batke, *150 Jahre 'Mabinogion' – Deutsch- Walisische Kulturbeziehungen*, Tübingen, Niemeyer, 2001, p. 171.

48 *MG* 9 February 1923.

49 Evelyn and Henry also met in Berlin Robert Dell and Madame Vallentin, both writing for the *Herald*. See *DH* 8–14 February 1923 for Evelyn's arti-cles and quotations for this section unless otherwise stated.

50 HWN, *Last Changes*, p. 282.

51 Violet Bonham Carter noted that the Adlon Hotel (where Henry stayed in 1914) was now the only one to serve meals to French and Belgian custom-ers. Pottle, *Champion Redoubtable*, p. 142.

52 See too HWN, *Last Changes*, p. 283.

53 Violet Bonham Carter also noted shops full of jewels, Pottle, *Champion Redoubtable*, p. 142.

54 HWNP, e621/4, 13 February 1923, ES, *UA*, p. 273, HWN, *Last Changes*, p. 288.

55 ESNP, MSS. Eng. Misc. f403, 14 February 1923.

56 *Ibid.*, 12 February 1923.

57 *MG* 7 March 1923.

58 *Ibid.*, 21 February 1923.

59 *Ibid.*, 8 March 1923.

60 Huw Richards, *The Bloody Circus: The Daily Herald and the Left*, Pluto Press, 1997, p. 42.

61 *NL* 2 March 1923.

62 *DH* 16 July 1923.

63 HWNP, e621/4, 13, 24 April 1923.

64 Quoted in Pottle, *Champion Redoubtable*, p. 140.

65 ESNP, MSS. Eng. Misc. f403, 31 October 1923 for quotations for this visit unless otherwise stated.

66 HWN, *Last Changes*, p. 291.

67 ES, *UA*, p. 277.

68 *DH* 5, 7 November 1923.

69 *MG* 6 November 1923. Evelyn also noted colour prejudice, ES, *UA*, p. 291.

70 ES, *UA*, p. 281.

71 *DH* 5 November 1923.

72 See too John, *War, Journalism*, p. 185.

73 HWNP, e623/1, 4–5 November 1923.

74 ESNP, MSS. Eng. Misc. f403, 5 November 1923

75 *Ibid.*, 23 November 1923.

76 *Ibid.*, 7 November 1923. The *MG* series included Evelyn's article (21 November) about this Ruhr hospital.

77 Morgan Philips Price, *Dispatches from the Weimar Republic: Versailles and German Fascism*, Pluto Press, 1990, p. 169.

78 *NL* 16 November 1923.

79 *Ibid.*, p. 175.

80 ESNP, MSS. Eng. Misc. f403, 15 November 1923

81 *Ibid.*, 6 March 1931.

82 See Chapter 8.

83 ESNP, MSS. Eng. Lett. d278, 29 April 1932.

84 EWVRC, General Committee, 27 February 1923.

85 *New Statesman and Nation* 2 May 1931.

86 ES, *UA*, p. 301. See Chapter 11.

87 ESNP, MSS. Eng. Misc. f403, 18, 19 March 1931.

88 *Ibid.*, 23 March 1931.

89 HWNP, e625/2, 14 April 1931.

90 *New Statesman and Nation* 2 May 1931.

91 See Chapter 10.

7 Irish Rebels

1 See Chapter 1.

2 Stephen Gwynn, *Experiences of a Literary Man*, Thornton Butterworth, 1926, p. 138.

3 For the influence of Nannie and Ireland on Henry see Angela V. John, *War, Journalism and the Shaping of the Twentieth Century: The Life and Times of Henry W. Nevinson*, I. B. Tauris, 2006, chapter 9.

4 ES, *UA*, p. 213.

5 MS 33 605 (1) and (5), Sheehy Skeffington Papers, National Library of Ireland, Dublin. She also deplored the fact that Hanna was not permitted legal representation at the court martial.

6 On 12 March 1921 Evelyn's appeal for support for this organisation appeared in the *DH*, *MG* and *Nation*.

7 HWNP, e621/3, 25 August 1920.

8 See his uncompromising article 'The Desecration' in the *Nation* 18 December 1920.

9 ES, *UA*, p. 214. The following account is based on Chapter XII and *DH* 9 January 14, 24 February and 2 March. Violet Bonham Carter spent a fortnight investigating conditions in Ireland in March 1921.

10 Evelyn, along with other journalists, tended to refer to England rather than Britain.

11 In a story written just before her visit Evelyn tells of an army cadet serving in Ireland home on leave. He believes it 'every Englishman's duty to stamp out these murderous savages' and that it is far better sport keeping them on the run than 'big game shooting or punishing Huns in Belgium'. Yet this 'unimaginative man' is shown not to be beyond redemption, perhaps because he is with the British Army rather than with the special forces. After a dream, in which a leprechaun puts him in his place, he decides to leave the army. His wife attributes this to the effects of shell-shock from the war. *DH* 15 December 1920.

12 ESNP, MSS. Eng. Misc. e631, 4 June 1921. The following account is based on this diary.

13 33 606 (7), Sheehy Skeffington Papers.

14 *DH* 9 September 1921.

15 ESNP, MSS. Eng. Misc. e631, 25 July 1921.

16 ES, *UA*, p. 229.

17 HWNP, e622/1, 21 December 1921.

8 Somewhere in Russia: fiction and famine

1 *DH* 9 August 1919. See too Chapter 7.

2 ES, *UA*, p. 231.

3 HWN, 'The Dayspring in Russia', *Contemporary Review*, CXI, April 1917, pp. 409–17.

4 G. Bernard Shaw, *The Intelligent Woman's Guide to Socialism and Capitalism*, Constable, 1928, p. 14, criticises the press for giving the impression that Communism was 'a wicked invention of Russian revolutionaries and

British and American desperadoes', rather than a 'highly respectable way of sharing wealth, sanctioned and practised by the apostles'.

5 This was the sub-title to *But Why Not?* the play of her novel, ESNP, MS. Eng. Misc. d672/8. The following discussion is based on this and on ES, *Somewhere in Christendom.*

6 Tritonia was Minerva, goddess of wisdom, Hygeia the goddess of health. Ethuria seems to be an Anglicisation of Etruria. Etruscan culture was dominant in Italy by 650 BC. Under the Republic of Rome Etruria was finally conquered though the Etruscans continued to rule Etruria/ Tyrrhenia until 283 BC.

7 HWNP, e621/1, 12 May 1919.

8 *Christian Science Monitor* 30 June 1920.

9 Allen & Unwin correspondence with ES, 1919–20, MS 3282, AUC, 5/25, University of Reading Archives.

10 *Ibid.*, Reader's Report, 8 July 1919, AURR, A/1/02.

11 *DH* 18 March 1920.

12 Evelyn criticised proprietors owning groups of newspapers, thereby narrowing opportunities for differing viewpoints and imposing their own propaganda. *MG* 27 February 1927.

13 See Chapter 10 below and articles such as 'Sermons in Toys', *MG* 31 January 1923.

14 Serialised in Gilman's own periodical, *Forerunner.* See Ann J. Lane, *To Herland and Beyond: The Life and Works of Charlotte Perkins Gilman*, New York: Pantheon Books, 1990, chapter X.

15 Charlotte Perkins Gilman, *Charlotte Perkins Gilman's Utopian Novels*, ed. Minna Doskow, Associated University Presses, 1999, p. 37.

16 *Ibid.*, p. 54. There are other interesting comparisons with Evelyn's vision: the only kind of prison left is called a quarantine though that punishment is unknown. Output has grown though nobody needs to work more than two hours daily and most work four.

17 In *Jane Dunmore or a Socialist Home* (1888), by the Scots novelist Jane Clapperton, mothering and housework are accorded equal status with other work in a middle-class commune. The gendered division of labour is not, however, challenged. See Sally Ledger, *The New Woman: Fiction and Feminism at the Fin de Siècle*, Manchester: Manchester University Press, 1997, pp. 50–3.

18 HWNP e623/1, 25 October 1923.

19 Gilman could also be very funny. See Lane's comments on her book *The Home* in *To Herland and Beyond*, pp. 264, 272.

20 *Punch* 158, 11 February 1920.

21 The USSR was not established until after Evelyn's visit and it was recognised diplomatically by Great Britain only in February 1924.

22 See Chapter 10.

23 F. M. Leventhal, 'Seeing the Future: British Left-wing Travellers to the Soviet Union, 1919–32' in J. M. W. Bean (ed.), *The Political Culture of Modern Britain: Studies in Memory of Stephen Koss*, Hamish Hamilton, 1987, pp. 209–27.

24 See Orlando Figes, *Peasant Russia, Civil War: The Volga Countryside in Revolution (1917–1921)*, Oxford: Oxford University Press, 1989, Lewis H. Siegelbaum, *Soviet State and Society between Revolutions, 1918–1929*, Cambridge: Cambridge University Press, 1992, chapter 2.

25 Quoted in David Randall, *The Great Reporters*, Pluto Press, 2005, p. 173.

26 ES, *UA*, p. 233.The following account is based on A. Ruth Fry, *A Quaker Adventure*, Nisbet, 1926, chapters XXIII and XXIV, John Ormerod Greenwood, *Friends and Relief*, William Sessions Ltd, 1975, pp. 240–9, David Mcfadden and Claire Gorfinkel, *Constructive Spirit: Quakers in Revolutionary Russia*, Pasadena: Intentional Productions, 2004, and FEWVRC/10/1/9, Report to the Yearly Committee 1922, Friends House Library, London. For Evelyn's previous work with the Quakers see Chapter 6.

27 Fry, *A Quaker Adventure*, p. 169.

28 ES, *UA*, p. 233, A. Ruth Fry, *Three Visits to Russia 1922–5*, James Clark, 1942, p. 8.

29 Unless otherwise indicated, the following account of Evelyn's travels is from her Russian Diaries, ESNP, MSS. Eng. Misc. e632 and d667 and ES, *UA*, chapter XIII.

30 ES, *UA*, p. 233.

31 ESNP, MSS. Eng. Lett, c277, 9 January 1922.

32 Fry, *Three Visits*, p. 11.

33 ES, *UA*, p. 241.

34 ESNP, MSS. Eng. Lett. c277, 9 January 1922. See Chapter 10 for her work on London children.

35 See Evelyn's accounts of these schools in *DH* 27 March, 10 April 1922.

36 *MG* 24 February 1922.

37 ES, *In the Volga Valley*, p. 4.

38 *MG* 6 February 1922. See too Tom Copeman's account in *The Friend* 6 January 1922.

39 ESNP, MSS. Eng. Lett. C277, 25 January 1922.

40 *Ibid.*

41 ES, *In the Volga Valley*, p. 6.

42 *MG* 24 February 1922.

43 ESNP, MSS. Eng. Lett. c277, 25 January 1922.

44 ES, 'The Camel', *Labour Weekly* 7 November 1925.

45 For an account of this see *MG* 30 March 1922.

46 Evelyn included him in a somewhat fanciful story 'The Man Who Wanted to Die', ESNP, MSS. Eng. Misc. d671.

47 ES, *In the Volga Valley*, p. 24.
48 ES, *UA*, p. 267.
49 According to Henry, HWNP, e622/3, 1 April 1922.
50 ESNP, MSS. Eng. Misc. c499b/6.
51 *DH* 30 October 1922, also 23 October 20 November, 4, 18 December 1922.
52 *Ibid.*, 7 November 1922.
53 *Ibid.*, 27 November 1922.
54 *Ibid.*, 23 October 1923.
55 Arthur Ransome, *The Autobiography of Arthur Ransome*, Jonathan Cape, 1976, p. 303.
56 Queen Victoria's favourite poet, she had also helped found the *English Woman's Journal* in the 1850s.
57 *Ibid.*, MSS. Eng. Lett. c277, 12 February 1922.
58 Alex M. Sidney, Diary, October 1922, Temp. MSS. 683/1, Friends House, London.
59 Beatrice Harraden, *Rachel*, Hodder, 1926, pp. 103–9, ESNP, MSS. Eng. Lett. C277, 16 September 1928. Here Harraden admits that the relief worker 'is indeed you', adding 'for I know how you worked with the Friends and in other ways'.
60 In the summer its work was transferred to the Council for International Service.
61 John Shepherd, *At the Heart of Old Labour*, Oxford, Oxford University Press, 2002, p. 362.
62 HWNP, e623/6, 5 December 1924. This forged letter appeared in British newspapers just before the general election called by Labour's Ramsay MacDonald. The government had recognised the Soviet Union and the letter, urging revolutionary activity, purported to come from Zinoviev, President of the Third International, whom Evelyn had briefly met in Moscow. For a disagreement between Evelyn and Henry on this subject see HWNP, e622/2, 31 March 1922.
63 *Ibid.*, e626/2, 19 December 1934.
64 *Ibid.*, e622/2, 10 April 1922.
65 ES, *UA*, p. 233. On 8 March 1940 *The Friend* published Evelyn's story 'Nine O'Clock News'. Anna listens to the radio with neighbours in her English village. She hears, to her consternation, how a division of Russian soldiers has been wiped out. She recalls a snowbound village in the Volga valley where, seventeen years earlier, she had saved lives 'in that one vivid chapter' of her life. Though many had perished in the famine, Anna and her comrades had saved some. But these Russians were now of an age to be slaughtered. As she muses on the past, a neighbour shouts out as the football results are announced (in the same tone as a thousand deaths), 'Didn't you once go out to one of those outlandish places, to relieve some famine or plague or something?' She does not enlighten them.

9 Still rebelling: women, writing and politics in the 1920s

1 *DH* 5 September 1922. Mrs Coombe Tennant, who stood (unsuccessfully) as a National Liberal in the 1922 General Election, stated 'I do not want anyone to vote for me solely because I am a woman – nor to vote against me solely for that reason'. Quoted in Cheryl Law, *Suffrage and Power: The Women's Movement, 1918–1928*, I. B. Tauris, 2000 ed., p. 148. See too www.oxforddnb.com, article 70/700091 by Deirdre Beddoe, Peter Lord, *Winifred Coombe Tennant: A Life through Art*, Aberystwyth: National Library of Wales, 2007.

2 Mary Stott (ed.), *Women Talking: An Anthology from the Guardian's Women's Page 1922–35. 1957–71*, Pandora Press, 1987, p. xvii.

3 See Rosemary T. Van Arsdel, *Florence Fenwick Miller: Victorian Feminist, Journalist and Educator*, Aldershot, Ashgate, 2001.

4 For this correspondence see A/538/13–20, January to December 1923, MGA.

5 HWNP, e6223/5, 11 December 1923.

6 See Chapter 10.

7 *MG* 5 September 1923

8 *Ibid.*, 1 July 1922. See Chapter 6.

9 *Ibid.*, 4 July 1923.

10 *Ibid.*, 24 October 1923. See too 'The Rebel on the Hearth', *MG* 4 March 1924.

11 *MG* 13 February 1929.

12 *Ibid.*, 16 November 1932. See too *ibid.*, 30 July 1924.

13 Quoted in Marion Shaw, *The Clear Stream: A Life of Winifred Holtby*, Virago Press, 1999, p. 145, and p. 248, for Holtby's comments about psychologists' influence on women writers.

14 *DH* 20 August 1923.

15 *MG* 11 April 1933.

16 *NL* 23 July 1926, *DH* 16 October 1922.

17 *MG* 27 May 1925.

18 *NL* 27 June 1924. For the book's arguments see Angela V. John, *Elizabeth Robins: Staging a Life*, Stroud: Tempus, 2007, pp. 287–9.

19 *NL* 25 July 1924.

20 HWNP, e623/5, 28 March 1925. It was rejected by Chatto & Windus.

21 For her achievements see James A. Tattersall and Shawnee L. McMurran, 'Hertha Ayrton: A Persistent Experimenter', *Journal of Women's History* 7/2, 1995, pp. 86–112.

22 ES, *Hertha Ayrton 1854–1923*, pp. 137, 139.

23 ESNP, MSS. Eng. Lett. c277, 15 May 1917.

24 Laura E. Nym Mayhall, 'Creating the "Suffragette Spirit": British Feminism and the Historical Imagination', *Women's History Review* 4/3, 1995, p. 332.

25 HWNP, e624/4, 21 May 1928, *MG* 23 May 1928.

26 ES, 'Mary Wollstonecraft 1759–1797', pp. 680, 688. Only three out of the thirty-six individuals were women. Henry contributed a chapter on Edward Carpenter.

27 See Evelyn's article in *Nineteenth Century* CVII, April 1930, on 'Emmeline Pankhurst and Militant Suffrage' written soon after witnessing Mrs Pankhurst's statue unveiled in Westminster, close to where she had been ejected from Parliament. Paula Bartley, *Emmeline Pankhurst*, Routledge, 2002, pp. 229–30.

28 See Elizabeth Crawford, *The Women's Suffrage Movement: A Reference Guide 1866–1928*, Routledge edition, 2001, p. 703.

29 A thinly disguised sketch of Henry by Evelyn in the *NL* (6 November 1925) called 'The Traveller's Joy' told of the international traveller's infatuation for his cat.

30 *DH* 19 March 1920.

31 *MG* 24 October 1934.

32 *Ibid.*, 29 June 1924. The Performing Animals Defence League tried to reform the situation.

33 ES, *Daily Bread*, pp. 8, 11. It was in a sixpenny series (with contributions from Beatrice Webb and Leonard Woolf) examining how social and economic issues affected consumers.

34 Compare Evelyn's words with Virginia Woolf's Introductory Letter, written in 1930, for Margaret Llewelyn Davies (ed.) *Life As We Have Known It*, Virago Press ed., 1977, pp. xvii–xxxx, [*sic*]. See too the unease Woolf provoked: Hermione Lee, *Virginia Woolf*, Vintage ed. 1997, pp. 360–1.

35 ES, *Buyers & Builders*, p. 8

36 *DH* 10 November 1919.

37 *Ibid.*, 24, 27 November 1919.

38 *MG* 8 June 1922.

39 DMar5/3, Catherine Marshall Archive, Cumbria Record Office, Carlisle.

40 *NL* 27 April 1923.

41 *DH* 17 May 1920.

42 ES, *UA*, pp. 295–6.

43 Andrew Charlesworth, David Gilbert *et al.*, *An Atlas of Industrial Protest in Britain 1750–1990*, Macmillan, 1996, p. 140.

44 HWNP, e623/6, 3 May 1926.

45 ESNP, MSS. Eng. Misc. f405, f406.

46 Originally due to appear on 13th (an urgent personal request was delivered to Evelyn's flat late at night) but news of the victimisation of the miners, and their decision to reject the terms, delayed the resumption of the paper. Her article was abbreviated to fit a skeleton issue.

47 Margaret Morris, *The General Strike*, Harmondsworth, Penguin, 1976, p. 252.

48 *NL* 21 May 1926.
49 *Ibid.*
50 ES, *UA*, p. 95, ESNP, MSS. Eng. Misc. f406, 10 May 1926. See Henry's long *NL* article on the same day (21st) as Evelyn's diary. When the strike ended, the *MG*'s 'How the War Won the Strike' commented on the comradeship and 'the new habit of executive capacity of the middle classes', 3 May 1926.
51 *NL* 21 May 1926.
52 ESNP, MSS. Eng. Misc. f405, 3 May 1926.
53 *Ibid.*, f406, 13 May 1926.
54 *Ibid.*, f407, 29 August 1926.
55 Chris Williams, *Democratic Rhondda: Politics and Society 1885–1951*, Cardiff: University of Wales Press, 1996, p. 26, *Christian Science Monitor* 27 May 1930, ESNP, MSS. Eng. Misc. f408.
56 See Alun Burge, '"A Subtle Danger"?: The Voluntary Sector and Coalfield Society in South Wales 1926–1939', *Llafur* 7/ 3 & 4, 1998–99, pp. 127–41.
57 See too her article in the *MG* 17 May 1932.
58 *Christian Science Monitor* 26 May 1930.

10 The Child Grows Up: configuring childhood in the interwar years

1 ESNP, MSS. Eng. Misc. e632, 21 January 1922.
2 See Harry Hendrick, *Children, Childhood and English Society 1880–1990*, Cambridge, Cambridge University Press, 1997, pp. 28–30, Cathy Urwin and Elaine Sharland, 'From Bodies to Minds in Childcare Literature: Advice to Parents in Inter-war Britain' in Roger Cooter, (ed.), *In the Name of the Child: Health and Welfare 1880–1940*, Routledge, 1992.
3 See Anna Davin, 'Imperialism and Motherhood', *History Workshop Journal*, Spring 1978.
4 ES, *The London Child*, pp. 168–72.
5 *MG* 21 March 1923. An article on 10 March 1926 lamented the constant pontificating on types of childhood and ridiculed those who saw a connection between defective digestion and schoolroom 'dunces'. Evelyn thought it amusing and bizarre that too much suet pudding might affect a child's aptitude in class.
6 *Ibid.*, 23 December 1909.
7 *Ibid.*, 16 May 1923.
8 See Chapter 9.
9 In 1907 (*Votes for Women* November 1907) Evelyn had lamented the way that, lacking the vote, women were powerless to influence the shaping of legislation. The State Children's Association promoted child legislation and had advocated Children's Courts.

10 *MG* 29 April 1925.

11 *Ibid.*, 13 June 1928

12 *Ibid.*, 27 October 1926. Her first piece on the subject was written as early as 13 February 1907 (*MG*).

13 See for example 'Man to Man', *DH* 9 May 1921.

14 *NL* 9 March 1923.

15 In *The London Child* Evelyn tells the tale of Elsie, a docker's daughter who goes to a doctor's family and proudly defends her lifestyle. The story first appeared in the *DH* in 1921.

16 *MG* 7 July 1925.

17 *Ibid.*, 6 September 1922, 7 March 1923, 25 November 1925.

18 *Ibid.*, 13 October 1926

19 ES, *The London Child*, p. 81.

20 Sarah King, 'Technical and Vocational Education for Girls: A Study of the Central Schools of London, 1918–1939' in P. Summerfield and E. Evans (eds), *Technical Education and the State since 1850*, Manchester: Manchester University Press, 1990, p. 78.

21 ES, *The London Child*, p. 159.

22 *MG* 16 June 1926. She mentioned the London County Council's renewed ban in *ibid.*, 17 February 1926.

23 See *ibid.*, 21 May 1925.

24 Hendrick, *Children, Childhood and English Society*, pp. 70–1.

25 *MG* 6 May 1925.

26 ES, *The Child Grows Up*, p. 92.

27 MS 206, The Bodley Head. John Lane/B11, 1926, University of Reading Archives.

28 Carolyn Steedman, *Childhood, Culture and Class in Britain: Margaret McMillan 1860–1931*, Virago Press, 1990, chapter 7, and 'Margaret McMillan and the Late Nineteenth-century Remaking of Working Class Childhood' in Cooter, *In the Name of the Child*.

29 ES, *The London Child*, pp. 40–1.

30 *NL* 23 July 1926.

31 *Nation* 23 April 1927.

32 ES, *The London Child*, Author's Note.

33 *Ibid.*, p. 102.

34 *Ibid.*, p. 198.

35 From seven extracts from reviews reprinted at the end of *The Child Grows Up*.

36 John Lane/B11, 9 November 1931.

37 ES, *The Child Grows Up*, p. 275. See John R. Gillis, *Youth and History: Tradition and Change in European Age Relations, 1750–Present*, New York: Academic Press, 1981 ed.

38 *Ibid.*, p. 3.

39 E.g. *MG* 7 May 1924, 13 January, 14 July 1926.

40 A duke's daughter, she had 'electrified her family by joining the Labour Party as a girl' according to Mary Agnes Hamilton, *Remembering My Good Friends*, Jonathan Cape, 1944, pp. 171–2.

41 The term was used by the American social psychologist G. Stanley Hall to define a period lasting for about a decade from the ages of twelve to fourteen.

42 See Sally Alexander, 'Becoming a Woman in London in the 1920s and '30s' in *Becoming a Woman and Other Essays in 19th and 20th Century Feminist History*, Virago Press, 1994, which draws on oral history.

43 ES, *The London Child*, p. 214.

44 ES, 'The Juvenile Criminal' in *A Communion of Sinners*.

45 ES, *Who Was Jane?* p. 54. This book was briefly considered as the basis for a film in 1936. In 1920 Evelyn had published a story for younger children called *John's Visit to the Farm* in which a middle-class city child meets country cousins.

46 The Children's Act of 1908 empowered magistrates to deal with those under sixteen separately from adults. Probation for young offenders had been instigated in 1907.

47 *MG* 17 January 1923.

48 *Ibid.*, 19 March 1924.

49 *Ibid.*, 24 January 1923.

50 HWNP, e623/3, 9 December 1923.

51 *Ibid.*, e624/4, 13 May 1928. He did, though, call her adventure story *Young James* 'really first-rate', *ibid.*, e623/5, 21 June 1925. It included the somewhat androgynous Miss Popinjay, an intrepid traveller who had travelled in Angola and had a pet zebra named after a Zulu king.

52 *MG* 12 December 1923.

53 See Jane Lewis, *The Politics of Motherhood*, Croom Helm, 1980, p. 225.

54 *MG* 30 June 1930.

55 John Springhall, *Youth, Empire and Society: British Youth Movements 1883–1940*, Croom Helm, 1977, pp. 113–14.

56 HWNP e622/6, 20 May 1923.

57 *Ibid.*, 29, 30 April 1924. The following year saw the establishment of the Woodcraft Folk. Never a large organisation, Kibbo Kift became a Social Credit Party. A Kibbo Kift Foundation still exists: see www.kibbokift.org. Its archives (BLPES) do not suggest that Evelyn or Henry played a very active role in the society in the 1920s.

58 *MG* 1 April 1934.

59 The title of Jebb's biography (Francesca Wilson, *Rebel Daughter of a Country House*, George Allen & Unwin, 1967) suggests what she shared with Evelyn. Both also had religious faith and believed in humankind's international responsibility. Unlike Evelyn, however, Jebb had studied history at Oxford.

60 ESNP, MSS. Eng. Misc. f407, 10 September 1926.
61 *MG* 7 April 1926.
62 ES, *The African Child*, p. 2.
63 *Ibid.*, pp. viii and 27. Note his addition of an exclamation mark when quoting Evelyn.
64 *MG* 20 March 1929.
65 ES, *The African Child*, p. v.
66 *Ibid.*, p. 5.
67 *Ibid.*, p. 12.
68 'Children's Rights in Imperial Political cultures: Missionary and Humanitarian Contributions to the Conference on the African Child of 1931', *International Journal of Children's Rights* 12, 2004, p. 294.
69 ES, *The African Child*, pp. 44–5.
70 Marshall, 'Children's Rights', p. 275.
71 Dominique Marshall, 'Humanitarian Sympathy for Children in Times of War and the History of Children's Rights, 1919–1959' in James Marten (ed.), *Children and War*, New York: New York University Press, 2002.
72 ESNP, MSS. Eng. Misc. c499.

11 Defying time and the times

1 HWNP, e624/1, 29 August 1926.
2 *MG* 17 February 1932.
3 For Cecil Sharp see http://www.oxforddnb.com article 36040 by Michael Heaney.
4 Cecil Sharp correspondence. Box 3, 8 August 1913, Vaughan Williams Library, Cecil Sharp House, London.
5 Henry had published a review in the *Nation* of Sharp's book on *The Sword Dances of Northern England* as early as 25 March 1911.
6 Not 1923 as she states in *UA*.
7 ES, *UA*, p. 293. Her newspaper articles do not mention that he was her brother. He has been criticised for neglecting the industrial north-west and whatever lay outside his definition of folk, and for monopolising the collection of material. However, his dedication and vital retrieval work should not be underestimated. See Heaney's *ODNB* entry and Dave Harker, 'May Cecil Sharp Be Praised?' *History Workshop Journal* 14, 1982, pp. 44–62.
8 *The School Music Review* 15 January 1929.
9 This article (on 4 May) led to disagreement between Evelyn and the editor of the Women's Page. It is not clear what caused this but, unlike all her other contributions, it is signed ES, not Evelyn Sharp.
10 ESNP, MSS. Eng. Misc. f407, 25 April 1927.
11 *MG* 2 May 1928.
12 Peter Ackroyd, *London: The Biography*, Vintage ed., 2001, p. 657.

13 HWNP, e625/4, 16 March 1933.

14 *DH* 4 April 1928. Although in the name of Marion Allison, it was by Margaret Morris.

15 *Ibid.*, 6 April 1928, *EFDS News* 18, October 1928, p. 137. By the end of 1932, with sales of just over a thousand, the publisher Gerald Howe proposed remaindering it at 6d. Evelyn protested and he agreed to keep it on the list. Soon afterwards she complained to the Society of Authors about his treatment of her work. Society of Authors correspondence, Add 56804 British Library, 1932–33.

16 She also did a talk on folk singing in this series of summer talks that included speakers such as Malcolm Sargeant.

17 Maud Karpeles, 'Henry Nevinson', *English Dance and Song* VI/2, December 1941, p. 16.

18 HWNP, MS. Eng. Misc. c496.

19 *Ibid.*, e625/1, 4 November 1929.

20 Interviewed by the author 11 December 1999.

21 *Ibid.*, e625/3, 3 May 1931.

22 ESNP, MSS. Eng. Misc. f407, 17 May, 2 June 1930.

23 *Ibid.*, MSS. Eng. Misc. e631.

24 See Chapter 3. HWNP, e625/4, 1 July 1932.

25 ESNP, MSS. Eng. Misc. f410. She called this 'The Busy Woman's Rest Cure', *MG* 8 September 1932.

26 Elizabeth Robins 2B/19/136, 9 August 1932, Fales Collection, Elmer Holmes Bobst Library, New York University.

27 ESNP, MSS. Eng. Misc. b102. See, for example, Sybil Thorndike's encouraging letter about the importance of this experimental subject but awareness of the difficulties she might encounter with commercial management. ESNP, MSS. Eng. Lett. c277, 27 July, ny.

28 Published by the Labour Publishing Company Ltd as part of its Plays for the People Series. In 1951 the American composer Henry Leland Clarke published an opera with the same title based on this.

29 HWNP, e625/1, 4 April 1930.

30 ES, *UA*, pp. 9–10.

31 *Ibid.*, p. 306.

32 HWNP, e625/4, 8 June 1932.

33 ESNP, MSS. Eng. Lett. c279, 15 December 1932.

34 *Western Mail* 29 December 1932.

35 ESNP, MSS. Eng. Misc. c499a.

36 *Daily Telegraph* 29 December 1932.

37 ES, *UA*, p. ix.

38 ESNP, MSS. Eng. Lett. d278, 27 January 1931.

39 Carpenter MSS. 386–422, 11 November 1923, Sheffield Archives.

40 HWNP, e622/3, 31 March 1922, e625/1, 29 June 1930.

41 ESNP, MSS. Eng. Misc. f405, 7–19 September 1925.
42 HWNP, e625/4, 1 April 1929.
43 ESNP, MSS. Eng. Misc. f407, 19 April 1929. The Suvla reference is to Henry's description in his book *The Dardanelles Campaign*, Nisbet, 1918.
44 HWNP, e624/5, 19 April 1929.
45 ESNP, MSS. Eng. Lett. c279, 25 December 1932.
46 Henry explained their reasoning in his diary. HWNP, e626/1, 27–8 December 1932.
47 HWNP, e626/1, 29 May 1933.
48 ESNP, MSS. Eng. Misc. f409.
49 *Ibid.*, MSS. Eng. Misc. f407, 18, 28 August. 1934.
50 For Nevinson family relationships see Angela V. John, 'A Family at War: The Nevinson Family' in Michael J. K. Walsh (ed.), *A Dilemma of English Modernism: Visual and Verbal Politics in the Life and Work of C. R. W. Nevinson (1889–1946)*, Newark, DE: University of Delaware Press, 2007, pp. 23–35.
51 HWNP, e626/1, 12, 16 December 1932.
52 John L. Nevinson's diary, 20A, 11 June 1932, the Society of Antiquaries of London.
53 ESNP, MSS. Eng. Misc. f407, 20 April–12 May 1934 for this and following description.
54 Turkish women won the right to vote that year.
55 For this cruise see ESNP, MSS. Eng. Misc. f407, 3–24 April 1937.
56 Another lecturer was the historian Margaret Cole. HWNP, MSS. Eng. Misc. c497.
57 The Bodley Head. John Lane/B11, MS. 2606, 31 July 1927, University of Reading Archives.
58 Sub-titled *The Empress and the Necromancer*. Score published by Oxford University Press.
59 HWNP, e624/5, 8 July 1929.
60 ES, 'Island Magic', *Contemporary Review* 133/1, May 1928, pp. 638, 640.
61 Vaughan Williams Letters, MS. Mus. 161C ff. 20–2, Vaughan Williams to ES, nd, Music Collections, British Library, London. The correspondence is partly in Adeline Williams's hand, singed by the composer. See also *Letters of Ralph Vaughan Williams 1895–1958*, edited by Huge Cobbe, Oxford: Oxford University Press, 2008.
62 Music by M. E. Marshall. Lillian Braithwaite performed it. ESNP MSS. Eng. Misc. c499b/7. See too ES's 1922 correspondence about copyright in the Society of Authors Papers, British Library Add.56804.
63 ES to R. Vaughan Williams, MS. Mus. 161C, ff. 20–2, 14 September 1928.
64 *Ibid.*, Vaughan Williams to ES, nd.
65 *MG* 12 October 1942.
66 Vaughan Williams to ES, MS. Mus. 161C, ff. 20–2, 3 January 1930.

67 Since his music currently lasted almost one and three-quarter hours and the dialogue fifty minutes, Evelyn had to cut the most. But Vaughan Williams pointed out that since this was a work of fantasy, much could be taken for granted. Vaughan Williams to ES, MS. Mus. 161C, ff. 20–2, 24 December 1935. According to reviewers the performance actually lasted for three hours.

68 HWNP, e626/3, 12 May 1936. Produced by Camille Prior.

69 *Ibid.*, 18 May 1936. The music critic of the *Liverpool Daily Post* thought it a 'delightful work', but Fox Strangways in the *Observer* (17 May 1936) was grudging about the 'clever repartee'.

70 Two CDs with the Chandos label.

71 See John Stevenson, *British Society 1914–45*, Harmondsworth, Penguin, 1984, chapter 10.

72 *MG* 2 March, 2 November 1932.

73 *Ibid.*, 2 March 1932.

74 *Ibid.*, 25 November 1932.

75 *Ibid.*, 30 March 1932.

76 *Ibid.*, 23 May 1933. The Welsh National Council of the League of Nations Union appealed to Evelyn to publicise the eighteenth World Radio Message of the Children of Wales in 1939. ESNP, MSS. Eng. Misc. c499c.

77 *Ibid.*, 20 June 1934.

78 *Ibid.*, 5 August 1931, 30 March 1932, 5 April 1933.

79 *Ibid.*, 22 March 1933.

80 *Ibid.*, 22 February 1933.

81 Six others were co-opted. Within months, 'finding herself unable to attend committee meetings', Evelyn resigned and became a vice-president. University of Hull Archives, NCCL, Annual Report for 1934, DCL/73A(ii).

82 *MG* 25 February 1934.

83 HWNP, e626/2, 25 February 1934.

84 ESNW, MSS. Eng. Lett. d280, 10 November 1941.

85 HWNP, e627/3, 15 March 1939.

86 Society of Authors Papers, BL Add. 56804, 19 October 1938. Henry also wrote. Both participated in a deputation to the German Embassy in London in July 1934 to protest against the trial of the Communist Thalmann before the People's Court in Germany.

87 ESNP, MSS. Eng. Misc. f407, 10 September 1926. See Chapter 10.

88 The wording differs slightly from the original diary entry. ES, *UA*, p. 299.

12 War and widowhood: Chipping Campden and Kensington

1 B/N81A/4, 28 October 1940, MGA.

2 For Henry's account of the Blitz see HWNP, e628/1 and e628/2.

3 Quoted in Angus Calder, *The Myth of the Blitz*, Pimlico, 1997 ed., p. 33.

4 ESNP, MS. Eng. Misc. f409, 15 March 1934. They stayed at Rita House, Park Road.

5 G. M. Trevelyan, *English Social History*, Longmans, Green & Co., 1942, p. 35.

6 ESNP, MSS. Eng. Lett. d278, 12 September 1937.

7 *Ibid.*, 4 April 1941.

8 *Ibid.*, d279, 22 February 1942.

9 HWN, *Visions and Memories*, Oxford University Press, 1944, p. 179.

10 *MG* 31 October 1941. For Arcadia see Angela V. John, *War, Journalism and the Shaping of the Twentieth Century: The Life and Times of Henry W. Nevinson*, I. B. Tauris, 2006, chapter 1. Henry's autobiography opened with the words 'I was not born in Arcadia'. Marie Belloc-Lowndes had been a journalist in the late nineteenth century.

11 ESNP, MS. Eng. Lett. d278, 29 June 1941.

12 HWNP, e628/4, 8–9 November 1941.

13 *The Times* 10, 12 November 1941.

14 Quoted in Norman and Jeanne MacKenzie, *The Diary of Beatrice Webb. Volume One 1873–1892. Glitter Around and Darkness Within*, Virago Press, 1986, xiii.

15 For this see John, *War, Journalism*, Afterword. *PEN News* January–February 1942, p. 15.

16 26 December 1941, Isle of Wight Record Office, Newport,

17 ESNW, MS. Eng. Litt. d280, 10, 11, 12, 17, 27 December 1941.

18 *Ibid.*, 16 June 1942.

19 Society of Authors, BL Add. 56804, 12 December 1941.

20 ESNP, MSS. Eng. Lett. d279, 22 February 1942

21 For correspondence on this see the Penguin Archives, Pelican, 02.0095, University Library, Bristol.

22 Broadcast on 24 February 1942. Correspondence of 19, 21 June, 1, 5 July 1942, RCONT, BBC Written Archives Centre, Caversham Park. The BBC also wrote to Evelyn in 1948 about the possibility of a further broadcast but received no reply: 1, 4, 5 November 1948.

23 *Listener* 2, 9 July 1942.

24 Vere Hodgson, *Few Eggs and No Oranges: The Diaries of Vere Hodgson 1940–45*, Persephone Books, 1999 ed., p. 323.

25 ESNP, MSS. Eng. Misc. d668, 23 October 1942.

26 *Ibid.*, 2 August 1942.

27 *Ibid.*, e634, 2 May 1943.

28 ESNP, MSS. Eng. Lett. d279, 23 March 1842.

29 *Ibid.*, 24 August 1942.

30 In 1943 she contributed to a PEN fund-raising scheme to produce a book of sixty-three short stories of five hundred words covering different generations. Eleanor Farjeon asked Evelyn to write about the 1870s to

1930s. Evelyn's story 'Aunt Sarah' was about a 'venturesome' woman who rebelled against her country upbringing, becoming a journalist and campaigner before eventually returning home. She defied convention once more by refusing to die. The book does not seem to have been published. ESNP, MSS. Eng. Lett. d279, June 1943.

31 *MG* 25 November 1942.

32 *Ibid.*, 6 February 1943.

33 ESNP, MSS.Eng. Lett. d279, 21 September 1942.

34 Within five months it sold again for £1,150.

35 ESNP, MSS. Eng. Misc. d668, 14 August 1942.

36 Paper shortages and other difficulties had led to small print runs and many books selling out quickly.

37 For these reviews see HWNP, MS. Eng. Misc, c497.

38 ESNP, MSS. Eng. Lett, d279, 7 September 1946.

39 Society of Authors, BL Add. 56804, 30 August 1943, British Library, London.

40 ESNP, MS. Eng. Lett. 16 September 1944.

41 *Ibid.*, MSS. Eng. Misc. e635, 8 October 1944.

42 *Ibid.*, MSS. Eng. Misc. e634.

43 *Ibid.*, e635, 26 October 1943.

44 *Ibid.*, e634, 31 May 1943.

45 Gilbert Murray Papers, MSS. 410, 31 May 1943, The Bodleian Library, University of Oxford.

46 ESNP, MSS. Eng. Lett, d279, 29 November 1944.

47 Hodgson, *Few Eggs*, pp. 213, 232.

48 *Ibid.*, p. 274.

49 ESNP, MSS. Eng. Misc. e634, 11 February 1943.

50 *Ibid.*, MSS. Eng. Lett. d278, 26 March 1942.

51 The following account draws on Philip Ziegler, *London at War 1939–1945*, Mandarin, 1995 ed.

52 Hodgson, *Few Eggs*, p. 460.

53 *Ibid.*, p. 453.

54 ESNP, MSS. Eng. Misc. e635, 10 August 1944.

55 *Ibid.*, 21 October 1944.

56 D/2532/1, 21 January 1944, MGA.

57 Hodgson, *Few Eggs*, p. 502.

58 ESNP, MSS. Eng. Misc. e636, 22 December 1944.

59 *Ibid.*, 25 February 1945.

60 *Among You Taking Notes: The Wartime Diary of Naomi Mitchison 1939–1945*, Dorothy Sheridan ed, Phoenix, 2000, p. 321. This diary was part of the important Mass-Observation project. Although she spent most of the war on the family's Scottish estate, her perspectives were often similar to Evelyn's.

61 ESNP, MSS. Eng. Misc. e636, 6 June 1945.
62 *Ibid.*, 5 July.
63 She also sat on the Society of Authors' Pension Fund Committee from 1937.
64 ESNP, MSS. Eng. Lett, d278, 9 December 1942.
65 ESNP, Eng. Misc. e636, 7 August 1945.
66 *Ibid.*, e635, 3–8 December 1943.
67 *Ibid.*, 14 June, September 10 1945. This did not result in any further publications.
68 *Ibid.*, e635, 3–8 December 1943.
69 ESNP MSS. Eng. Lett. d278, 26 March 1942.
70 ESNP, Eng. Misc. e635, 20 December 1943.
71 ESNP, e636, 9 March 1947.
72 *Ibid.*
73 *Ibid.*, 24 March 1945.
74 *Ibid.*, 27 August 1945.
75 ESNP, MSS. Eng. Lett. d279, 22 January 1946.
76 *Ibid.*, 16 February 1947.
77 *Ibid.*, 12 January 1948.
78 H. N. Brailsford (ed.) *Essays, Poems and Tales of Henry W. Nevinson*, Victor Gollancz, 1948, p. 7.
79 Daniel George in the *Daily Express* 10 November 1948.
80 ESNP, MSS. Eng. Lett. 29 June 1948.
81 ESNP, MSS. Eng. Misc. e636, 28 April 1946. Her executors Barbara Ayrton Gould and Percy Beaumont Shepheard (her solicitor) predeceased her so the will was proved by her niece Joan Sharp.
82 The electoral roll shows her living in Russell Road for the last time in 1948. On 10 May 1956 Evelyn's niece confirmed that she had spent 'many years in a nursing home'. Evelyn Sharp, 4001, Joan Sharp letter to National Portrait Gallery Picture Library, London.
83 *MG* 20 June 1955. It was headed 'Mrs. Evelyn Nevinson' despite the fact that she had written for decades in the paper as Evelyn Sharp. See too *The Times* and *Daily Telegraph* for 21 June 1955. She left £7,641 4s 9d.
84 *Women's Bulletin* 16 July 1955.
85 *Times Literary Supplement* 22 June 1933.
86 ESNP, MSS. Eng. Lett, d279, 14 October 1945.

Index

Page numbers in italics refer to illustrations.